THE VISION OF WORLD PEACE
IN SEVENTEENTH AND
EIGHTEENTH-CENTURY FRANCE

THE VISION OF WORLD PEACE IN SEVENTEENTH AND EIGHTEENTH-CENTURY FRANCE

BY

ELIZABETH V. SOULEYMAN

KENNIKAT PRESS
Port Washington, N. Y./London

THE VISION OF WORLD PEACE IN SEVENTEENTH
AND EIGHTEENTH-CENTURY FRANCE

First published in 1941
Reissued in 1972 by Kennikat Press
Library of Congress Catalog Card No: 76-118454
ISBN 0-8046-1585-3

Manufactured by Taylor Publishing Company   Dallas, Texas

TO THE MEMORY OF
MY FATHER

FOREWORD

The considerations and conclusions offered in this study often required reference to original sources. Quotations in Old French, references given in Latin, French, and German would appeal to academic readers alone. The thought that this study may interest a wider group has induced the author to give all references in English. With regard to well-known writers, some standard translations have been available, and the name of the translator has been given in each particular case. In other instances the author has given her own version. It must be understood that the footnotes refer the reader to the primary sources except in few cases when the original work was not available.

The subject of this study was suggested by Professor G. L. van Roosbroeck shortly before his death. I am indebted to Professor John Lawrence Gerig who encouraged me to continue the subject and kindly directed my investigations from the beginning and to Professor Norman Lewis Torrey under whose guidance this study was brought to its present form. Professor Torrey made available some firsthand material from the libraries of Europe and gave invaluable help both in the organization of the material and in matters of style. The author takes this occasion to express her gratitude to Professors Horatio Smith, Henri François Müller, Jean-Albert Bédé, Jeanne Vidon Varney, and visiting Professor Daniel Mornet, who in different ways and at different times have been of aid to her during her work at Columbia University.

I would like to acknowledge the services of the staff of the Main Public Library and to express my sincere gratitude to the staff of the libraries of Columbia University—in the Department of International Law and especially in the various Departments of the Main Library—where helpful assistance and every research facility were generously offered.

Elizabeth V. Souleyman

CONTENTS

ix

INTRODUCTION

NEVER in the course of bygone centuries have nations lived through trials and terrors equal to those of our time. The hope for a permanent peace established at last through "placing it upon the foundation of international understanding, international appreciation, and international co-operation," [1] this firm hope, bought at the price of the disasters of the World War, seems to recede into a more and more distant future and may have even to be abandoned. In the face of the wholesale destruction of life and wealth, of the widespread havoc brought about through the pressure of the arbitrary will of a few individual leaders of nations, the bonds forged by religion, philosophy, science, art, industry, and trade do not prove strong enough to compel one people, or rather its government, to respect the rights of another people. Yet the recognition of certain inalienable rights of even the smallest nation is essential if peace is to prevail in the sphere of international life, the universal peace of which men vaguely dreamed of old. If this dream, changed by the course of centuries into an idea characterized by all the driving power an idea can have, has still not brought the expected results, if war, more ruthless than at any time, threatens to destroy civilization, where lies the cause of the failure of so many efforts?

Mr. Clarence K. Streit, in his work published in 1938,[2] explains this failure by the fact that all forms of international governments planned up to our day have been governments for states, and not for the individuals of which a state is made. He points out that the principle on which the League of Nations was founded is the equality of political bodies, not that of men; that a league is a government of governments, by governments, and for governments, and not a "govern-

[1] N. M. Butler, *Introduction* to Kant's "Perpetual Peace," 1932.
[2] C. K. Streit, *Union Now*, 1938.

ment of the people, by the people, and for the people." [3]   He affirms that, in establishing the League of Nations for the purpose of securing the freedom, rights, independence, and sovereignty of the member states, the creators of this institution had not been true to the principles of democracy. Like those writers whose visions, planning, and efforts to clear the road leading towards the establishment of perpetual peace, the author of *Union Now* sees the possibility of the creation of a "Great Republic . . . spreading peacefully round the earth as nations grow ripe for it." [4]   The beginning, he thought, was to be made by fifteen democracies : the American Union, the United Kingdom, France, Australia, Belgium, Canada, Denmark, Finland, Holland, Ireland, New Zealand, Norway, Sweden, Switzerland, and the Union of South Africa.[5]   It was his proposal that they unite into a great federal republic closely following the lead given at the end of the eighteenth century by the thirteen original colonies that established the American Union wrongly called, he asserts, the United States of America.[6]

In the course of this study we shall come across a political scheme built on the fundamental principles recently advocated by Mr. Streit. Written during the most feverish years of the French Revolution, the plan for the organization of a universal federal republic of A. Cloots [7] is less a worked out political scheme than a declaration of principles on which the human race should be organized into a permanent union. He envisioned no independent, national, sovereign states in this future union, but individuals alone.[8]   His main idea was that if the whole world became one political body there would be

[3] A. Lincoln, *Oration at Gettysburg*, Nov. 19, 1863.

[4] C. K. Streit, *op. cit.*, p. 3.

[5] At the time this study goes into print, five of these democracies, Denmark, Holland, Belgium, Norway, and France have already lost their independence, while Finland, Sweden, and Switzerland are living under the perpetual threat of losing theirs.

[6] C. K. Streit, *op. cit.*, pp. 2-5.

[7] A. Cloots, *La République universelle* ou *Adresse aux tyrannicides,* Paris, l'An quatre de la Rédemption.

[8] *Bases constitutionnelles* . . ., 1793, pp. 3, 37, 42. [The full titles of the works mentioned in the text of this study or in the footnotes are given in the bibliography.]

no conflict between patriotism and love for mankind, nationalism and cosmopolitanism, ethics and politics. From his point of view, all peace plans based upon the recognition of the sovereignty of states (and such was the type of world organizations furthered by all French peace plans but his own) were doomed to fail.

Contemporary events, the ruthless war which, at this very time, is being fought between the British Empire, on one side, and the German and Italian dictatorships, on the other side, seem to testify in favor of Cloots' conceptions.

What is necessary, even in the midst of the present turmoil, is a further study of the old subject of war and peace, a new light thrown upon all its aspects, political, economic, moral, and historical. It is hard to believe that the seeds sown by so many generations in so many countries will not one day yield a rich harvest.

In France during the seventeenth and eighteenth centuries men of very different walks of life were actively interested in the peace problem. Among them we find jurists, writers, preachers, philosophers, scientists, statesmen, and economists. France has been the country where many of the pacifist ideas, still occupying the minds of men, have either originated or have received their full development. To her is due the credit for the first project for a world organization and the first plan for an international court of justice. Not satisfied with vague aspirations for peace, French writers have designed fully developed political schemes where every detail has been thoroughly examined or have directed the searchlight on the terrible or absurd aspects of war.

Many factors seem to account for the leading rôle French pacifists have played in the development of the peace idea. The geographical position of France makes her a desirable prey for her neighbors and forces her to concentrate her thought on the issue of political security. Already at the time of Pierre Dubois (1255-1312c.), the author of *De recuperatione Terre Sancte* which contains the first plan for an international organization, France was a powerful monarchy fully conscious of her national unity. She must have been likewise conscious of the value of her culture since the Sorbonne had become, almost from the time of its foundation (12th century), a center of knowledge which attracted scholars and students from every European country. The French jurists (*légistes*), who did so much to strengthen the power of kings in their struggle against the opposition of feudal lords and helped the sovereigns to enforce the principles of law and order, were pupils of the Sorbonne.

The influence of the brilliant French men of letters, especially of such great thinkers as Montesquieu, Voltaire, Rousseau, was felt and will be steadily felt until the ideals they served find their realization, and their ideals had never taken the form of aspirations for acquiring territory, for military glory and conquests. French patriotism, as a rule, is not directed against foreign countries; it combines very well with cosmopolitanism. The principles of liberty, equality, and brotherhood, proclaimed by the French Revolution, have in view all men, not the people of France alone. France does not separate her interests from those of other nations; the writings of French philosophers, encyclopedists, and moralists have a universal character.[9]

This study will summarize French pacifist thought of two centuries, covering the period from 1611—year of the publication of Dubois's *De recuperatione Terre Sancte*—until 1794—year of the publication of Condorcet's *Esquisse du tableau des progrès de l'esprit humain.*

The authors of the peace projects have been grouped according to the time of the publication of their political schemes.

The place of the representatives of French literature has been determined not only by the time of the appearance of their works in print, but mainly by their particular approach to the issues of war and peace. Some writers saw the main cause of war in the wrong policies of the government, others in religious intolerance. A theological pattern of thought is strongly noticeable in the works of Guez de Balzac, Pascal, and Bossuet. The moralistic approach sharply separated

[9] See Gustave Lanson, *L'Idéal français dans la littérature de la Renaissance à la Révolution,* 1927.

Rousseau and his followers from the philosophers and the encyclopedists. The economists considered free trade as the best remedy against all evils. However different was the approach, the efforts of all these writers were directed toward the attainment of the same goal, the abolition of war, the greatest obstacle in the path leading to the realization of the true ideals of human life.

THE VISION OF WORLD PEACE
IN SEVENTEENTH AND
EIGHTEENTH-CENTURY FRANCE

CHAPTER I

EARLY SEVENTEENTH-CENTURY POLITICAL SCHEMES

THE end of the sixteenth and the first half of the seventeenth centuries in France saw besides her wars against Spain a more dangerous struggle, that of political parties within her own borders. The policies of these groups were determined mainly by the religious denomination of the members. The Edict of Nantes had appeased the dissensions only to a certain point; it did not put an end to them. France longed for peace. This aspiration became particularly evident in 1611, 1623, and 1638, years of the publication of three remarkable plans for world organization, those of Dubois, Crucé, and Sully. These early political schemes seem to testify that already in the seventeenth century, when religion had a powerful hold on hearts, people looking for the establishment of peace sought means towards its realization outside the immediate realm of the Church.

The rôle of the Pope in Dubois's plan, written in the fourteenth century, is very important: the Pope should have the power to call together an International Council, to choose its president, to initiate reforms, and to make the ultimate decision in case the arbiters did not succeed in solving a conflict. Crucé, who wrote three centuries later, assigned the Pope or his legate the first place in the Council; he evidently wished to emphasize the part moral force should play in international politics. In Sully's plan the Pope is merely a member of the General Council on an equal footing with the others. The moral level seems highest in Crucé's plan : contrary to Dubois, he does not allow considerations of economic or imperialistic character to come into the foreground, and the urge for revenge, very apparent in Sully's work, is absent from that of Crucé. While discussing the problem of military sanctions, Crucé hesitates to take a definite stand; he seems to think that war, even in case of extreme urgency, is not a remedy against diseases of political bodies.

PIERRE DUBOIS (1255c.-1312c.), whose name was almost unknown until the second half of the nineteenth century and who is considered now one of the most remarkable men in the history of the peace movement, was born at Coutances or in the suburbs of this Norman town. He studied law at the University of Paris where he had the chance to attend some lectures of the great theologian Thomas Aquinas and of the renowned scholar Siger de Brabant. He evidently took advantage of the opportunities afforded by this institution and he left it a man of sound scholarship and rare culture. Some years after his student life in Paris, we find him back at Coutances, established as a lawyer and consulted especially by people who were menaced by excommunication. He contributed to the triumph of the lay courts over the ecclesiastical tribunals and soon became one of the counselors to the King of France Philippe le Bel. He suggested to the sovereign the weapons the latter should use in his struggle against the Pope; the most powerful of these was the convocation of the States-General (Etats-Généraux). The first assembly of the delegates of all classes of the French people took place in 1302, and unanimous support was given to the King against the Pope. Dubois played a prominent part in this assembly. He became a member of the second assembly of the Etats-Généraux in 1308. His reputation must have been considerable, for he was appointed lawyer to Edward I, King of England and sovereign of Guyenne, an appointment which, however, did not prevent him from carrying on his activities in France as "lawyer of the King for ecclesiastical cases."

The work that made him one of the most famous men in the history of the peace movement was *De recuperatione*

Terre Sancte written in 1305-1307 and published for the first time in 1611, in Bongar's *Gesta Dei per Francos* (II, 316-361), and afterwards by Charles Langlois in 1891. The latter used for his critically revised edition the manuscript of the Vatican. All references have been taken from this edition and translated into English.

The title of Dubois's work, characterized by him as a *Treatise on General Politics,* suggests that the author was preaching a new crusade. E. Renan does not admit it; he thinks that the recovery of the Holy Land was for Dubois only "a pious pretext, an implement of war which allowed him to suggest very bold reforms . . . a utopia which permitted him to develop plans the realization of which in Europe could not be proposed without danger." [1] The following considerations might have led Renan to this conclusion: Dubois was not merely a lawyer in the service of the French King, but a *légiste,* one of those scholars in law who, from this time on, began to use their knowledge for the strengthening of royal power, supporting the kings in their struggle against the all-powerful feudal lords as well as against the overbearing attitude of the Roman Church. The *légistes* were lending to the sovereigns a strong hand in their efforts to create a united France. For them the king, independently of his personal qualities, was a divine being, the symbol of political unity, the embodiment of the nation. With Dubois himself, the cult of the royal power went even further: he was anxious to see the king of France at the head of a universal federation (Dubois repudiated the idea of a universal monarchy). The Pope stood in the way, and Dubois was looking for means to force him into a secondary rôle. According to him, a new crusade against the Turks should be undertaken, this time on the initiative of the French King; the Pope should be deprived of his temporal power, and the greatest part of the revenues of the Church, of the clergy and, above all, of the religious orders should pass into the French treasury and form the basic fund for the crusade. The King of France

[1] E. Renan, "Pierre Du Bois légiste," *Histoire littéraire de la France,* XXVI, 479.

would thus become the defender of the interests of Christianity in the place of the Pope. These considerations possibly led Renan to look at the crusade planned by Dubois as "a pious pretext and an implement of war."

Robert Barroux does not share this opinion. He points to the fact that at the beginning of the fourteenth century many people gave serious thought to a new crusade and did not consider the fall of Saint-Jean d'Acre (1291) the end of Christian domination in the Holy Land. He reminds us of the traveler Marino Sanuto who at this same time was speaking of all the economic advantages which would result from the conquest of Palestine. He mentions also Raymond Lully who, too, at this time, had handed over to the King his plan for the conquest of the Holy Land. Dubois thus was not the only one who thought of a new crusade, but his plan outstripped all the others because it carried with it a whole set of important political, international, and social reforms. "Dubois," says Barroux, finds at one stroke in his thought what modern pacifists at Geneva are trying to find once more half a millennium later, and with what effort?" [2]

One is inclined to share Barroux's opinion and to admit that Dubois was perfectly serious and sincere in proposing a new crusade; he was writing only twelve years after the capture of the Château des Pèlerins, the last Christian stronghold in Palestine. Since the Crusades were mainly inspired by France, it is not surprising that the idea of a new campaign was once more suggested there. Besides, it is not to be forgotten that the plan for taking the Holy Land from the Turks was a general preoccupation in Europe even in the eighteenth century and became a reality through the peculiar political conditions of our own time. Dubois, as a child, had probably heard some of the fascinating stories of the deeds of French knights in the distant East, and those far-away lands could not fail to appeal to his imagination. The *Drang nach Osten* seems to have been in the blood of the men of his time. Religious considerations probably remained in the background of Dubois's thoughts. He saw a new goal of greater value: namely, the

---

[2] "Un Projet français de fédération européenne," *Revue d'histoire diplomatique*, année 47, 1933.

possibility of establishing perpetual peace among the nations of the world united under the hegemony of France. In the strengthening of the position of this country he saw a guarantee for peace.

The edition of 1891 of *De recuperatione Terre Sancte* has 140 pages and consists of 142 paragraphs, plus an appendix. Langlois sees in the first part, paragraphs 1-109, a kind of circular which, according to the hope of the author, was going to be read, besides the King of France, by the King of England, the Pope, and many Christian European sovereigns. The rest of the book, paragraphs 110-142 and the Appendix, was intended only for the French King. Forwarding his work to Philippe le Bel, Dubois asked him to send it to the King of England whom he considered to be the most powerful vassal of the French crown; at the head of the book he had written for the latter a special dedication. He wished his work to be afterwards forwarded to the Pope.

Dubois thought that a common military undertaking of European nations against the Turks would never be successful unless lasting peace could be established among them and a strong union of Catholic nations be formed: "Let no Catholic take up arms against a Catholic, let none spill Christian blood." [3] Dubois speaks of Catholic nations, but he admits as a member of the Union the emperor of Constantinople, although he writes after the separation of the Churches which had taken place in the ninth century. He wants the Catholic nations to form a Republic governed for the furtherance of common interests by a Council of the chiefs of various states or their representatives. It is evident that Dubois does not dream of a universal monarchy; he is even opposed to this idea which he characterizes as insane; the free development of individual activities of various nations seems to him essential:

There is no man of sound mind, I feel certain, who truly thinks that it could be brought about in this secular world, which is the whole world, a condition in which there would be only one ruler

[3] P. Dubois, *De recuperatione Terre Sancte,* éd. Ch. Langlois, 1891, (IV)3, p. 7.

who would govern everything as far as temporal matters are concerned.[4]

Dubois leaves to the Pope, in whom people have always seen a peacemaker, the initiative for calling together an international Council, the choice of its president, and the right to propose reforms.   The idea of peace is the central idea in his work; he even asserts that peace is the end of all human activity: "So truly is universal peace the goal which we try to attain, which we hold of first importance in our thoughts."[5] Peace is not only the aim of war, it presupposes war, he asserts.   Being the great aim of Catholic nations, peace is the immediate objective in their expedition against the Turks. The Council must publish a decree that no Catholic be allowed to take up arms against another Catholic; the penalty for those who dare to disobey will be loss of property and transportation with their family and friends to Palestine, where they will receive a tract of land lying on the border of some savage settlement, so that they can wage useful war against the Mussulmans:

Those who are anxious to fight should direct their efforts against the enemies of the Christian faith and the holy places of our Lord in the Holy Land, not against their brothers, a state which can only result in the ruin of body and soul.[6]

"To make pugnacious people work toward a peaceful end is to create order through the very makers of disorder," Barroux says.[7]   Dubois is of the opinion that the above-mentioned punishment will prove more effective than excommunication:

Let them be punished, but let them not be excommunicated or anathematized, for this imperils the salvation of the soul; the number of the damned should not be increased; it is far better that they receive a worldly rather than an eternal punishment. Granted that a temporal punishment is of less importance than an eternal one, it will, nevertheless, be more greatly feared; besides, it will

[4] *Ibid.*, (XLI), p. 54.
[5] *Ibid.*, 28, p. 21.
[6] *Ibid.*, (IV) 3, p. 7.
[7] *Op. cit.*, p. 240.

be more profitable for the Holy Land and less dreadful for the family and relatives of the accursed.[8]

It is obvious that Dubois is far from opposing war in general; he does not approve of war for the sake of war; he draws our attention to the fact that every war bears in it the seeds of a future war:

Because, the more often they wage war, the greater becomes their desire to fight. . . . Every war in itself is evil and unlawful; war waged for the sake of war is the ultimate of wickedness.[9]

Eliminating war as a means of settlement of conflicts between the members of his Christian Republic, Dubois tries to find a way of settling disputes; he proposes to establish an International Court of Arbitration (he was the first to suggest this) to which the members of the Christian Republic should pledge themselves to appeal in case of a conflict. The arbiters, six in number, three clergymen and three laymen, were to be chosen by the Council among wise, capable, and wealthy men whom it would be impossible to corrupt or to tempt through greed, hatred, fear, or affection. The defendant and the plaintiff would be asked to furnish a detailed statement of the case. Unacceptable claims would be rejected, but if the claims were found worthy of consideration, the parties concerned would be summoned to appear, and the depositions of witnesses would be carefully examined by two jurymen of known probity. In order that the case might be considered from every point of view, the Court would have the right to invite men of experience and knowledge to give their opinions on different questions arising in the course of the procedure. These men should be persons well known for their integrity and impartiality. The records of the cases would be carefully preserved so as to prevent fraud or forgery. Dubois is an advocate of written procedure, for he believes that it saves time and prevents abuses.[10] This International Court planned by him would answer the need of a uniform procedure for all nations; it is one of the ideas most dear to his heart the reali-

[8] Dubois, *op. cit.,* 4, p. 8.
[9] *Ibid.,* (III), p. 4..
[10] *Ibid.,* (IV) 3, p. 7 and (VII) 12, p. 11.

zation of which he, as a lawyer, could appreciate more than any one else. If the parties submit to the decision of the Court readily, the difficulty is solved; if they do not, the arbiters must forward the record to the Pope. The record of his decision must be kept in the archives of the Roman Church. There shall be no further appeal.[11]

If a member of the Republic forfeits his engagements or does not submit to the decision of the Court, he incurs the punishment of excommunication; the signatories are invited to suspend commercial relations with him, and military sanctions may take place.[12]

As it was mentioned above, Dubois does not favor the idea of a universal monarchy, yet the prominent position he assigns in his project to France permits the questioning of a real balance of power in his Christian Republic. He claims for the sovereign of France the throne of the Eastern Roman Empire; he suggests the marriage of the King's brother, Charles de Valois, to Catherine de Courtenay who claimed to have hereditary rights in Constantinople. Through his pamphlets and the influence he exercises as a member of the Etats-Généraux in 1302 and 1308 he does everything in his power to ruin the prestige of the Pope and the clergy; he denies to them any right to *temporalia,* except what is needed for their existence; he helps the Crown to seize the immense riches of the religious orders, especially those of the Templars. In one of his *Memoirs* he advises the King to place his grandson on the throne of Spain and to found a new Eastern Kingdom of which his son, Philippe le Long, would be the sovereign. As for the colony of the Holy Land, it would have Charles II of Anjou for King with the title "King of Jerusalem." This colony would be used by the Christian Republic as an experimental ground for a set of reforms.

It is difficult to judge how much influence Dubois had in his own time since his *De recuperatione Terre Sancte* did not appear in print until 1611. From the fact that the paragraphs 1-109 of this work are a kind of circular addressed to Euro-

[11] *Ibid.,* (VII) 12, pp. 11-12.
[12] *Ibid.,* 101, p. 82.

pean monarchs we may conclude that it might have been known to George Podiebrad (1420-71), King of Bohemia, and Marini, a Frenchman who, from 1460 to 1465, was acting as his envoy to European sovereigns. It is to Podiebrad and Marini that we owe the second scheme for an international organization. It was composed about one hundred and fifty years after Dubois's plan. Marini was commissioned by the King to prepare the draft, copies of which were to be made for the reigning potentates. In this second plan, the conquest of the Holy Land was likewise given as the ultimate goal of the Union planned by the King. The work speaks also of a judicial body which would settle the disputes by arbitration. The Pope would be one of the representatives of the Italian States, but he would play a less important rôle than that allowed him by Dubois.

The envoys of Podiebrad received a very cordial welcome at the Court of Louis XI to whom they handed over the manuscript. There is a copy of it in the *Mémoires de Messire de Commines,* tome II, pp. 424-431, éd. Lenglet du Fresnoy, Londres, 1747.[13]

It seems impossible to find out whether Dubois's work was known to the pacifists of the sixteenth century. They have not suggested definite plans for peace. Erasmus and Suarez believed in arbitration, so urgently recommended by Dubois.

It seems significant that Dubois' work appeared in print in the year following the tragic death of Henry IV. Had it not the power to remind Europe, divided by differences in religious worship, broken up into independent national states, of the benefits of unity and peace?

The publication of Dubois's *De recuperatione Terre Sancte* (1611) was followed in 1623 by that of the outstanding work of EMERIC CRUCÉ (1590-1648), *Le Nouveau Cynée.*[14]

[13] Quoted from J. ter Meulen's *Der Gedanke der intern. Organisation . . .,* 1917.

[14] E. Crucé, *Le Nouveau Cynée* ou *Discours d'Estat représentant les Occasions et Moyens d'Establir une Paix Generale et la Liberté du Commerce par tout le Monde. Aux Monarques et Princes Souverains de ce temps.* Em. Cr. Par. M. DC. XXIII.

In many passages of his book we find thoughts and feelings
to which the century of the Renaissance and Reformation had
given rise. We notice the influence of Rabelais who taught
that every means leading toward a peaceful settlement of an
international dispute should be used before war is made; of
Montaigne, who asserted that our duties to mankind should
prevail over those to individuals, our country, or some particular cause. Besides the influence of French writers one
feels that of such humanists as Erasmus, Thomas More, John
Colet, and, above all, that of the Spanish theologians de Vitoria and Suarez. De Vitoria believed in *ius gentium,* the universal inalienable rights of man; Suarez envisioned a vast
federation of peoples governed by international law.

In his work Crucé, following the example of Cyneas, the
pacifist adviser of the belligerent Pyrrhus of Epirus, tries to
arouse in sovereigns to whom he dedicates his work, the desire
to establish peace among nations:

> Let us lay down arms and put an end to eternal enmities. We
> have stirred up enough storms. It is time to restore calm and
> serenity to this big ocean, pouring into it the oil of perfect recon-
> ciliation. . . . This rests with you, Great Monarchs. You have
> the power to appease the agitations of the world and force your
> peoples to obey natural law and submit to your will. . . . Even if
> you succeed in bringing the whole world under your dominion, a
> thing which was never yet accomplished or ever will be achieved,
> .still you will have to stop, since war is made for the sake of peace.
> What you would do for a universal monarchy, do it now for the
> one which is in your hands.[15]

In speaking thus to the monarchs, Crucé, contrary to
Dubois, has not in view the sovereigns of the Christian nations
alone; he embraces in his conception the whole human race
"formed in the same mould and by the same workman." [16]
He regards all the peoples of the world as one body, the different members of which are in such close interdependence
that the happiness or misery of one affects the whole. Differ-

[15] The pages in the footnotes refer the reader to the latest edition of
Crucé's *Le Novveav Cynée* given with an Introduction and translation
into English by Th. W. Balch in 1909, pp. 135, 137.
[16] *Ibid.,* p. 93.

ences in race or nationality should never, he thinks, be considered adequate reason for war. To those who assert that a Turk and a Persian, a Frenchman and a Spaniard, a Chinese and a Tartar, a Christian and a Jew or a Mahometan can not be on friendly terms, Cruce answers that enmity between them is mainly due to the fact that they belong to different political bodies; they should never be enemies, there is so much likeness between them; they are of the same nature and are closely related by the ties of blood:

Why should I, a Frenchman, bear ill will to an Englishman, a Spaniard, or an Indian? I could not, because I know that they are men, as I am a man, that I am liable to err and sin as much as they, and that all nations are in close relationship through natural and, consequently, indissoluble bonds. Inveterate tradition alone is responsible for the fact that man often sees in his fellow-man a stranger.[17]

There are people, Cruce says, who regard the sowing of dissensions among neighbors as political wisdom. He absolutely refuses to share their point of view:

When the house of your neighbor is afire or is tumbling down, there is plenty of reason for fear and compassion because human society is one body, the organs of which are in such sympathy with each other that the sickness of one affects the other.[18]

Neither can difference of religion be offered as an excuse for bloodshed. All religions, Christian and non-Christian, have for their foundation the same principle: the acknowledgment of the existence of a Supreme Being and His worship. At the source of every religion we find the same belief in supernatural forces; each claims the possession of the whole truth and considers those who belong to other faiths victims of error.[19] Christians laugh at the superstitions of the Mahometans, only to be despised by the latter. Pagans boast of the antiquity of their faith and persist in offering sacrifices. Jews mock the followers of any religion whatever; they are sure they are the chosen people of God since, hated and perse-

17 *Ibid.,* pp. 83, 85.
18 *Ibid.,* pp. 7, 9.
19 *Ibid.,* p. 87.

cuted as they have been at all times, they have yet maintained their position in the world.[20] All those peoples are sincere in their beliefs; their errors are due to their ingenuousness and their lack of knowledge; they deserve pity, not hatred:

It is necessary above all to uproot the most common vice which is the source of all the others, I mean inhumanity.[21]

We must bring about the reign of reason and justice, and not that of violence which is suited only to beasts.[22]

The adoration of God is not a mere outward worship, it is an attitude of mind. Why then should people fight on account of the differences in religious ceremonies? The latter are not to be disregarded, but we must not persecute the persons who do not wish to worship in the same way as ourselves.[23] We should not forget that there is no physical force that has the power to compel a man to change his opinion and no method of gaining assurance that he has done so. Therefore, tolerance should be the guiding principle in the relations between individuals and nations of different religious creeds:

Since it [religion] is a supernatural gift, it must come from God, and not from men who, with all their arms, have not the power to force their fellow-men to believe its mysteries. . . . Let those who profess true religion thank God for this Grace and do their best to show this by their good deeds. Let them not try to subdue imperiously the beliefs of others. . . . It is not for men to punish and correct the errors of faith. It is for Him who sees the hearts of men and their most secret thoughts. The faults of the will are punishable by the civil law; those of knowledge, namely, false doctrines, have God alone for judge.[24]

Besides, is not religion, in the so-called religious wars, merely a means to cover the other real reasons of conflict?[25] The sovereigns, while waging war, often try to find an excuse for doing so; they allege the necessity of defending or of up-

20 *Ibid.*, p. 85.
21 *Ibid.*, Préface, pp. 1, 3.
22 *Ibid.*, p. 133.
23 *Ibid.*, p. 87.
24 *Ibid.*, p. 97.
25 *Ibid.*, pp. 17, 19.

holding their honor. The word "honor," according to Crucé, covers many things besides dignity and integrity of reputation. Ambitious plans, a longing for domination, for triumph, for glory are usually implied in that word; and yet glory does not often crown a war; failure is more common than success. Sovereigns are foolish in putting their honor at stake, in listening to those who speak of what may be acquired by war; they forget to mention what may be lost. "Not triumphal arches, but ignominious subjection may be the consequence of war." [26]

A wise sovereign, then, will not invade the state of another prince, afraid as he will be of losing his own. If ambition induces him to risk his life and that of his subjects, let him at least spare his good name. . . . Those who wage wars place themselves on the brink of ruin; a slight wind, and they are hurled into the abyss of perdition; and when they think they are at the height of their prosperity, a reverse of fortune will make them, former sovereigns, slaves. . . . War hazards the reputation of a sovereign rather than augments it. And even if his name should become as great as was the fame of Caesar; if his victories should make him the ruler of a universal empire, would it not be a cruel thing to obtain it in so despicable a manner? What a miserable thing is honor if it must be bought by the shedding of blood? [27]

As for the profit one hopes to gain by war, it is very illusory, for even a victorious war is a loss for the victor: "For two soldiers who will enrich themselves in it, there will be fifty who will gain in it nothing but blows and incurable disease." [28]

The attraction which war, as a kind of sport, has for some men should have as little weight as the opinion that lasting peace weakens men. Every one knows that in time of peace as well as in time of war a country needs men of physical strength, courage, and abounding vitality. "Cursed nature which seeks rest in worry, honor in infamy, and amusement in inhumanity." [29]

[26] *Ibid.,* pp. 25, 27.
[27] *Ibid.,* pp. 27, 29.
[28] *Ibid.,* p. 31.
[29] *Ibid.,* p. 43.

According to Crucé, among the main causes underlying foreign wars there is only one that may be called excusable; namely, the desire for reparation of a wrong that has been committed, and even this excuse, he says, is hardly acceptable, since victory is not necessarily for the victim.   One may ask then: Must a nation submit supinely to the will of an aggressor?   Crucé seems to preach the doctrine of non-resistance, for he says that God has established the division of lands and can take them away or transfer them as he wills; the prince who has lost his territory has to reconcile himself to the decree of the Almighty:

The Princes . . . must know that God is not held to continue his blessing in one place, that if He transferred their scepter to another hand, He has done the same favor to their predecessors . . . in giving them an absolute power to enjoy it as long as it should please Him, and not otherwise.   Let them, therefore, not complain of a misfortune common to all States, let them not complain of an usurpation which . . . is authorized by the will of God; let them renounce their vain hopes and restrain their useless desire for vengeance.[30]

and in another place he writes:

Let every prince be satisfied with the territory he possesses and not go beyond its frontiers under any pretext. . . . Let him consider that the boundaries of kingdoms and seignories are set by the hand of God who takes them away and conveys them when and where He thinks fit; let the prince not try to regain the possession God had granted to his race for a limited period of time.[31]

Do we not notice in these lines the influence of Greek Stoics? They taught that man should be unsubdued by misfortune. The train of thought of Roman Stoics (Seneca, Marcus Aurelius) is also strongly felt, for they envisaged the world as a common dwelling of the human race and considered as absurd its division into separate provinces and peoples. From the point of view of the Christian Church (Crucé, according to some statements, was a Catholic priest or monk) which affirms that all men are children of the same Father, the shift-

30 *Ibid.*, p. 39.
31 *Ibid.*, p. 129.

ing of power from one sovereign to another should not appear a tragically important event. Such especially seems to be the point of view of the Roman Church which, after Constantinople and the Eastern Greek Orthodox Church had fallen into the hands of the Turks (1453), became naturally the only link tying separate European Christian peoples together.

After recommending non-resistance to violence as a matter of principle, Crucé discusses this policy from a practical point of view:

He [the prince] had better try to keep what he still possesses, not running the risk of losing it for a doubtful gain.[32]

The wisest policy, however, in case of a conflict, is recourse to arbitration:

Even if they [the princes] could avenge themselves, they should take another course and, before having recourse to arms, resort to the arbitration of Potentates and Sovereigns. In doing so, they would gain the friendship of the latter to prevail over the enemies in case they did not agree to submit to the judgment of the third party.[33]

The lines in which Crucé explicitly recommends non-resistance to violence and arbitration allow one to conclude that of the five causes which, according to him, lead to war—difference of race or nationality, difference of religion, desire for profit, the attraction which war has for those who see in it a kind of sport, the desire for reparation of a wrong that has been done—not one is either excusable or admissible. War has had its day and should be abolished for ever. Crucé speaks with irony of people who make plans for new crusades:

Some exhort the Christian Princes that by their union they fortify themselves against their common enemy; and even a famous personage has shown the means to exterminate the Turks in four years or in approximately that time.[34]

[32] *Ibid.*, p. 129.
[33] *Ibid.*, p. 39.
[34] *Ibid.*, p. 7, Préface. Crucé may well be referring here to Dubois. See M. Vesnitch, "Emeric Crucé," *Revue d'hist. diplomatique*, 1911.

In full harmony with his principles is Cruce's statement that the main task of a sovereign is the establishing and maintaining of peace. This explains the fact that he dedicates his work to the monarchs and sovereign princes of his time. He tries to make them understand that the greatness of a prince does not rest on the vastness of his dominions or the glory of his conquests; it rests on the ready submission of his subjects to his will, on his ascendency over them which may easily be lost in time of war.[35] The greatest ambition of a sovereign should be, therefore, the preservation of peace on the basis of the *status quo*. Cruce is of the opinion that it is much harder to keep a territory than to subdue it. Conquest depends only on the strength of the army while three conditions are needed for the preservation of the subdued country: the conqueror must be endowed with great circumspection; he must know how to make the conquered people love him and must be in a position to make them happy.[36]

Though the history of mankind seems to be mainly the history of war, there were periods of lasting peace of which the most significant was the first two centuries of the Roman Empire. Under the *Pax Romana* all nations belonging to the Empire enjoyed a lasting peace. What took place once can take place again, in more perfect form; centuries have not passed in vain.

Taking peace as the essential condition for the advancement of civilization, Cruce develops a vast plan of reforms. He is above all interested in activities which bring men into close relations. His suggestions regarding trade, currency, construction of roads, bridges, canals were very valuable for his time. He was one of the first to draw attention to the necessity of uniting the seas.[37]

Cruce was an advocate of free trade; he felt sure that this policy would greatly promote international relations; at the same time, being cautious, he did not endorse it fully; he wished a system of limited protection which, not preventing the freedom of trade, would at the same time allow the sov-

[35] Cruce, *op. cit.*, p. 49.
[36] *Ibid.*, pp. 157, 161.
[37] *Ibid.*, p. 61.

ereign to draw some revenue from foreign commerce. The drawback to international trade being piracy, he invited all the European states to unite in an effort to suppress it. In order to transform pirates into good citizens, he suggested that they be settled on the land and turned into farmers.[38]

It is also in the *Nouveau Cynée* that we find, perhaps for the first time in world literature, the thought that it is the duty of every man, regardless of his position and his wealth, to do his part in a common effort to benefit the community—it being the duty of a sovereign to see that this principle is carried out.[39]

Crucé wants every young man, as soon as he leaves school (Public Academy), to be forced to choose a profession. In blaming the Egyptians and Lacedaemonians for having compelled their sons to carry on the profession of the father, he declares himself, in principle, on the side of free vocational choice. But afraid as he is that certain professions may be overcrowded, that there may be too many judges, lawyers, physicians, and, above all, too many soldiers, priests, and monks who, if too numerous, weaken the state, he insists on the establishment of a quota based on the general census of the population. He does not think it necessary to establish a quota for farmers, craftsmen, laborers, and merchants, since the greatness and the wealth of a state rests with them. All those measures are recommended in order to maintain peace inside the state.[40]

The above is but a rapid sketch of the general trend of Crucé's thought. We pass now to the discussion of the most important contribution made by this writer to the idea of an international organization of the world.

After giving his reasons for the abolition of war, Crucé offers a plan for the establishment of permanent peace. He suggests calling together in some city the representatives of all sovereigns, without any discrimination as to race or creed. He suggests the inclusion of India, China, Persia, Ethiopia, Morocco, etc., the only provision being that the reigning

---

[38] *Ibid.*, pp. 69, 71, 73.
[39] *Ibid.*, p. 293.
[40] *Ibid.*, pp. 293, 295, 297.

princes be independent. He thinks that it would be proper for the Pope to take the initiative with the Christian sovereigns; for the king of France, with the others:

There is no one more capable of that than the Pope. It is his duty to bring about a general concord among the Christian princes. And in regard to the Mahometans, who form a considerable part of the world, the king of France, on account of the reputation and the prestige he has among them, will more easily make them condescend to peace.[41]

Whatever the case may be, it is more becoming that the Christians should speak of peace first, if it were only to enjoy the freedom of going to the Holy Sepulchre.[42]

The Council of Representatives should constitute a permanent body, ready at any moment to take care of any menacing situation that might arise on the political horizon. Crucé stresses again and again the necessity of an uninterrupted activity on the part of the Council. Treaties can never ensure peace:

Suppose that peace is announced today to the whole world. Can we be sure that our successors will ratify its articles? Opinions are changeable, and the actions of the men of the present time do not bind their successors.[43]

Crucé suggests Venice as the seat of the Council. It has a central location, situated as it is between the Papal States and the Holy Roman Empire. Persia, China, Ethiopia, the East, and the West Indies are, no doubt, very far from Venice, but every step forward in the art of navigation cuts down the distance; and he adds that one should not refuse to take the trouble of a long voyage for the sake of a great end.[44]

Every ambassador would plead the cause of his own country, and those who would not be parties in the dispute would act as arbiters. We see that Crucé evolves a definite plan for an international court of arbitration. The final decision would be based on the majority of votes. If there were a tie, depu-

[41] *Ibid.*, p. 341.
[42] *Ibid.*, p. 343.
[43] *Ibid.*, p. 101.
[44] *Ibid.*, p. 103.

ties of the Republics of Venice and Switzerland would be invited to vote. Crucé does not seem inclined to make republics regular members of his Union. He sees in republics a tendency toward revolution and is more afraid of the rule of the populace than of the tyranny of the sovereigns. Military sanctions are anticipated for the signatories who would refuse to submit to the decision of the court of arbitration.[45] But he does not really think there would be many cases of recourse to armed force. He has faith in human nature and thinks that, with few exceptions, moral compulsion would prove quite sufficient.

Crucé's work is an outstanding one in many ways: while Dubois's Union was planned to include Christian nations only, Crucé's Union was of a universal character. To have thought of a political body which would accept on equal footing members of different races and creeds testifies to an unusual broadness of mind and an amazing tolerance, especially at a time when the Inquisition was still claiming numberless victims. Cannot his tolerance be explained by his somewhat deistic convictions? Many lines in his work can be taken for early expressions of deism. He cannot see any excuse for bloodshed among men "formed in the same mould and by the same workman." He condemns war because he loves men and pities their sufferings; but he condemns it also as being in contradiction with the dignity of human nature and man's worth, and as something which ruins the economic welfare of the world. Crucé believes to a greater extent than did Dubois in the power of moral compulsion, but his knowledge of man and of life forces him to admit the necessity of securing submission to the decrees of the Council through armed force in certain exceptional cases. Contrary to Dubois, he is not at all anxious to give France a dictatorial power in the Union; he wants to see her merely one of the many members of his organization.

Crucé was credited with having given the first positive plan for an international court of arbitration. It seems, however, that our tribute with regard to this particular point should go to Guillaume Aubert (1534-1601), whose *Oraison de la Paix*

[45] *Ibid.,* p. 121.

et les Moyens de l'entretenir was published in Paris in 1559, and above all to Dubois.

Two years after the publication of *Le Nouveau Cynée,* namely, in 1625, appeared in print the *De Jure Belli ac Pacis* of Grotius. The latter, living in France as an exile while he was working on his famous treatise, might have been influenced by Crucé.

While Crucé had taken the *status quo* for the starting point of his scheme for a world organization, SULLY (1559-1641), on the contrary, in his peace project of 1638 which he speaks of as *Le Grand Dessein de Henri IV,*[46] stressed the thought that to admit the existing political organization of Europe meant to renounce every hope for a lasting peace, and this for three major reasons: a glance at the map of Europe, he asserted, is sufficient to make one realize that the territories which were in the possession of different states were so unequal in size and natural resources that there could not be any question about the balance of power—the cornerstone of a society aiming to maintain peace. Another cause of eternal unrest lay in the fact that the peace treaties, in allowing a territory to become an integral part of a state, did not take into consideration the principle of nationality, and, finally, one could hardly hope for lasting peace before freedom of religious thought and worship was guaranteed.

The first and only reference to the *Great Design* during the life of Henry IV is in a letter written to the King by Sully in 1593. He asks his master to form a Union of all sovereigns who fear the ever-growing power of the House of Austria. Years after the death of the King, reconstructing in his memory his life and work during the past reign, Sully saw himself talking to his master and, full of devotion to his memory, he ascribed to the King the scheme which had ripened by and by in his own mind.

[46] Sully, Maximilien de Béthune, "Mémoires des sages et royales Oeconomies d'Estat . . .," *Nouvelle Collection des Mémoires relatifs à l'Histoire de France,* éd. Michaud et Poujoulat, 1854, vol. XVI et XVII.

Your plan, Sully sees himself saying to the King, is to have Europe divided in such a way that the balance of power and the principle of nationality be maintained: small states should receive some parts of the large ones with a population homogeneous to that of their main territories. The domain of the Pope, for example, should have the Kingdom of Naples; the Venetian Republic—Sicily; the Duc of Savoy—Milan and Lombardy; the Helvetian Republic—Tyrol, Franche—Comté, Alsace, Trent, Istria, and Trieste; Hungary—Transylvania, Moldavia, and Wallachia. Your plan is that all closely associated states solemnly request the Emperor of the Holy Roman Empire and the King of Spain (the two sovereigns who embody the spirit of domination of the House of Austria) to prevent forever the possibility that the title of Emperor become hereditary or that two princes of the same House be elected to the throne. They would request them to agree to the organization of a new Italian Republic and of two elective kingdoms which probably would play an important part in the defense of Europe against the Turks. The King of Spain would be requested to give up his claim on the Low Countries and establish them as a sovereign republic. In this manner Europe would be divided into fifteen dominions of about the same size, strength, and wealth; there would be:

Six hereditary monarchies: France, Spain, Great Britain, Sweden and Norway, Denmark, Lombardy (Piedmont, Milan).

Five elective states: The Holy Roman Empire, The States of the Pope, Hungary, Bohemia, Poland.

Four republics: Venice, The Netherlands, The Helvetian Republic, The Italian Republic (Florence, Genoa, Parma, Modena, Mantua, Lucca).

Your plan, Sully sees himself saying to the King, is to have the borders of the European states so placed that powerful and ambitious princes would realize the vanity of any effort toward expansion and thus spare other monarchs the torments of suspicion, jealousy, and fear. Maps upon which the borders of each state would be carefully indicated, the estimate of the revenues of each state, and the determination of the form of its government would prevent conflicts.[47]

It is obvious that the main idea of the political plan of Sully was the altering of the map of Europe at the expense of the Habsburgs. It is, however, noteworthy that his plan did not aim to reduce the enormous colonial empire of Spain. Sully hoped that this powerful State would be satisfied with the territory properly called Spain inclusive of Navarre, with the islands of Sardinia, Cape-Verde, the Baleares, the Canaries, and the Azores, with its possessions in Africa, in America (Mexico and many islands), and in Asia (the Philippines, Goa, the Moluccas, etc.).

France, in the thought of Sully, would not play the part of an aggressor or declare war. Her ambition was to assume the rôle of mediator and peacemaker on the continent of Europe without aiming at any prerogatives or territorial acquisitions, as one can see from the following lines:

No military aggression, no declaration of war . . . will take place either for establishing new states or increasing or decreasing the size of those already in existence.[48]

Those who are to belong to your party must be well aware of the fact that you do not aim at any other prerogative or title than that of protector and defender of all legitimate rights or such that have been legalized by long possession or universal approval.[49]

In order to prevent every occasion which might fill anyone with distrust, jealousy, or arouse suspicion that you might be aspiring to a greater title, power, authority, wealth, or enlargement of territory, it is advisable that you exhibit in the enjoyment of your privileges the greatest modesty so that you may be an example worthy of imitation.[50]

It is desirable that you show the greatest wish to establish peace among all European potentates. As soon as you see the least dispute or contention arise among them, your intention should be to try to find a way of maintaining tranquillity and peace among them . . . making it clear to those with whom you are negotiat-

[47] *Ibid.*, XVII, pp. 150-154.
[48] *Ibid.*, XVII, 329.
[49] *Ibid.*, XVII, 151.
[50] *Ibid.*, XVII, 153.

ing that your generous decision is to do everything for others and to disregard your own advantages.[51]

Sully saw, however, that the House of Austria would never subscribe to a plan which was likely to assure the predominance of its rival, the House of France; therefore, a last European war seemed to him unavoidable and he praised the wisdom of his master for the treaties of mutual assistance signed with England, Sweden, and the Protestant princes of Germany.

King Henry's most natural ally was Queen Elizabeth of England. "She was no more devoted to Protestantism than Henry to Catholicism. They were both philosophical statesmen who saw that various religions could be used as agencies of civilization." [52] She supported the Low Countries in their struggle for freedom of religion and their political independence. An interview between these two sovereigns was planned for the time when Elizabeth would come to Dover and Henry to Calais (1601). It did not take place "owing to certain difficult questions of protocol raised by their malevolent advisers," as Sully says.[53] The plan for peace was not abandoned, however, and the deliberations took place in England where Sully went as the representative of the King of France.

The death of Queen Elizabeth (1603) was a terrible blow to Henry IV, for it threatened to ruin his great design. He decided, however, not to abandon the project and win to his ideas James I. A solemn embassy was sent to England with this objective and strong allies were gained in Germany. Sully asserts that on the untimely death of the King in 1610, an army of thirty-six thousand infantry and eight thousand cavalry, inured to the hardships of war, well disciplined and trained, was ready to take to field at the first sign of the King.

Sully thought that if this last war against the House of Austria had been waged, peace among the European nations would have been assured for ever. They would have formed one Christian Republic "always pacific with all Christians,

[51] *Ibid.*, XVII, 151.
[52] E. York, *Leagues of Nations Ancient, Mediaeval, and Modern,* 1919, p. 86.
[53] Sully, *op. cit.,* XVII, 327.

always militant with infidels." [54] Since reciprocal oaths and pledges once given cannot be retracted, the guilty member would bring upon himself the righteous wrath of the Union, possibly aggression and war.[55]

Speaking of the "Christian Republic," Sully became quite a dreamer : he anticipated the brotherhood that would prevail among the members ; none would be inclined to cherish ambitious plans in a society where ambition was not likely to lead anywhere.[56]

Full freedom of commerce would strengthen the mutual bonds.[57] All matters of general interest, especially those that might lead to conflicts, would be under the jurisdiction of the General Council.[58] Consisting of the plenipotentiaries from all governments, it would be a permanent organization ; the delegates, constantly assembled, would deliberate on the political, civil, and religious affairs of Europe ; above all, they would try to pacify the disputes.

The Assembly itself would determine the manner of proceedings.[59] On different pages of his *Mémoires* Sully gives different numbers of the representatives to the Senate : 40, 60, 66, and 70, one of the many contradictions in his work that can be easily explained by the fact that certain parts of it were written by his secretaries. The number 66 is referred to more often than the others. France, England, Spain, Germany, and the Holy See would send more delegates and have more votes than the other members. Elections would take place every three years. Every member-state would choose in turn the seat of the General Council among the following fifteen important cities of central Europe : Paris (or Bourges), Metz, Nancy, Cologne, Mayence, Trèves, Frankfort, Würzburg, Heidelberg, Spire, Worms, Strasbourg, Basle, Besançon, and Luxembourg. If need should arise, the General Council might separate into three sections which

[54] *Ibid.*, XVII, 428.
[55] *Ibid.*, XVII, 330.
[56] *Ibid.*, XVII, 153, 329.
[57] *Ibid.*, XVII, 329.
[58] *Ibid.*, XVII, 154.
[59] *Ibid.*, XVII, 154.

would hold their sessions simultaneously in three cities: Paris (or Bourges), Trent, and Cracow.

The General Council would be assisted by six Local Councils; their seats would be: Danzig, for the northeastern part of the Republic; Vienna, for the eastern part; Nüremberg, for Germany; Bologna, for Italy; Constance for Switzerland; and one yet to be chosen, for France, England, Spain, and the Netherlands.[60] Those Local Councils would regulate matters of secondary importance. If need arose for appeal, they would refer the questions to the General Council, the decisions of that body being irrevocable.

The Councils would be the most important institutions in the new organization of Europe; they would be in a position to settle all differences between the members of the Republic; in this respect the rôle of the General Council could never be overestimated: it was to take note of all proposals, interpellations, designs, amendments, dissensions, wars, in short, of everything which might be of concern to the Christian Republic.[61]

One of the most important functions of the General Council would be the choice of senators who, in matters of dispute among the member-states, would constitute a Court of Arbitration; in case of non-submission to the sentence, international armed force would be used. This force would be placed in the hands of the General Council by the Allied Powers who would make contributions, according to their ability, to provide for all the needs of the Union.[62]

The bloody religious wars of the sixteenth century and the horrors of the Spanish Inquisition had taught the nations of Europe (to a certain extent) the folly of intolerance. In the new Republic three Churches were to be admitted on equal footing: the Catholic, the Lutheran, and the Calvinist. A certain order and a definite procedure were to be established to secure the peaceful coexistence of these three denominations. In case of disputes among them, they would be

[60] *Ibid.*, XVII, 350.
[61] *Ibid.*, XVII, 350.
[62] *Ibid.*, XVII, 153, 154.

obliged to refer to arbitration.[63] In states like France where
the population is divided between two Churches one of
them would be considered as gover 'ng as long as the ruler
neither changed his denomination nor was succeeded by a
ruler of a different denomination.   Those who disliked this
kind of regulation could leave the country. "Sully's view on
toleration is simply the orthodox 'cujus regio, eius religio.' " [64]
Since the Moscovites belong to the Greek-Orthodox Eastern
Church, war against them is permissible, perhaps even desirable. "Le puissant Knès Scithien," as Sully calls the Russian
monarch, might conceivably nourish the ambition to possess
Constantinople which, at the dawn of the history of this country, was once invaded by Oleg (911), the reigning Prince of
Russia.   One might read this consideration between the lines
of Sully's *Mémoires*.   The fact is that Sully did not invite
Russia to become a member of his Christian Republic, at least
not for the time being:

> In spite of the fact that the powerful tzar of Russia (Knès
> Scithien) rules far more absolutely than any other sovereign over
> his subjects among whom in the boundless expanses of northern
> Scithia is found the greatest diversity of peoples, languages, char-
> acters, and colors; in spite of the fact that for more than five hun-
> dred years he has been one of the Christian potentates; we do not
> find it wise to invite him to become a member of our Association
> . . . and this for many reasons.[65]

1. A considerable part of Russia lies within the borders of
Asia.

2. It comprises a great number of different peoples some of
whom are on an extremely low level of culture.

3. Russia borders on the powerful empires of Tartary,
Turkey, and Persia; the Christian Republic, accepting Russia
as member, might be involved in her wars against her neighbors.

4. Many of the peoples of Russia are heathen.

5. There are too many superstitious practices in this coun-

[63] *Ibid.*, XVII, 154, 327, 329, 330.
[64] "Sully's Grand Design of Henry IV," *The Grotius Society Publications*, II, 33, editor's footnote.
[65] Sully, *op. cit.*, XVII, 348.

try, and the religious ceremonies of the Orthodox Church differ too much from the rituals of the three denominations which are to be regarded as State Churches.[66]

The wise policy, in the opinion of Sully, would be to wait for the time when Russia herself would express the desire to join the Republic and, consequently, be more ready than before to consider the principles on which the Union would be built. Strangely enough, Sully did not seem to consider a change of religion a hopeless proposition in so far as the Turks were concerned:

The Turks will have to choose: either to leave Europe, taking with them all they possess, or to join one of the three Christian denominations. If they refuse, a merciless war will be waged against them until they return to Asia.[67]

And this war was so strongly anticipated that certain military actions were planned by Sully beforehand: an international army would defend Hungary against the Turks, Poland against the Tartars and the Moscovites. He even spoke of a joint interallied command and of the strength of the army and navy.[68]

War against those who were not members of the Union was for Sully also a means of getting rid of restless, seditious, and criminal elements in every state of the Union as well as a means of acquiring new lands. It should be, however, noted that the author was in favor of conquests only on the condition that they would be undertaken as response to the vote of the Senate, who would have to decide later on the division and use of the acquired territory.[69]   Speaking of a common campaign, Sully did not forget to remind all the members that peace among them could be preserved only on the condition that no harm would be done to the population of the allied country through whose territory the army would have to pass.[70]

[66] *Ibid.,* XVII, 348.

[67] See J. Hodé, *L'Idée de fédération internationale dans l'histoire,* 1921, p. 77.

[68] Sully, *op. cit.,* XVII, 351-353.

[69] *Ibid.,* XVII, 329-330.

[70] *Ibid.,* XVII, 330.

The question as to whether we owe the *Great Design* to
Henry IV or to Sully occupied the mind of many people.
A. H. Fried,[71] Elizabeth York,[72] and some others are inclined
to believe Sully's assertion that the plan was conceived by
his master.   Some other scholars, J. ter Meulen,[73] Jacques
Hodé,[74] Sir Geoffrey Butler,[75] and Theodor Kükelhaus[76]
whose doctoral dissertation aimed at solving this problem do
not admit it.   At the present time, after much laborious research, it is generally believed that *Le Grand Dessein de
Henri IV* is Sully's plan conceived and written about twenty-
five years after the King's death.[77]   This question remains,
however, a matter of secondary importance; there is hardly
anyone who would not be ready to share the opinion of E. D.
Mead who says:

Whether Shakespeare or Bacon wrote Hamlet, our chief interest is in the possession of Hamlet.   Whether the King or his minister conceived the *Great Design,* our chief interest is in the fact
that this broad and bold program of world organization was
worked out in that critical period of history.[78]

Unlike the *Nouveau Cynée, Le Grand Dessein de Henri IV*
did not aim to establish a universal union; it had only Europe
in view, and in Europe only countries whose inhabitants were

[71] *Handbuch der Friedensbewegung,* 1911-1913.
[72] *Op. cit.*
[73] *Op. cit.*
[74] *Op. cit.*
[75] *Studies in Statecraft,* 1920.
[76] *Der Ursprung des Planes vom ewigen Frieden in den Memoiren des
Herzogs von Sully,* 1893.
[77] Dr. ter Meulen, in the above cited work, advances the following
points in support of this opinion: 1) The contradictions one finds in
the *Mémoires.* 2) The lack of connection between the different parts.
3) The well-known fact that people often use a name of great prestige
to impress readers or listeners in order to force them to give credence
to their opinions.   4) Sully's effort to show that the ideals of his time
were superior to those of Louis XIII and Richelieu.   5) The treaty
which Henry IV, Elizabeth Tudor, and the Government of the Netherlands were about to sign in 1597 was not meant to have as a result the
creation of the Federated States of Europe.   It was rather an attempt to
form an alliance against the powerful House of Austria.
[78] E. D. Mead, *The Great Design of Henry IV,* 1909. Introduction, p.
xi.

either Catholics or Protestants. The Eastern Church to which belongs most of the population of the lands where Christianity was established by the Apostles was not admitted by Sully, and Christian Russia was excluded from membership in his Christian Republic. This would leave great possibilities for war in the world at large. There is another reason why some internationalists question Sully's pacifist trend of thought: like Dubois, though to a lesser extent, he gives too prominent a place to France in his plan, and his scheme, as Thomas Balch says in the *Introduction* to his edition of the *Nouveau Cynée* (1909) "is based upon the idea of building up a great league of smaller European Powers around the French monarchy."

Nevertheless it must be admitted that the *Grand Dessein* was not inspired by egotistic considerations alone. No doubt, it aimed above all at the safety and happiness of France, but her safety was dependent on the safety and happiness of the other European countries. The road to this goal lay through the creation of an International Tribunal before whom the particular interests of individual states would give way to those of the Union.

Many thoughts in the political schemes of Dubois, Crucé, and Sully were real revelations in the then untrodden field of world organization. The necessity for having a permanent body of delegates to represent the members of the league of independent national states, the settling of international disputes through arbitration, the obligatory recourse to it for every member state—are not those the basic ideas upon which the attention of the League of Nations has been centered in our day? Closer to their own time, in the seventeenth century, their influence could be traced in the works of J. A. Komensky and William Penn.

John Amos Komensky (1592-1670), the famous Moravian bishop and educationist, wrote after the Thirty Years' War. In his *Panegersia* (General Awakening) and *Angelus Pacis* he appeals to monarchs, scholars, and preachers entreating them to direct their efforts towards the establishment of peace.

He points out the necessity for giving the right of self-determination even to the smallest national groups; he insists on abandoning secret diplomacy; in that he anticipates the Abbé de Saint-Pierre.   He insists also on the unification of Churches in order to assure the triumph of the Christian religion, on the creation of a universal "pansophic" language, on the opening of a universal college to promote intellectual cooperation, and on the establishment of periodical meetings of the representatives of all European nations in a congress to meet half-way any conflict that might arise.   He thinks that peace might be brought about by education.[79]

In 1696 William Penn (1644-1718), a man who knew from the moment he had settled in America and to the end of his life how to retain the affection of Indians and how to deal with them without having recourse to arms, published his *Essay Toward the Present and Future Peace of Europe.*[80] Son of an English admiral, he was won during his years at Oxford, at Lincoln's Inn, and at Saumure in France, to the doctrine of the Quakers, a doctrine of tolerance and brotherliness which made him opposed to any discrimination as to race and creed. As a Quaker, he protests against war.   In his *Essay* he shows himself a proponent of the establishment of a European Diet in which the number of delegates would be in accordance with the importance of the state, but in which no country would have more than one vote. All differences would be brought before this sovereign assembly.   The decision, requiring a majority of three-fourths, would be taken after a secret ballot and supported by armed force in case of nonsubmission of the party concerned.   That is the only kind of war W. Penn does not refuse to sanction.   We see that he has many ideas in common with the French pacifists of his century.

[79] See A. Heyberger, *Jean Amos Comenius* (Komensky), 1928.
[80] William Penn, *An Essay Toward the Present and Future Peace of Europe,* 1912 [1696].

CHAPTER II

CRITICS OF THE POLICIES OF LOUIS XIV

HOWEVER significant and convincing the arguments in favor of peace brought up in the early seventeenth-century political schemes, there is no trace of their direct influence during the reign of Louis XIV (1643-1715). The persecution of all dissenters and thirty-two years of war are undeniable features of this in other respects epoch-making reign. Official praise of the King's military achievements, in which he, faithful to the tradition among monarchs, saw his greatest glory, was not lacking; however, hardly any voices exulting in the ruler's triumphs could be heard among the best representatives of French literature: the thoughts of RACINE (1639-1699) were for the victims of war.[1] LA FONTAINE (1621-1695) deplored the fate of the humble whose right he saw crushed by might.[2] In his fables he frequently used the lion as a symbol of the King; he spoke of his tremendous force, yet he did so without enthusiasm or admiration; he knew too well how easily force becomes a menace to independence which he valued the most highly among all blessings. In his fable *Les Compagnons d'Ulysse,* Ulysses tries to make the wolf feel ashamed of being a bloodthirsty beast. The wolf answers:

> You treat me like a savage beast,
> But what are you? Do not you feast
> At flying at each other's throat
> When lured by slightest hope to gloat?
> You act like wolves among yourselves.[3]

[1] "Lettre écrite à Boileau le 21 mai 1692," *Oeuvres, éd. Mesnard,* 1870, VII, 34.
[2] *Oeuvres,* éd. Régnier, 1892, "Le Loup et l'Agneau."
[3] *Ibid.,* III, 178.

In his *Ode pour la paix* we find the following lines:

> Dearest Peace, source of all that is good,
> Come to bless and enrich our earth,
> To erase every slightest trace
> That recalls the passed terrors of war.[4]

One must admit that some of the works of BOILEAU (1636-1711) were written with the aim of celebrating the victories of Louis XIV; this writer might have been quite sincere in his praise: exploits of war, which at all epochs of history had enchanted masses of people, aroused enthusiasm also in his heart; however, in moments of quiet thought, and especially in times when a new war promising to give birth to a thousand evils was on the point of being declared, his attitude was not the same. In his *Satire VIII* he points to the fact that men, unfortunately, are very prone to find their honor in the extermination of their fellowmen.[5] He looks on the thirst for conquests as upon a kind of madness and regrets that the tutor of Alexander of Macedonia had not restrained in good time the young man and kept this conqueror from setting on fire the whole of Asia.[6] In his *Epître I* he clearly shows himself opposed to war.[7] Boileau pictures Cyneas, the wise adviser of the King of Epirus, trying to cool his master's ardor for military adventures; then, giving up the form of a parable, he openly expresses to Louis XIV his ideal of a peaceful and peace-making ruler of a state. The following quotation illustrates this point:

> I understand, all is to be subdued:
> We'll cross the boundless Libyan sands,
> Bring under our control Egyptian and Arabian lands,
> Obtain the shores where flows the Ganges toward the East,
> Lay down the Scythians camped the Pontus banks along,
> Thus bringing endless tracts beneath our sway.

[4] *Ibid.*, VIII, 380, "Ode écrite avant la conclusion de la paix des Pyrénées (1659)."

[5] N. Boileau, *Oeuvres*, éd. Berriat Saint-Prix, 1830, I, 171, "Satire VIII."

[6] *Ibid.*, I, 168.

[7] By means of this work Boileau hoped to give support to Colbert, the Minister of Finance, who was trying to dissuade the King from declaring a new war.

But those great deeds achieved, what lies ahead of us?
—Oh then, dear friend, oh then, victorious, satisfied,
Our mind released from care, we'll lead a merry life . . .   ▪
—From this time on, great King, here in your castle,
Enjoy in peace your days from morn till night!

. . . . .

Widespread the fame of those renowned in siege and battle,
While those who sacrifice for peace—they go unsung.
The names of conqu'rors, sword in hand, are legion,
Each cent'ry boasts its own.
Yet are there not more worthy deeds
Than those of warring heroes?

. . . . .

How rare are kings intent on peace
And subjects' happiness! How rare are they!
A search through score on score of years
Yields scarce a name.[7a]

It is perfectly clear what trend of thought Boileau would like to stir up in the King's mind, but he is very reserved in his criticism. Some other writers sounded more discordant notes

[7a] *Ibid.*, II, 13, "Epître I."
Je vous comprends, Seigneur, nous allons tout dompter:
Nous allons traverser les sables de Libye,
Asservir, en passant, l'Egypte, l'Arabie,
Courir de là le Gange en de nouveaux pays,
Faire trembler le Scythe au bord du Tanaïs
Et ranger sous nos lois tout ce vaste hémisphère.
Mais, de retour, Seigneur, que prétendez-vous faire?
—Alors, cher Cinéas, victorieux, contens,
Nous pourrons rire à l'aise et prendre du bon temps;
—Mais, Seigneur, dès ce jour, sans sortir de l'Epire,
Du matin jusqu'au soir, qui vous défend de rire?

. . . . .

Mais quelques vains lauriers que promette la guerre,
On peut être héros sans ravager la terre.
Il est plus d'une gloire. En vain aux conquérants
L'erreur parmi les rois donne les premiers rangs;
Parmi les grands héros ce sont les plus vulgaires;
Chaque siècle est fécond en heureux téméraires;

. . . . .

Mais un roi vraiment roi qui, sage en ses projets,
Sache en un calme heureux maintenir ses sujets;
Qui du bonheur public ait cimenté sa gloire;
Il faut pour le trouver courir toute l'histoire.

in trying to analyze what was at fault in the policies of Louis XIV.

We meet [LA BRUYÈRE (1645-1696) writes] with certain wild animals male and female scattered over the country, dark, livid, and tanned by the sun, clinging to the land they are untiringly digging and turning up and down with dogged tenacity; they have something like an articulate voice and, when they stand erect, they show a human face, and indeed they are men. At night they withdraw to their dens where they live on black bread, water, and roots. They spare other men the trouble of sowing, tilling the ground, and harvesting for their maintenance and deserve, one could think, not to be in want of that bread they themselves sow.[8]

Such is the picture of the life of French peasants in the latter part of the seventeenth century, when this country was the leading power in Europe, when the splendor of its court life and the magnificence of the royal palaces were being admired everywhere and were disposing almost all European countries to fashion their lives according to the standards set by France.

Never mentioning Louis XIV, La Bruyère in his works speaks of sovereigns in general. He states that their erroneous ideas of honor, their unbounded thirst for glory, their eagerness for riches, for the annexation of territories make of them instigators of war in which lies the main cause of the degrading poverty of the masses. "The Topinambous, in spite of all their savagery, are happier than the French peasants." [9] In order to satisfy their ambition, the rulers are ready to pay any price; their subjects are for them mere money with which they hope to pay for their victories:

Eight or ten thousand men are to a prince like money; with their lives he buys a town or a victory; but, if he can obtain either at a cheaper rate, by sparing men, he is like a man who is bargaining, since he knows better than any other the value of money.[10]

8 J. de La Bruyère, *Oeuvres*, éd. Servois, 1865, II, 61, "Les Caractères: De l'Homme."
9 Cf. Pierre Pic, *Guy-Patin*, 1911, "Lettre du 2 sept. 1661."
10 La Bruyère, *Oeuvres*, I, 384, "Du Souverain ou De la République."

La Bruyère finds absurd the commonly accepted idea of a king as a "father" of his subjects, a "shepherd" tending his flock. Contrasting the poverty of the lower classes with the splendor of the Court of Versailles, he wonders of what use it is to the flock to see the shepherd clothed in gold and precious stones, with a golden crook in his hand; to see the dog wearing a golden collar. Does all this protect the sheep against wolves?[11] Poets, philosophers, and preachers, from ancient days to our time, like to emphasize the conception of a sovereign as a shepherd. If we agree with them, the sovereign's task is hard, one of unending service. He is responsible for the happiness of his people, and since all the power is in his hands, there is no excuse for him if they are miserable: "How happy is that post which every minute furnishes opportunities of doing good to thousands of men! How dangerous is that post which every moment gives its occupant the power to injure millions![12] This is exactly what a sovereign does when he wages war. He harms millions of men; he forgets that the most glorious victories do not give any advantages to the rank and file, to the humble martyrs whose lives are being sacrificed:

Indeed, what benefits and what increase of pleasure would accrue to a people if their prince extended the boundaries of his empire into the territories of his enemies; if the neighboring sovereignties became provinces of his kingdom; if he overcame his enemies in sieges and battles, so that neither plains nor fortifications of the strongest kind afforded any security against him. . . . What signifies it to me, in a word, or to any of my countrymen that my sovereign be successful and overwhelmed with glory . . . that my country be powerful and dreaded if, sad and worried, I have to live in oppression and poverty.[13]

During the year following that of the first publication of *Les Caractères* (1688) appeared an anonymous pamphlet *Les Soupirs de la France esclave*[14] in which, trying to show how

[11] *Ibid.*, I, 385-386.
[12] *Ibid.*, I, 386.
[13] *Ibid.*, I, 382-383.
[14] *Les Soupirs de la France esclave*, Amsterdam, 1689.

little the interests of the ruler and of men in power agree with those of the common people, the author exclaims:

How does all this benefit the common people? Are they less miserable for all that? Is their yoke lightened? Is their wealth and honor increased thereby? Do they not languish in misery and servility and, consequently, in shame?

And yet a good government is supposed to have in view not only the greatness of the state, but also the happiness of the citizens. "No one but a flatterer dares to affirm that the lives of the subjects and all they possess belong to the sovereign, and even a flatterer will deny it with his last breath." [15]

War is our inheritance from the remotest times, but, against all expectation, it has become more cruel with the advance of civilization, which has made suffering more acute and the destruction of lives more rapid:

Like rational creatures and to distinguish yourselves from those which only make use of their teeth and claws, you have invented spears, pikes, darts, sabres, and scimitars and, in my opinion, very judiciously; for what could you have done to one another merely with your hands, except tearing your hair, scratching your faces and, at best, gouging one another's eyes? Whilst now you are provided with convenient instruments for making large wounds and letting out the utmost drop of your blood, without there being any fear of your remaining alive? But as you grow more rational from year to year, you have greatly improved the old fashion of destroying yourselves; you use certain little globes which kill at once if they but hit you on the head or chest. . . . Fancy a man of the size of Mount Athos. . . . If such a man's sight were piercing enough to discover you somewhere upon earth, with your offensive and defensive arms, what do you think would be his opinion of a parcel of little marmosets thus equipped and of what you call war, cavalry, infantry, a memorable siege, a famous battle? Shall I never hear any other sound buzz in my ear? Is the world only filled with regiments and companies? Has everything been changed to battalions and squadrons? "He takes a town, then a second, then a third; he wins a battle, two battles; he

[15] La Bruyère, *Oeuvres*, I, 384-385.

drives away the enemy, he conquers by sea, by land." Do you say these things of one of you or of a giant, a Mount Athos? [16]

The main character of war, from the point of view of La Bruyère, is its absurdity:

If any one should come and tell you that all the cats of a large country met in a plain in their thousands and tens of thousands, and that after they had squalled to their hearts content, they had fallen upon each other tooth and nail; that about ten thousand of them had been left dead on the spot and infected the air for ten leagues around with their evil-smelling carcasses; would you not say that it was the most disgraceful row you ever heard?

If you see two dogs barking at each other, provoke, bite, and tear one another to pieces, you say they are foolish creatures and take a stick to part them.

And if the wolves acted in the same way, what a butchery would there be, and how it would be heard!

Now, if these two kinds of animals were to tell you they love glory, would you not come to the conclusion that this glory consists in their meeting together in such a way to destroy and annihilate their own species? And if you have come to such a conclusion, would you not laugh heartily at the folly of these poor animals? [17]

La Bruyère's clever argumentation in favor of peace as well as his cutting, witty attacks against war could not fail to create a current of thought in favor of a more peaceful sovereignty than that of Louis XIV during whose reign his works were written.

An analogous line of thought is noticeable in VAUBAN (1633-1707), an eminent economist and one of the most remarkable thinkers of his time. Chief engineer of the army, the principal assistant of Louvois, he had built or reconstructed hundreds of fortresses and directed some fifty sieges. Through this kind of activity he had come into close contact

---

[16] *Ibid.,* II, 130-131, "Des Jugements." [The translation is taken from *The Characters of the Age,* made English by several hands, London, 1705.]

[17] *Ibid.,* II, 130-131. [The English text has been taken from *The Characters of Jean de La Bruyère,* transl. by Henry van Laun, 1885.]

with all classes of people. The high position he occupied and the title of "Marshal of France" which had been bestowed on him never led him to forget the distressing conditions under which the greatest part of the population of his country lived. Guided by a strong sense of justice, he looked for some means which might alleviate the life of the lower classes. It seemed to him that a reform in the way of levying taxes would answer the purpose. In his work *La Dîme royale* (1707),[18] in which he shows himself a fearless reformer, we find a detailed account of this plan. He draws the attention of the King to the fact that taxes are unequally and unjustly portioned out; that they lie heavy on the poor people, while the rich, the nobility and the clergy, are exempted therefrom. He suggests that the poll-tax be replaced by the tithe, so that one-tenth of the produce of land, industry, and commerce be used to meet the needs of the country and to cover the costs of the Court and the Government. He does not provide for any exceptions to the general rule.

The *Dîme royale* aroused against its author the privileged feudal classes as well as those who were deriving great profits from industry or commerce; it also threatened to undermine the tremendous fortunes made by contractors and purveyors in time of war. Vauban presented a copy of his work to Louis XIV, but the King refused to consider the advantages he might derive from the suggested reform. An order to destroy the whole edition was issued. Vauban died a short time after.

Notwithstanding the fact that his activity was one unceasing effort to strengthen France in her war against other European nations and that all his life was spent in close contact with soldiers of every rank, Vauban had a profound dislike for war. A man with a generous heart, he could not help meditating on the very essence of war. Here are some lines he writes on this subject:

War has for father self-interest, for mother ambition, and for near relatives all the passions that lead us into evil. She made

[18] S. Vauban, "La Dîme royale," see *Eugène Daire, Economistes financiers du 18e siècle,* 1844.

her appearance in the world with the first men. She was born with them and, like them, she took possession of all habitable parts of the globe of which she made her heritage and in the enjoyment of which she has maintained herself and will maintain herself as long as there will be men on earth with a tyrannical power over the wealth and lives of their fellowmen. . . . Her ordinary occupations are . . . the destruction of mankind, the disruption of states, the ravaging of towns and the countryside, and the bringing of general desolation upon all the peoples of the world. . . . All states which have been and are still in existence are dependent on her; there is not one that does not owe to her its origin, its highest success, its continuance, or its downfall. It is she who makes and unmakes kings, who lifts them up, casts them down, and singles them out from other men. Ambition and injustice have brought it about that she has become an evil so necessary that one might observe that princes who ignore her and neglect her teachings do not reign in security and are ordinarily so little respected that their subjects can hardly observe the veneration and obedience that is due to them. . . . In the beginning, war had for rules only lawlessness and brutality; but, necessity having taught the feeblest to join cunning to force . . . she very soon became a science to which the greatest men applied their closest attention; this made her less brutal little by little and—sordid and ferocious as she still was—she was brought under certain rules; experience has so many times amended them that at last we have succeeded in creating what is called "the great art of war." [19]

Does Vauban believe that a time may come when war will be merely a reminiscence of the past? He does, and this will be the era when no man will ever be in possession of despotic power over the property and lives of his fellowmen. The normal condition of existence for a state as well as for an individual is peace. Wars of conquest, according to Vauban, bring nothing but disaster. France should never try to expand beyond the size of ancient Gaul; her natural borders should be the Rhine, the summits of the Jura, the Maritime Alps, the Pyrenees, and the two seas: "It seems that common sense forbids the thought of reaching beyond those boundaries." [20]

[19] *Oisivetés et Correspondance,* 1910, I, 267, "La Guerre."
[20] *Ibid.,* I, 50, 508, "Projet de paix."

The acceptance by Louis XIV of the throne of Spain in favor of his grandson, Philip of Anjou, according to the will of Charles II, King of Spain, is regarded by Vauban as a great mistake. "The Pyrenees no longer exist," says Louis XIV, meaning by this that France and Spain are going henceforth to be close and faithful allies forever. Family relationships between sovereigns, thinks Vauban, have never prevented war between nations. France should renounce her rights rather than be involved in war against the whole of Europe at a time when, after forty years of war, it is almost impossible to raise soldiers; when fields are lying untilled for lack of laborers, and money is scarce.

Vauban was not in favor of acquiring new territory unless the new land could be incorporated into the mother-country; with regard to colonies, he valued only "les colonies de raison," as he called lands occupied in accordance with a decision of the government for the purpose of settling there the surplus population or for political or commercial ends.

The author absolutely condemns religious intolerance and the conflicts it brings about. In 1689 he made a report to the King in favor of the re-establishment of the Edict of Nantes. He pointed out all evil the Revocation had entailed: from eighty to one hundred thousand of the best citizens had left France, carrying to foreign lands about thirty million pounds; France had lost all her Protestant alliances; industry and art had suffered a great decline; a very great number of emigrants had joined the army and navy of the enemy; therefore, the only wise thing to do would be to allow the Huguenots to return, restoring to them all their rights, because "where there are no subjects, there cannot be any question of a sovereign, a state, or domination. . . . Religion is a matter of conviction, not of command.[21]

Stressing the importance of establishing peace in the country as well as in its relations with other countries, Vauban expressed the opinion that the best way to avoid war with other nations is to be prepared for it; therefore, he directed all his activity toward giving France this preparedness.

[21] *Ibid.*, t.I, "Mémoire pour le rappel des Huguenots."

Vauban was the great designer and strengthener of the natural frontiers that separate France from turbulent neighbors. Behind the great French "Chinese Wall" he attached masonry works, dug ditches, rounded bastions, in a word, closed the gate: "On ne passe pas." His work holds good to this day in many of its parts.[22]

Vauban had a high opinion of the French: he found them, as a rule, men of extensive capacity, clever, intelligent, making fearlessness a point of honor, ready to embrace the military profession every time it promised them an opportunity of gaining distinction; this feature once noticed, the merit system becomes indispensable.   In his letters to Louvois, Vauban stressed the necessity of bringing the appointments and promotions in the army into harmony with merit, not with birth. He was indignant every time he learned that a very young nobleman with no training at all had been appointed to a high position while a man of knowledge and experience but belonging to the *tiers-état* was doomed to serve under his command. Vauban shared the opinion of La Bruyère who thought that valor might in exceptional cases counterbalance want of training, but that, on the whole, "War has its rules, there is a science of war." [23]

Vauban felt that France can have the best troops in the world, but she must use them for defense only.   This opinion is very consistent with his general tendency to consider matters from the angle of right and justice.   From the fact that he was wounded eight times one may conclude that he did not consider his own life; he spared, on the contrary, as much as it was possible, the lives of his officers and soldiers.   He opposed the bombardment of besieged towns: "Let us burn more gunpowder, but shed less blood." [24]   The ideal of peace was deeply rooted in his mind and heart.   The greatness of a state rests, according to him, upon the prosperity of the laboring masses which is thinkable only during the reign of peace.

[22] See Léandre Vaillat, "Vauban," *National Review*, 100, janv.-juin 1933.

[23] La Bruyère, *Oeuvres*, II, 186-187, "De quelques usages."

[24] "Discours prononcé par M. de Rochas d'Aiglun à l'inauguration du monument de Vauban à Bazoches le 26 août 1900," *Revue Scientifique*, Séries 4-14, janvier-décembre 1900.

It is, however, in the works of FÉNELON (1651-1715) that we find the most violent criticism of the policies of Louis XIV.

Fénelon, one of the heads of the Roman Catholic Church in France, was before all and above all a Christian. In his opinion, ethics should be subordinated to religion, and politics to ethics. The principle, "I am the state," adopted by this King, is inadmissible, Fénelon thought, because it puts the private interest of the monarch above the welfare of his people. The laws intrust a nation to a sovereign that he be her father; his duty is to defend her against an aggressor and, in time of peace, to make his subjects wise, good, and happy. It is not for his own benefit that God has made him king; he deserves to be the leader of his people only if, forgetting his own interests, he devotes his time and his cares to the well-being of his subjects.[25]

Analyzing from this point of view the reign of Louis XIV, Fénelon finds that it has been a time of aggressive wars, made often in breach of a treaty, wars that have not had the excuse of being fought in order to defend the vital interests of France. On the contrary, they have been putting the very existence of the country in danger. The author sees the European nations take up arms against France which in that critical moment, exhausted as she is by all the preceding wars, has no power and no means for self-defense:

Your peoples are dying of hunger. The cultivation of the land has been almost abandoned; town and country lie depopulated; crafts languish and can no longer support the craftsmen; commerce is destroyed. The whole of France is like a desolate hospital, left without food.[26]

Fénelon reminds the King of the danger of allowing the greatest part of the population to lead a life of misery; people may refuse at last to sacrifice their lives in unjustifiable wars and to starve in order to be able to contribute to the splendors of court life. Fénelon is strongly opposed to revolutionary

25 F. Fénelon, *Les Aventures de Télémaque,* éd. Cahen, 1923, Livres II, 49 et V, 103, 119.
26 Fénelon, *Oeuvres,* éd. Lefèvre, 1835, III, 443, "Lettre à Louis XIV."

methods, preferring established order no matter how bad it is; however, he finds it useful to remind the King that revolutions are historical facts,[27] that in engaging in fierce battles and besieging fortresses, he fights on a ground that is sinking under his feet.

Thus the power which struck united nations with terror fell in a moment, totally and forever. So the ground that is gradually undermined, in appearance maintains its stability; the slow progress of the work below is disregarded or despised; nothing shakes, nothing is broken and, in appearance, nothing is weak; yet the secret support is certainly, though insensibly, destroyed, and the moment at last arrives when the whole falls at once into ruin, and nothing remains but an abyss in which the surface and all that covered it is swallowed up. Thus an unjust power, an illegal authority, however founded, is gradually subverted by fraud and cruelty: whatever degree of prosperity it may reach through fraud, it gradually undermines itself. It is gazed at with admiration and terror, and everyone trembles before it till the moment when it sinks into nothing: it falls by its own weight, and it can rise no more, for its support is not only removed, but annihilated —justice and integrity are wanting which alone can produce confidence and love.[28]

Kings should never forget that, in the long run, it is always justice that triumphs by virtue of the law which maintains order in the moral world in the same way in which the forces of gravity and attraction maintain order and balance in the physical world.

Reading the above mentioned and some other similar passages in the works of Fénelon, one might think that he was endowed with a kind of prevision which allowed him to foresee the future destinies of France, the downfall of the French monarchy, and the terrors of the Revolution.

He tried to educate his pupil, the Duke of Burgundy, heir to the throne, not to see a hero in every successful conqueror; he tried to impress upon him that there is but one moral law, and this should be our guide in our appreciation of men:

[27] *Ibid.*, III, 383, "Essai philosophique sur le gouvernement civil."
[28] *Les Aventures de Télémaque*, L. XV, p. 456, transl. by Dr. Hawkesworth.

The poor wretch who, from extreme necessity, steals a purse upon the highway, is hanged, while the man who unjustly subjugates a neighboring state, is called hero. . . . To take a field from an individual is a great sin; to take a country from a nation is an innocent and glorious action. Whence are these ideas of justice . . . ? Ought we to be less just in great than in little things . . . ? Should we not have some scruples about committing a crime against a million men, against a whole country, when we dare not injure an individual? [29]

Before being a great man, one must be an honest man and not allow oneself to commit crimes unworthy of man.[30]

Fénelon wants the future King to understand the importance of being true to political treaties; he impresses upon him that it is more infamous to deceive in a treaty of peace than in a private contract with an individual. He points out that a peace treaty should never contain ambiguous terms: "To insert in a treaty ambiguous and insidious terms is to sow the seeds of a future war or to place powder-chests under homes." [31]

Fénelon's hatred for war has for basis his religious convictions and his love for man: "All mankind is but one family spread over the face of the earth. All peoples are brothers and should love one another as such." [32] This concept of the universal brotherhood of man makes him look on war as an evil which dishonors mankind; he would like to bury for ever all books of history in order to conceal from posterity that men have been capable of killing one another. From his point of view all wars are civil wars: the parties, shedding each other's blood, are members of the same human family.[33] Besides, why should we try to draw near the mournful hour? Death is in store for each one of us; there is so much suffering in life that it seems foolish to increase it. Why should we kill our brothers in trying to usurp their lands, whereas there are

[29] *Oeuvres*, III, 354, "Examen de conscience sur les devoirs de la royauté." Translation taken from the English edition of this work, London, 1747.

[30] *Ibid.*, II, 574, "Dialogues des morts: Romulus et Rémus."

[31] *Ibid.*, III, 354, "Examen de conscience sur les devoirs de la royauté."

[32] *Les Aventures de Télémaque*, Livre IX, p. 241.

[33] *Oeuvres*, II, 584, "Dialogues des morts: Socrate et Alcibiade."

boundless uninhabited territories? [34]   Sovereigns are prone to excuse their wars by the fact that the annexation of a new land increases the wealth of the country; yet they should remember that no one has the right to attain prosperity by sacrificing the well-being of another man; this rule applies to nations as well as to individuals.   That our coexistence here, on earth, be a worthy human life, the following principle should be upheld : the interests of the individual should be set aside for those of the family, the interests of the family for those of the community, those of the community for those of the nation, the ends of the nation for those of mankind.[35] Any one nation is as much a member of the human race as any one family is of a particular nation.   Every man is far more obliged to mankind in general than to his own country; it is therefore far more unjust for a people to attack another than for any family to act against the state.[36]

The kind of war to which Fénelon could never reconcile himself is war for the sake of glory: "Oh, kings, do not say that you are bound to wage war for the sake of glory.   True glory is never divorced from humanity.   He who places his glory above love for man, is not a human being, but a monster of pride." [37]   Honor and glory are fine things; happy are those who know how and where to find them.[38]   In his letter to Louis XIV he accuses the King, point-blank, of waging war for the sake of glory:

So much frightful turmoil that has disturbed Europe for the last twenty years, so much bloodshed, so many provinces sacked, towns and villages reduced to ashes are the baneful consequences of the war of 1672 undertaken for your glory.[39]

Has not he, who is ambitious of glory, sufficient opportunities of acquiring it by taking good care of things intrusted to him?   To be ambitious of governing nations against their

[34] *Ibid.*, II, 469, "Mandement pour des prières."
[35] *Ibid.*, III, 368, "Essai philosophique sur le gouvernement civil." [We find the same idea in the works of Montesquieu, cf. p. 104, note 5.]
[36] *Ibid.*, II, 584, "Dialogues des morts: Socrate et Alcibiade."
[37] *Les Aventures de Télémaque*, Livre IX, p. 241.
[38] *Oeuvres*, II, 578, "Dialogues des morts: Solon et Pisistrate."
[39] *Ibid.*, III, 442, "Lettre à Louis XIV."

will is more than unwise, good administration not being an easy task. Happy is the man who is free from the desire to make slaves of other men:

A conqueror is a man whom gods in their wrath against the human race have sent to the earth to lay waste kingdoms, to spread terror, misery, and despair everywhere. . . . The great conquerors, extolled so much, are like overflowing majestic rivers that ravage fertile plains instead of irrigating them.[40]

It is in the fourteenth book of the *Aventures de Télémaque* that Fénelon has summed up all he had to say about unworthy rulers. In search of the shade of his father, *Télémaque* descended into Tartarus. He was astonished at the great number of kings he saw there. They were those who during their earthly life had abused their power, had satisfied their ambition of false honor at the expense of the blood of men whose happiness should have been the first object of their attention. Their chastisement consisted in seeing themselves faithfully represented in a mirror with their vain parade and ostentatious splendor in which the public welfare was consumed. Some rulers were punished not for the mischief they had done, but for the good they had neglected to do. As ministers of the law, they had been found guilty of crimes committed by their subjects; as public servants, they had been accused of not having realized that they had no right to prefer ease and leisure to the painful labors of government. They had forgotten that kings must live not for themselves, but for those they govern.

The severest punishment was, however, inflicted for war of conquest. Only one kind of conquest found excuse in the eyes of Fénelon: if war made in self-defense fails to establish peaceful relations with one's aggressor, the conquest of the latter's land seems to be the only way out of the difficulty, but the duty of the new ruler is to do everything in his power to secure the welfare of the conquered country.[41]

Contrary to Montesquieu, Fénelon, like Voltaire, does not find any excuse for a war made with the aim to prevent a

[40] *Les Aventures de Télémaque,* Livre VII, p. 185.
[41] *Oeuvres,* II, 584, "Dialogues des morts: Socrate et Alcibiade."

neighbor from becoming powerful: "Would you like to see your neighbor take from you anything he feels he needs for his security? The consideration of your security does not give you a right over the property of others." [42] History shows, however, that the powerful are very prone to take advantage of their strength. In Fénelon's opinion, defensive leagues could unite the smaller nations into a kind of general republic; enabling it this way to face the danger of an attack from the strong, each nation would become an arbiter called to participate in the decisions to be reached by the members of the league. If all nations would always keep in mind the memory of the evils caused by conquests, they would try hard to establish this equilibrium, the only condition that can secure happiness to each of the nations and guarantee their common interests. [43]

The mere existence of leagues of states would make war of less frequent occurrence; yet the necessity of preparedness for it remains: Fénelon recommends sending young noblemen into foreign service that they might acquire an experimental knowledge of the art of war. Since the importance of the example given by the head of a nation cannot be overlooked, the greatest attention should be given to the military education of a prince. He should always be ready to answer the call of duty. His valor should never be doubtful; it is better for him to perish in battle than to bring his courage into question; his contempt for death should, however, never lead him to expose himself unnecessarily for the purpose of the gratification of an idle ambition. Never should he also forget to show the greatest deference to old commanders, men of knowledge and experience. [44] Being fully aware how destructive the unlimited competition in armaments is to the well-being of a people, Fénelon admits the necessity of armed peace with reluctance; he would prefer to see the issue of war depend on moral values, not on the strength of armaments. [45]

[42] *Ibid.*, III, 355, "Examen de conscience sur les devoirs de la royauté."
[43] *Ibid.*, III, 361, "Supplément à l'examen de conscience sur les devoirs de la royauté."
[44] *Les Aventures de Télémaque*, Livres X et XI, pp. 252-255, 272, 318-322.
[45] *Oeuvres*, II, 572, "Dialogues des morts: Confucius et Socrate."

There are not many pages in the works of this author referring to religious wars; his main objection to them is their uselessness; such is at least the impression of one who reads the account of his interview with the son of King James II at Cambrai in 1709.[46] He sees the essence of religion in thought and feeling which can be neither enforced nor suppressed:

Liberty of thought is an impregnable fortress which no human power can force. Violence can never convince; it only makes hypocrites. When kings take upon themselves to direct in matters of religion, instead of protecting it, they bring it into bondage. You ought, therefore, to grant to all people legal toleration, not as approving everything indifferently, but suffering with patience what God suffers and endeavouring to reconcile the misled by soft and gentle persuasion.[47]

Fénelon did not, however, raise his voice against the Revocation of the Edict of Nantes and the "dragonnades" (quartering of soldiers). Some of his convictions, if fate should have placed him in power, might even have brought about intense struggle instead of pacification: he was an ultramontane, an obedient son of the Holy See, an enemy of gallicanism; he placed Church above State and wanted sovereigns to submit to her decrees.[48]

Fénelon gave great attention to the problem of civil war, internal discord, and the relationship between a sovereign and his subjects. His opinions in regard to those questions were, on the whole, those of the Catholic Church. In spite of the fact that in many respects he shows himself to be a thinker of the eighteenth century, in the matters mentioned above he belongs to his own century: "To transgress the law of established subordination is a crime of high-treason against God." [49] He asserts his belief in the divine right of the anointed head of a nation, his readiness to consider every government as established by God, and patience and submission as the only permissible attitudes for subjects. Citizens may further the

[46] See A. M. Ramsay, *The Life of François de Salignac de La Motte Fénelon*, 1723, pp. 307-308.
[47] *Ibid.*, pp. 307-308.
[48] *Les Aventures de Télémaque*, Livre XVII, 494.
[49] *Oeuvres*, III, 374, "Essai philosophique sur le gouvernement civil."

development of a more perfect order of things only by peaceful means. If they suffer from despotic government, they must consider their suffering as a punishment inflicted by God. Under no condition may one make an attempt to take the life of a sovereign; God knows to what extent he will allow a tyrant to chastise a nation:

But, one will say, if it is possible to put an end to tyranny by sacrificing the life of one man, if it is possible to save the fatherland by killing the tyrant, should not the public good be put above the life of him who is a monster among men?

God will not allow that a people be forever oppressed by bad government just as he will not let continuous storms disturb the universe. One should therefore bear with bad sovereigns out of reverence for the Divine Providence who knows how long tyrants will be allowed to chastise a nation.[50]

The author does not mean to assert that despotism is lawful; the sovereign who places himself above law will be thrown down in due time, but "the chastisement for abuse of power should be left to God, who alone is omniscient." [51]

Such is the principle which, according to Fénelon, is justified by experience and practical considerations: despotism is bad, but anarchy and revolution are worse, the tyranny of the multitude is more cruel than that of one man.[52] Once the established order is overthrown, there is no possibility "of putting an end to the fickleness of the multitude and the ambition of turbulent individuals who will unceasingly carry away the mob under the plausible pretext of improving government and reforming abuses." [53] Besides, one should keep in mind, that the best form of government is not in itself a guarantee against abuses; the only guarantee can be found in moral principles which prevent men from wrongdoing, teach them to bear suffering patiently, and to find a remedy for all misfortunes in the peace and beauty of their inner life.[54]

[50] *Ibid.*, III, 382-383.

[51] *Ibid.*, éd. 1881, IV, 302, quoted from Mme. Constantinescu-Bagdat, "De Vauban à Voltaire," p. 102, and transl. into English.

[52] *Oeuvres,* éd. 1835, III, 375-376, "Essai philos. sur le gouvernement civil."

[53] *Ibid.*

[54] *Ibid.*, III, 403.

We see that the doctrine of sovereignty of the people is one that is alien to Fénelon. His trend of thought leads him in just the opposite direction: a man, he says, from the very moment of his birth, is a member of some community already existing; he is neither his own master, nor his own law; how can he delegate to anyone the rights he does not possess? [55]

Fénelon is, furthermore, a supporter of established order in the sphere of economics and social relations. Considering peace as the highest good, deeply believing that the good aspects of human nature are the stronger, he condemns all violent methods which, in the opinion of so many, are considered to be the shortest way of bringing about a better order of things. [56]

Fénelon's profound religious convictions gave him a wonderful moral balance. He believed that Divine Providence is leading the world toward ends unknown to us, but good and immutable. Every single event might be a necessary link in the chain of events leading to those ends. The words "might be" are meant to stress the fact that Fénelon was not a determinist. All his writings and his activity as bishop and as educator to the heir to the throne testify that his general attitude was not a passive one. He was not merely an observer of life; he took a passionate part in it and tried to direct it, but when he failed, he never lost his moral balance, for he was convinced that what happened was evidently necessary in the general plan of life directed by Divine Providence:

As in the physical constitution of man and in nature there is a hidden universal action of the initial motive power, the sole origin of all force, order, and movements we observe in nature, so in the government of the world there is an unseen sovereign Providence which regulates everything according to eternal and immutable designs.

All the different events which seem to ignorant human beings to be the works of mere chance or man's vain wisdom are linked one to another so as to contribute to the fulfillment of the designs

[55] *Ibid.*, III, 374.
[56] *Ibid.*, III, 379.

of the Supreme Being. He leads all things to their ultimate ends. Often the very matter that seems unworthy of our attention becomes the cause of great changes. The imperceptible motion of an atom can bring about numberless revolutions in the world.[57]

Fénelon's contribution to the development of the peace idea has been considerable. He was an early internationalist, who placed the interests of the human race above national interests. In a time of unceasing wars made by the most powerful and most dreaded of the European sovereigns he raised his voice to protest against a policy of conquests and violation of treaties; he did so, not only as a representative of the Christian Church, but as a philosopher, a writer, starting thus in literature this fight for peace which will be led with unequaled force in the eighteenth century by Voltaire.

Fénelon's philosophical works might be unknown to the public at large, but his work of fiction, *Les Aventures de Télémaque,* has found its way into every cultured home and has spread the author's ideas with regard to perfect government and universal brotherhood.

Jules Lemaître finds in this seventeenth-century novel all the humanitarian ideas of the following century and even some of the ideas of the nineteenth: The attitude of the "Manduriens" [58] and of the people of "Bétique" toward aggressive neighbors seems to anticipate Tolstoi's doctrine of non-resistance to evil.[59]

The life in Bétique and in Salente was in many respects that of the so-called "Tolstovtzi," the members of some Russian agricultural societies which could be found in South Russia and in Caucasus before the revolution of 1917. The members of those colonies were mostly disciples of Tolstoi, men and women who were trying to shape their lives according to the ideals of their master; it was a kind of life which G. Lanson might be prone to characterize as the "nostalgic life of primitive humanity." [60]

[57] *Ibid.,* III, 374.
[58] *Les Aventures de Télémaque,* Livre IX.
[59] Jules Lemaitre, *Fénelon,* 1910, p. 147.
[60] G. Lanson, "Fénelon," *Revue des Cours et Conférences,* 8 avril 1909.

The name of the Abbé de Saint-Pierre, whose *Projet de paix perpétuelle,* written in the eighteenth century, is analyzed in one of the following chapters, should be listed with those who felt opposed to the policies of Louis XIV. All these men had witnessed the disasters brought about by war; their longing for peace had thus a realistic basis. Peace was at the same time the aspiration of their hearts because they loved mankind. They did not care for the few chosen ones to whom war may bring fortune and honor, but for the mass of common people whose happiness and economic welfare it destroys.

CHAPTER III

STRICTLY RELIGIOUS ATTITUDE
TOWARD WAR

BESIDES the group of writers of seventeenth-century France who condemned war on practical grounds, there were others in whose works the condemnation of war bore the particular stamp of the philosophy of the Christian religion. To this group belong GUEZ DE BALZAC, PASCAL, and BOSSUET. The name of Fénelon might well be placed among them too, not only because he was a high official of the Catholic Church, but mainly because, as a convinced Christian, he was in his outlook an internationalist. His idea of human society embraced all mankind whom he saw in his dream as united by bonds of love and charity. The earliest writer of this group was Guez de Balzac.

BALZAC (1594-1654) notes with astonishment that the thoughts of most men are concerned with two interests only, state and family; and yet there is something above these two, the world. Men are primarily citizens of the world and must fulfill their obligations as members of one universal republic.[1] Casting a veil over this great truth, they are prone to behave not like Christians, but like followers of the Alcoran or to become "brigands of all lands and pirates of all seas," as have become the Spaniards.[2] A sovereign must never allow the spirit of conquest to take hold of him. Reason and equity should guide his policies. Why are small faults punished and great ones honored? Does the enormity of a crime excuse it?

[1] Guez de Balzac, *Le Prince*, 1631, p. 10.
[2] *Ibid.*, p. 354.

53

A poor man who as a pirate earns a meager livelihood is called a "sea-thief" and treated accordingly, while he who, taking advantage of his large navy, pillages and plunders on a large scale is called "emperor." A Christian can, to a certain extent, reconcile himself to this temporary triumph of evil; he knows that deeds of violence never pass unpunished; that right and justice shall claim their place not only in the life to come, but in this present life.[3]

Of all deeds of violence war of conquest is the greatest; it contributes rarely to the welfare and happiness of a people:

There are evil gains and ruinous acquisitions. . . . Princes, after having won battles and conquered peoples, must stand in fear of their own conquests, realizing that there are no more dangerous enemies than subjects who obey merely submitting to force. . . . Oppression arouses courage, and suffering sharpens valor. . . . The lamentations of oppressed nations, the outcries of persecuted innocent people . . . will reach the throne of God. . . . If the voice of the dying Abel reached His ears, will the blood of numberless Christians be shed silently and fall soundlessly to the ground? Will Justice permit their unjustifiable death without investigating who caused them to perish?[4]

The worship of war heroes or of conquerors is alien to Balzac. They are called to serve the designs of Providence, to be instruments of a punishment imposed upon a people for disobeying God's commandments. There is no need that those instruments of Providence be men of exceptional talents or power of intellect. God's infinite power allows humble, ignorant men to perform great things and explains the fact that foolish undertakings are often crowned with success, while apparently wisely planned enterprises fail:

When Providence has some plan, it cares little what instruments or what means it uses. In its hands even the smallest thing becomes a thunderbolt, a storm, a deluge, and even the weakest man an Alexander or a Caesar.[5]

[3] *Socrate chrestien,* 1652, pp. 99-100.
[4] *Le Prince,* pp. 384-385.
[5] Quand la Prouidence a quelque dessein, il ne luy importe gueres de quels instruments et de quels moyens elle se serve. Entre ses mains tout est foudre, tout est tempeste, tout est déluge, tout est Alexandre, tout est César. *Le Prince,* pp. 384-385.

God deliberately chooses small and feeble instruments to confound human grandeur.[6]

The main idea dominating the philosophy of Balzac is his profound belief that God takes an immediate part in all events of individual, national, and universal life:

The diseases that trouble political bodies are predestined. . . . In the high fever of rebellion, in the lethargy of servitude we recognize God's hand. Men are but actors: the great plays performed on earth have been composed in heaven, and it is often a mere puppet who plays the parts of Atreus or Agamemnon.[7]

Balzac does not suggest any remedy for the prevention of war; he deplores the fact that the spirit of conquest is inherent in rulers and that the ideal of peace is alien to the diplomats and statesmen of all countries. With regard to France, he seems optimistic to a certain degree; he hopes that this country which "espouses only righteous causes and successfully defends those which have been considered hopeless"[8] will, in times to come, contribute to the pacification of Europe.

In the works of PASCAL (1623-1662) there are only a few pages referring to war and peace. Were the plans for an international organization of the world written by Dubois, Crucé, and Sully and published in the first half of the seventeenth century known to him? He does not mention them; at all events, he does not seem to have been the kind of man disposed to espouse their ideas. He sees the source of a better life among men, citizens, and nations in the moral improvement of the individuals forming these groups.

The cornerstone on which social, civil, and international relations ought to be established is, according to him, justice; but, is there any reality behind this great word, he asks? There are no principles of justice universally acknowledged.

[6] Dieu choisit tout exprès les petits et faibles instruments pour confondre la Grandeur humaine. *Socrate chrestien,* pp. 99-100.
[7] *Socrate chrestien,* pp. 140-141.
[8] *Le Prince,* p. 388.

What we call "justice" rests upon mode, opinions, customs, all of which are changeable; hence the relativity of moral standards:

Theft, incest, infanticide, patricide have all had a place among virtuous actions.

The glory of true equity would have brought all nations under subjection. . . . We should have seen it set up in all the states on earth and in all times; whereas we see neither justice nor injustice which does not change its nature with change in climate. Three degrees of latitude reverse all jurisprudence; a meridian decides the truth. . . . A strange justice that is bounded by a river. . . . Truth on this side of the Pyrenees, error on the other side.

The result of this confusion is that one affirms the essence of justice to be the authority of the legislator; another, the interest of the sovereign; another, present custom, and this is the most sure. Nothing, according to reason alone, is just in itself; all changes with time. Custom creates the whole of equity, for the simple reason that it is accepted. It is the mystical foundation of its authority. . . . The art of opposition and of revolution is to unsettle established customs, sounding them even to their source, to point out their want of authority and justice.[9]

Because men have failed to establish a universal principle of justice which alone could guarantee peace, the sovereign good of mankind, they had to legitimize force, and in particular, its strongest manifestation, the law of the sword: "When a strong man armed keepeth his goods, his goods are in peace." [10] Nothing is left to the weak except to submit to the point of sacrificing life for ends unknown.

It is not only in the sphere of international relations that force supplants right:

Why do we follow the majority? Is it because they have more reason? No, because they have more power.

Why do we follow ancient laws and opinions? Is it because they are more sound? No, but because they are unique and remove from us the root of difference.[11]

[9] The "Pensées" are given in the translation of W. F. Trotter made from the ed. by L. Brunschvicg. See *Everyman's Library* (1931) ed. by Ernest Rhys, publ. by E. P. Dutton & Co., Inc., New York.

[10] *Ibid.*, No. 300.

[11] *Ibid.*, No. 301.

The government founded on opinion and imagination reigns for some time, and this government is pleasant and voluntary; that founded on might lasts forever. Thus, opinion is the queen of the world, but might is its tyrant.[12]

When one of the most important problems in the life of a nation comes up, that of the declaration of war, the decision is made by those whose personal interests are involved, most usually by the sovereign alone. The welfare of the people is not taken into consideration; thus, the very meaning of kingship is lost, and one is entitled to think that the main cause of war lies in the fact that almost all countries are governed by monarchs who are at the same time judges and executors in their own cause.[13]

This opinion might be easily inserted into a revolutionary speech, but Pascal is a man of deep religious feelings, and a convinced Christian for whom submission and patience in suffering are paramount virtues. He finds a way to reconcile what seems contradictory in his ideas: It would be almost a sacrilege and a violation of God's will to be wanting in respect to the sovereign in a kingdom because his right to the crown and his power have been established by God; at the same time, it would be wrong to change a state like Venice into a monarchy by depriving it of the freedom which God has given its people.[14] And yet one can hardly see a believer in the divine right of kings in him who asserts that men become kings "by the very force of events." In order to avoid anarchy, Pascal says, a nation needs a head, but it is force or accident, not merit, which places a man at the head of a government, and his power is transmitted by means of succession or election. Sovereigns as well as those belonging to the influential classes should not forget that they do not belong to a superior order of human beings: "There is no bond which ties your soul and body to the status of a duke rather than to that of a ferryman." [15] Accident gave them the position they

[12] *Ibid.*, No. 311.

[13] *Ibid.*, No. 298.

[14] See S. M. Melamed, *Theorie, Ursprung, und Geschichte der Friedensidee,* 1909, p. 161.

[15] Pascal, *Pensées et Opuscules,* éd. Brunschvicg, 1922, "Premier Discours sur la condition des Grands," p. 235.

are occupying; God does not place them in the position in which they are, but merely allows them to serve his ends; and they certainly do not serve his ends while they wage wars of conquests, sacrificing thousands of people to their thirst for glory, allowing thus the principle of right to become blurred and finally erased from the mind and conscience of men :

Can anything be more ridiculous than that a man should have the right to kill me because he lives on the other side of the water and because his ruler has a quarrel with mine, though I have none with him? [16]

Why do you kill me? What : do you not live on the other side of the water? If you lived on this side, my friend, I should be an assassin, and it would be unjust to slay you in this manner. But since you live on the other side, I am a hero, and it is just.[17]

Great suffering for an infinite number of people is the result of this absence of logic characteristic of men in all walks of life.   Pascal addresses subjects and sovereigns as individuals because, in his mind, a better society will be the result of the improvement of the individuals.   He objects to revolutionary methods; he hates war; peace is for him the highest blessing, unattainable, unfortunately, in his time in which the thirst for military glory is prevalent among monarchs.   He analyzes this inner drive and discovers in it something that attenuates its demerit: whatever advantages man may have on earth, he is not satisfied unless he enjoys the esteem of his fellowmen.[18]   It is only too unfortunate that sovereigns do not find a better way to merit this esteem than the way of arms.   Like most men they seek rest in a struggle against difficulties; and when they overcome these, rest becomes intolerable.   The advice given to Pyrrhus by Cyneas to take at once the rest which he was about to seek with so much labor was full of difficulties.   Men never seek things as ends in themselves, but for the sake of the search; thus passes away all man's life.   "I have discovered that the misfortune of

16 *Pensées*, No. 294.
17 *Ibid.*, No. 293.
18 *Ibid.*, No. 404.

man has only one source, namely his unfitness to stay quietly in his room." [19]

The future will prove whether to stay within its own borders would be the best policy for the state. Pascal has no definite scheme for the organization of international life; he merely points out the gulf which separates that which ought to be from that which is, and tries to show that the moral standards accepted as guiding principles in the life of individuals within a state should also be acknowledged in the sphere of international life.

The greatly venerated head of the Roman Catholic Church in France in the reign of Louis XIV, BOSSUET (1627-1704), being above all and before all a firm Christian, contemplated the human race as one whole; God who created it, being the source of life, is at the same time the object of human life and its ultimate end. Men have for their dwelling place the same terrestrial globe and are united by common interests; as children of the same Father, they are brothers called upon for mutual love and mutual care. The Christian Church, international in principle, strengthens this union, above all the Roman Catholic Church that points out the necessity of a common faith, common worship, and common action set against the individualism of the Reformation, as represented by Protestantism.

The religious convictions of Bossuet made him oppose the theories of those who, with Hobbes, saw in primitive man a kind of beast devoid of any notion of duty or dignity and submitting only to force. Bossuet thought of him as a sociable being ready to co-operate with his fellowmen—not necessarily with the strong alone, since skill and talent, though in a weak body, are as useful and as important as physical strength: "Each part has its assigned rôle, and the whole holds together through the co-operation of all the parts." [20]

Thus, taking for a starting point the teachings of religion,

[19] *Ibid.*, No. 139.
[20] Fortunat Strowski, *Bossuet et les Extraits de ses Oeuvres diverses,* 1901, p. 101.

Bossuet comes to the same conclusion as that revealed by
science—the necessity of co-operation among men not only
in order to be able to achieve something worth while, but also
to enjoy life. There are no unsurmountable obstacles to the
establishment of solidarity among men: "There is nothing
more sociable than man by his nature; nothing more intracta-
ble and unsociable if he becomes a prey to corruption." [21]

The unfortunate division of mankind into different
branches, due to geographical conditions and the subsequent
development of various languages, has led to conflicts. That
peace may prevail, the borders established by different peoples should not be infringed upon; a war of invasion, a war
for the sake of conquest are unjust wars:

If taking from one man the divine gift of life is like an attack
on God who has created man after his image, how much more
guilty must be in His eyes those who sacrifice millions of men
and so many innocent children to their ambition! [22]

Not every war is, however, illegitimate; the author makes
a strict distinction between just and unjust wars. The cases
in which he finds that war is legitimate and just are the following: (a) war of self-defense, (b) war waged by a people
in order to shake off the yoke imposed by an aggressor, (c)
war made in order to secure a passage refused by a nation
which, in holding it, forgets that "highways belong to all
men," [23] (d) war declared in case of an attempt on the life of
the ambassador of a nation, (e) war in defense of religion,
as it was in the case of the Maccabees, when to make war is
the positive command of God. The nation which has justice
on her side, has God on her side; if God wills her to be defeated, she must realize that to be defeated in a just war is
better than to triumph in an unjust one.[24]

To make war in breach of moral law is unwise: success or
defeat are predestined; men cannot change anything in God's

[21] J. B. Bossuet, *Oeuvres,* éd. Didot, 1852, I, 303, "Politique tirée des
propres paroles de l'Ecriture Sainte."

[22] *Ibid.,* I, 430.

[23] *Ibid.,* I, 429.

[24] *Ibid.,* IV, 775, "Pensées chrétiennes et morales."

plans, but the responsibility for immoral deeds is entirely theirs:

> This long chain of separate causes that build or destroy empires depends on the secret design of Divine Providence. God from His height in heaven holds the reigns of all kingdoms. . . . Let us not speak of accident or good luck, unless, in using these words, we agree that they are but expressions that hide our ignorance. What seems to be a mere accident in regard to our uncertain resolutions is a prearranged design in a higher council, in this eternal council in whom abide all causes and all consequences.[25]

> Absolute master of the earth, God uses it according to His will. If a nation is guilty in His eyes, He delivers it to a just vengeance.[26]

Bossuet sees in war the most effective instrument of God's justice and mercy. It offers individuals and nations the means of making reparation for their wrongdoings and allows them to start a new life.

To all religious denominations outside the Roman Catholic Church Bossuet shows little tolerance; he was an unrelenting Catholic who thought that it was the duty of a sovereign to eliminate from his state all "false" religions.[27] The Revocation of the Edict of Nantes had his approval; he was at this time a most influential person at the Court. He could not have approved the *dragonnades* organized by Louvois; unfortunately, some measures recommended by him could not fail to become a source of suffering to the Protestants: their children were either to attend Catholic schools or be separated from their parents; marriages between Protestants were to be performed by Catholic priests.[28]

He also reveals himself as a man of his time in his point of view with regard to slavery. It seems to him natural that a great many men are deprived of human rights by no fault of their own. The idea that slavery should be abolished once and forever is alien to him; he sternly criticizes Jurieu, the

---

[25] *Ibid.*, I, 297, "Discours sur l'histoire universelle."
[26] *Ibid.*, I, 428, "Politique tirée. . . ."
[27] *Ibid.*, I, 390.
[28] See M. Poujoulat, *Lettres sur Bossuet à un homme d'état*, 1854, "Lettre de Bossuet à l'Evêque de Mirepoix, à la date du 15 juin 1698."

Protestant minister, for his unwillingness to acknowledge the rights of a conqueror over the conquered. He goes even further, expressing the opinion that the conqueror has the right of enslaving a whole nation, and refers to the Roman law, the Old Testament, and the Gospels for the support of this opinion. He sees the origin of slavery in war: if the victor, who has the power to kill his enemy, spares him, he becomes through this act of mercy master of the person of his prisoner, of the family of the latter, and all his possessions.[29]   With regard to this question, Bodin, a sixteenth-century writer, proved to be a more advanced thinker, though, on the whole, before Montesquieu there was no abstract idea of the dignity of man.

Bossuet is also very conservative in his opinions concerning the relations between a sovereign and his subjects. He never speaks in terms of the rights of the subjects, but always in terms of their duties, of the blind obedience they owe the ruler.

The question arises: should Bossuet's name have a place on a list of pacifists? Some critics, besides calling him "the philosopher of Providence," speak of him as "the theologian of war." [30]   It seems, nevertheless, that his name should not be omitted in a study of this kind. He used the admirable beauty and power of his word to stir in the minds of sovereigns the idea that an unjust war will never remain unpunished, that he who has the ability to keep and strengthen his state shows greater wisdom than he who knows how to conquer or win battles; he urges upon the monarchs the idea that all their actions must meet the challenge of the equity of law, that justice must be pre-eminent. The brotherhood of men and nations is his ideal and the cornerstone of his philosophy. If his tolerance in religious matters can be questioned, if he has no sympathy with Protestantism, it is because he finds that the Reformation stirred the spirit of insubordination and

[29] Bossuet, *Oeuvres,* IV, 404-405, "Cinquième Avertissement sur les Lettres de M. Jurieu."

[30] See Pierre Fernessole, "Bossuet et la Guerre," *Etudes,* tome 143, avril-juin 1915.

sowed the seeds of enmity and strife between members of the same family, among citizens of the same state, and between nations. As tutor to the heir to the throne of France, he tried to mold in the mind of his pupil a trend of thought likely to promise Europe more peaceful times.

It must be admitted, however, that men whose outlook on life is that of the above-mentioned writers could not provide the world with a driving force strong enough to lead towards the abolition of war. In their opinion, personal or public misery is either a righteous chastisement inflicted by God or an opportunity sent by Providence that we may work out our moral improvement. We must not see in our misfortunes evils to be averted, but trials to be patiently endured. The foundation of the outlook of these writers is faith rather than reason; they place their ideal in the life to come. This made them less apt to contribute directly to the better organization of life on this earth.

CHAPTER IV

THE REACTION OF FREE THOUGHT

The freethinkers of seventeenth-century France did not agree with the group of writers whose outlook was based on the belief that every aspect and every event of human life is predestined. The freethinkers upheld the conviction that life within the broad limits of the laws of nature is shaped by the thought and will of man. The importance of freedom of thought, the necessity of personal, civil, and political liberty, and the need for peace in the sphere of international as well as national life were, therefore, held indispensable for unhampered and useful activity. Life as it was under a despotic government, an intolerant state religion, and an arbitrary administration did not answer those aspirations. The result was that a great number of educated men freed themselves, almost involuntarily, of the bonds of tradition and authority, above all of the recognition of religious dogmas. They were usually pointed out as *libertins*. Without any concerted effort, they made their influence felt in every sphere of life. No wonder that among other things, they found much to say about the foreign wars waged by France and about religious intolerance, the cause of persecutions, rebellions, and civil war. The insistence of the Church on the acceptance of certain dogmas was quite out of harmony with the deistic outlook of the *libertins*. They saw in deism a true religion of nature; as such, it did not contain anything that could not be readily accepted by any man: "Anything in thought limited to men of a special age, race, tradition is *eo ipso* without truth or value or importance. . . . Deism being not merely cosmopolitan but cosmical in its outlook could not admit the claim of one people and one planet to an exceptional or even distinctive rôle in religious history." [1] Its essential features were tolerance and aspiration for universal brotherhood.

Since times were dangerous and the Catholic clergy all-powerful, the *libertins* used to keep aloof from the crowd, meeting in a few *salons en vogue,* such as that of Ninon de Lenclos (1630-1705), in the homes of friends and, what was more usual in the eighteenth century, in cafés; there they were not afraid to unfold the ideas they held in the domain of religion, politics, and current events. Among the latter, war, forced conversions, religious dissensions and persecutions, and, now and then, trials accompanied by torture and death at the stake were topics worthy of being examined and discussed. The mass of the people accepted things as they were, with apathy or indifference, but the attitude of the *libertins* was vastly different. They felt that it was not justifiable to use force to attempt to gain a hold upon the inner life of man. What right, they asked, has any lay or Church official to persecute people on account of their religious convictions or the lack of them when, as GASSENDI (1592-1655) asserted, there is not and never will be the slightest possibility of proving by reason the existence of God or the soul; when, as SAINT-EVREMOND (1610-1703) thought, the source of human misery lies precisely in the impossibility of assurance that there is a life beyond the grave.[2]

There was, however, something very characteristic in the general attitude of the *libertins* towards the insoluble problems of human life. They met with humor a situation in which a man like Pascal, for example, was crushed by suffering; but their ready wit, their fine irony were sharp-pointed weapons against intolerance. Such were the characteristics of the *libertins* as a group. Individual reactions to the reigning ideas and events depended, of course, on the personality of each man.

[1] Arthur O. Lovejoy, "The Parallel of Deism and Classicism," *Modern Philology,* vol. XXIX, No. 3, Febr. 1932.
[2] Ch. Saint-Evremond, *Oeuvres,* éd. Giraud, 1865, I, 17-18.

The thoughts of LA-MOTHE-LE-VAYER (1588-1672) are comparatively little occupied with the issue of foreign wars, all his attention being centered upon the struggle between Catholics and Protestants. He asserts the futility of theological disputes:

If God had wished us to know one thousand things which are today the object of violent disputes, be sure that He would have revealed them to us; notice, however, that in these matters it is easier to attack than to defend, to destroy than to edify. In the matter of religion there is always something which goes beyond human understanding. All we can do is to build up in our soul some imperfect image of God. To wish fully to understand things of that nature is obstinately to persist in squeezing water.[3]

Le-Vayer refuses to understand the reasons which lead the authorities of the Christian Church to condemn scepticism. He sees in a sceptical attitude of mind the best preparation for becoming a Christian. Pascal was of the same opinion. He who distrusts the power of the human mind is likely to seek in religion the solution of the problems that torment him; only, as Jacques Denis says,[4] it does not mean necessarily that it will be the Christian religion that will satisfy his intellectual and moral needs. Le-Vayer finds so much similarity in all known creeds that he is prone to think that they were not due to any kind of revelation but merely to natural reason. He had traveled a great deal for his time, he had observed the customs of different peoples, had studied their beliefs and their culture; this accounts for the abundance of ethnological and geographical data in his argumentation.

CYRANO DE BERGERAC (1619-1655) in his *Les Estats et Empires de la Lune* (1656) and *Les Estats et Empires du Soleil* (1662) shares the general opinion of the *libertins* that man, keeping in mind the weakness of his reason, should avoid dogmatism and intolerance in his human relationships.

[3] La-Mothe-Le-Vayer, *Oeuvres*, 1756, VII, 251, "De la Connaissance des choses divines."

[4] J. Denis, *Sceptiques et Libertins de la première moitié du 17e siècle*, 1884, p. 222.

When during his stay on the moon Cyrano was facing capital punishment for having affirmed that the planet seen from the moon and called by the inhabitants of the latter *moon* is the *earth* whence he had come, one of the orators of the moon said:

You have no right to convict this man for his assertion that the Moon is the World whence he came, since you cannot make him see things as they appear to you. He will believe only if certain possibilities which are more in favor of an opinion than against it arise in his imagination. If these conditions do not exist, he will tell you that he believes, but in fact he will not.[5]

The issue of war seemed to have occupied Cyrano's mind more than that of the freedom of conscience. As a youth he had the reputation of being a fomenter of discord, a duelist, but at the same time a brilliant warrior. In his thirties he did not show the same enthusiasm for the military profession: a bad wound that caused him great suffering may have affected his outlook. In the course of the long conversation which took place between him and one of the inhabitants of the moon during the author's imaginary sojourn on this planet, Cyrano happened to mention to his interlocutor that in his world, that is, on the earth, the wearing of a sword was an outward sign that the wearer belonged to the nobility of the country.

Oh, my little man, [the dweller of the moon said] how strange that the lords of your world seem obstinately resolved to wear with pride an instrument denoting an executioner, a tool of destruction, a sworn enemy of all that lives.[6]

When Cyrano was taken to the Queen of the Moon, he was asked to explain the causes of the wars devastating his planet:

Why do not your Princes [the Queen said] choose arbiters to reconcile them? While they are causing the massacre of about 4,000,000 men who are better than they, they sit in their study and chaff about the circumstances of the killing of those fools

[5] *Les Oeuvres libertines de Cyrano de Bergerac,* éd. Lachèvre, 1921, p. 59, "Les Estats et Empires de la Lune."
[6] *Ibid.,* p. 88.

who die for their fatherland. . . . The matter is serious indeed, the problem to be solved being whether one has to be the subject of a king who wears a *fraise* or of the one who wears a *rabat*.[7]

In those lines the author speaks of the futility of the pretexts leading to war and of the mostly dynastic character of the latter.

Back from his dramatic adventures on the moon, Cyrano was spending happy days in the château of his friend Colignac, near Toulouse, a city renowned at this time for her autos-da-fé. The reputation of his manuscript, *Les Estats et Empires de la Lune,* added to the fact that he was known as a freethinker, put an end to his good fortune. He was cast into a prison cell at the top of a high tower. Being a physicist, he managed to build a kind of balloon and escape. He reached the sun and saw himself in a kingdom of birds. A magpie informed him that the state was ruled by a Dove, since their sovereigns were always elected from among the weakest and the meekest beings. This allowed everyone who had been wronged by the king to be avenged. The ruler, said the magpie, should always be of a sweet disposition in order to prevent war, "this channel of injustice." [8] Every week the king presided over the meeting of the states-general; every member was entitled to charge him with misgovernment; if rightly accused, he was removed from office.

Arraigned before the Court of Justice on the charge of being a *man,* the vilest of all the creatures, Cyrano anticipated a death sentence. The charges against him were heavy: not only had he allowed himself, "he, a nothingness, a bald beast, a plucked bird with neither beak nor claws," to treat animals as inferior beings, but he had been cruel to them. Created like all living beings for a life in society, he had repeatedly broken the laws of peaceful, friendly relations with his fellowmen and, above all, had engaged in wars. Fortunately, the Dove King had the right to set aside the judgment. Once more Cyrano escaped death and was free.

Cyrano indeed needed courage to write these pages against

[7] *Ibid.,* p. 88.
[8] *Ibid.,* pp. 147-156, "Les Estats et Empires du Soleil."

war. At a time when soldiers had to sacrifice their lives fearlessly in daily skirmishes or bloody battles, one needed courage to assert that those who do not fear death are a danger to their fellowmen: they make life too cheap.[9] Cyrano was human. Not being able to offer the consolation of religion to those thousands of men who were almost daily perishing in war, he offered what he had, thoughts which might reconcile them to the inevitable:

Do not be troubled at the thought that you have to do now what your companions will do later . . . and then, tell me, he who is not born is not unhappy; now you will be like one who is not born; in the twinkling of an eye, after life ends, you will be what you were an instant before life began, and when this instant is gone, you will be dead, as long ago as he who died one thousand centuries ago.[10]

We find an identical thought in the first dialogue of Oratius Tubero, a thought suggested to Le-Vayer by the reading of Seneca:

It is a great error to imagine that we die only after we have lived; we were dead before we were born; death of which we are so afraid has preceded our life and when it follows it, it will but take the place it occupied before. "A light is not more dark or dead when extinct than it was before it was lighted." [11]

To be resigned to the inevitable is wise, but war seems to be an unavoidable evil only to those who see in militarism the only guarantee of the security of a state. One glance at the dreary solitude of the place occupied in times bygone by the glorious Sparta reminds the nations of the world of the future prepared for them by the God of battles.[12]

The end of the seventeenth century was a particularly significant time in the history of free thought. In 1682 PIERRE

[9] *Ibid.*, p. 196.
[10] *Ibid.*, p. 162.
[11] Le-Vayer, *Oeuvres,* 1756, IV, 39, "Premier Dialogue entre Tubertus Ocella et Marcus Bibulus."
[12] *Ibid.*, t. VII, "Lettre CXXVII: De la Paix."

BAYLE (1647-1706) published his *Pensées diverses sur la Comète qui parut au mois de décembre 1680.*[13]

What is the right path, Bayle asks, that should be taken by a sovereign who hesitates over a decision between war or peace with a neighboring nation? The right thing to do, he advises ironically, is to consult the prophecies. With regard to King Louis, he adds, there are definite revelations from above, which promise him dominion over the entire world. To be convinced of this, it is enough to read the *Traité de l'Antéchrist,* ascribed to Saint Augustine, and the *Commentaire sur l'Apocalypse,* by Pareus,[14] and also to take into consideration the tradition prevailing among the Turks which predicts the destruction of their empire by the French. Will not the King avail himself of those good omens, he inquires, and, under their auspices, take possession of the parts of the Netherlands that are not yet under his rule as well as of all the territories in Germany that have some appeal for him? One should, of course, keep in mind that the Crusaders paid a heavy price for having lent an ear to the prophecy of a certain hermit of Mount Olivet. Bayle then proceeds in more serious vein; he admits that the unity of the French people, set off against the dissensions reigning in every other European State, is a great force, but the lethargy of Europe, he adds, may not last; the European nations may form a coalition. . . .

Nations are like the sea that is frightfully stirred up after the most profound calm. The influence of one man is often sufficient to give courage to half the world and to assure success to a party.[15]

Bayle, arguing from the point of view of natural law, refuses to sanction a war undertaken for conquest. Nothing seems to him more unjust or more infamous than to deprive of their lands those to whom they belong by the right of age-long possession. For a Christian, the only kind of legitimate war is a defensive war, and yet Christian nations have shown

[13] *Pensées diverses sur la Comète,* éd. Prat, 1912.
[14] Pareus, David (1548-1622), German theologian, professor at Heidelberg.
[15] *Pensées diverses* . . . , II, cclviii.

themselves in the course of bygone centuries equal to, if not surpassing, the Turks in warlike spirit. All progress in warfare, each new weapon of destruction, has been devised by Christian peoples:

Those who are acquainted with the rudiments of the Christian religion know well that it recommends quite particularly to put up with abuses, to be humble, to love our fellowmen, to seek peace. . . . I challenge all those who have a good knowledge of the art of war to make good soldiers of men determined to follow punctually all those maxims. . . . The most you could expect from them would be the decision to die for their country and their God. . . . It is most certain that our holy faith cannot impart a martial spirit, and yet there are no more warlike nations than those who profess the Christian religion. . . . I see therein the most convincing proof that in our worldly relationships we do not follow the principles of our religion since . . . the Christians use all their wit and all their energy to improve in the art of war, while their knowledge of the Gospels does not check in the least their cruel design.[16]

Bayle comes, as we see, to the same conclusion to which came Le-Vayer: a man's morals are very little dependent on his religious convictions; he fully realizes the bearing of this assertion and reaffirms it not only in his works, but in some of his letters.[17] The source of a man's morals, according to Bayle, is in his temperament, his passions, more or less held in check by the dictates of law. He even wonders whether an ardent devotion to a creed is not likely to lead one away from the path of virtue; it can easily rouse him to acts of fanaticism and violence against those who refuse to become his proselytes.

Neither Cyrus nor Alexander nor Caesar had ever inquired of what creed were the peoples they vanquished; Christian nations, unlike these conquerors, prefer to set their own land afire, to make their countrymen suffer all the calamities of

---

[16] *Ibid.*, I, cxli.

[17] With regard to this point, see Bayle's letter of June 29, 1694, found in the University Library of Leyden, Collection Papenbroeck, no. 15. "Unpublished Letters of Pierre Bayle" by J. L. Gerig and G. L. van Roosbroeck in the *Romanic Review*, vol. 23, 1932, pp. 117-128.

war rather than to allow a new form of the Christian faith
to be introduced into their states.

When the Revocation of the Edict of Nantes in October
1685 made political exiles of some hundred thousand French
Huguenots and applied oppressive measures to all those who
were not allowed to leave the country or were unable to do
so, the calm tone that characterized the early writings of
Bayle gave way to a vehement protest. He was aware of the
indifferent attitude with which French people were witnessing
the sufferings of their countrymen; Maimbourg's *Histoire
du Calvinisme* (1682), together with the influence of the
Catholic clergy, might have been responsible for it to a certain extent. They saw in the Revocation of the Edict a political measure that aimed at the preservation of the unity of
the French nation. In twenty-two letters Bayle issued his
General Criticism of Maimbourg's work and, after the Revocation of the Edict had taken place, his violent pamphlet *Ce
que c'est que la France toute Catholique sous le règne de
Louis le Grand* did much by way of creating a sympathetic
understanding of the trials to which the Huguenots were submitted. Then (1686) came his powerful work, *Commentaire philosophique sur les paroles de Jésus-Christ: "Contrains
- les d'entrer."* Already the title of the work shows that
Bayle saw the source of the erroneous effort to make France
all Catholic in the wrong interpretation of the words of
Jesus Christ: "Go out into the highways and hedges and
compel them to come in, that my house may be filled." [18]

The more earnestness Bayle puts into his plea for the toleration of an erring conscience, the more stress he lays on man's
right to independent thought, the less value he is inclined to
see in the dogmas of a creed. Far above dogmas he puts
moral conscience, "the true light which lighteneth every man
that cometh into the world." [19] This moral conscience is for
him the supreme judge; every action, every doctrine that is
in contradiction to this inner voice should be rejected. This
thought was expressed by Bayle years before the publication

[18] The Gospel according to Saint Luke, XIV, 23.
[19] The Gospel according to Saint John, I, 9.

of Kant's *Grundlegung zur Metaphysik der Sitten* (1798). Kant writes:

. . . it is clear that all moral conceptions have their seat and origin completely *a priori* in the reason . . . in the commonest reason just as truly as in that which is the highest degree speculative; that they cannot be obtained by abstraction from any empirical and therefore merely contingent knowledge; that it is just that purity of their origin that makes them worthy to serve as our supreme practical principle.[20]

Bayle fully realizes that our conscience can be blinded by prejudice, egotism, and passion; there is, however, for every one of us an infallible means of finding the right path; in a moment of doubt we should put ourselves above our personal interests or the ideas of our environment and ask ourselves:

Is such a thing just and, if it were a question of introducing it into a country where it was not in practice and where it might be possible to introduce it or not, could this thing, if examined dispassionately, justify its adoption?[21]

And the German philosopher in the same work mentioned above says:

There is therefore but one categorical imperative, namely, this: "Act only on that maxim whereby thou canst at the same time will that it should become a universal law."[22]

It is evident that, considered from the point of view stated in this maxim, dissensions and wars inspired by a difference in religious outlook as well as wars waged for the sake of glory, conquest, profit, inspired by ambition or national pride must be declared inexcusable.

The *Commentaire philosophique* (1686) preceded by three years Locke's *Letters on Toleration* (1689). Bayle was, consequently, the first to claim for man complete freedom of conscience; it was he who put this important idea into circu-

[20] I. Kant, *Fundamental Principles of the Metaphysik of Ethics,* ed. 1929, transl. by Th. K. Abbott, p. 33.
[21] P. Bayle, *A Philosophical Commentary* . . . ed. London, 1708, I, 48-49.
[22] Kant, *op. cit.,* p. 46.

lation and, by its influence, was to contribute, though indirectly, to the cessation of religious wars and persecutions.

The long life of FONTENELLE (1657-1757) seems to speak in favor of an impassioned attitude in regard to the reigning beliefs and ideas, the social and political events, and the tribulations of one's personal life. "I never laughed nor wept," [23] he is quoted as saying. In full harmony with this statement is the witty remark of Mme de Tencin: "Where you should have a heart, you have brains." [24] Fontenelle was a renowned writer, a very influential member of the French Academy; he held an enviable position in social circles; therefore, his poise and calm judgment must have exercised a pacifying influence at a time of dissensions and wars. Like Bayle, he was not the kind of man from whose lips an exhortation inviting men to love one another would seem in place. In both great writers brain outweighed heart; they were profound sceptics, "De las cosas mas seguras, la mas segura es dudar" (of all maxims the one which recommends doubt is the most secure); Voltaire states that such was, for example, the motto of La-Mothe-Le-Vayer; [25] such was probably their motto. They realized the limitations of the human mind and the inaccessibility of absolute knowledge, but their scepticism served to confirm in them the conviction that the only right attitude for any man is forbearance towards his fellowmen; to demand universal love would seem to them an exaggeration which would defeat itself.

While Le-Vayer was prone to defend the principle of tolerance from the point of view of racial, national, and religious differences, Fontenelle pointed to the possible existence of an infinite number of worlds of which many might be inhabited and more advanced in civilization than our earth. To the geographical data in favor of tolerance, advanced by Le-Vayer, Fontenelle added an argument based on astronomy.

[23] See Jean Jacquart L'Abbé Trublet critique et moraliste, p. 291.
[24] Ibid., p. 76.
[25] Oeuvres, éd. Moland, XIV, 86.

If one considers the fact that the climax of the so-called *libertinage* had coincided in France with the disturbances of the *Fronde,* the almost continuous foreign wars of Louis XIV, and the acute religious differences of the seventeenth century, it becomes evident that the tolerant pacifism of the French sceptics was a valuable philosophical background for more practical projects of peace than those of Dubois, Crucé, and Sully.

CHAPTER V

EARLY EIGHTEENTH-CENTURY PROJECTS

THE dislike of any kind of violence whether moral or physical, characteristic of the representatives of free thought, became particularly strong in the course of the eighteenth century. This century opened, in the field of pacifist ideals, with the *Projet de paix perpétuelle* of the Abbé de Saint-Pierre.

The path traced by this work was closely followed by the plan of 1745. The anonymous author of this new scheme published it shortly after the death of the Abbé (1743), as if to give a new force to the ideas expressed in the *Projet de paix perpétuelle*. This fresh call to peace came at a time when France under Louis XV had engaged in a war the sole purpose of which was, as it seemed, to benefit Frederick II. "We are fighting for the King of Prussia," French soldiers used to say.

The work of Ange Goudar (1757) was written during the Seven Years' War (1756-1763). France took part in it for dynastic reasons at a time when she should rather have been defending her possessions in North America and India.

This group of writers belonging to the first part of the eighteenth century approached the issues of war and peace mainly from a utilitarian point of view. They knew well the economic conditions prevailing in France; they realized that foreign wars impel the government to neglect the internal affairs of the state, whereas the intellectual, moral, and economic interests of the nation and her general welfare depend precisely on this branch of government. The most significant of the three plans for world peace is that of the Abbé de Saint-Pierre.

In the brilliant phalanx of French writers of the eighteenth century the ABBÉ DE SAINT-PIERRE (1658-1743) holds a modest place. While centering all his attention on the ideas he wished to promote, he neglected the form of his writings: "I am not afraid of being a poor writer provided I be a good citizen," he used to say. Most of his ideas were in advance of his age; they were directed toward the betterment of government, the amelioration of the lot of the lower classes, reforms in educational methods, the abolition of privileges and hereditary titles. Like Dubois, the Abbé saw the necessity of a universal law for all the different parts of France. There was hardly a field of social or political life which he had not observed and studied. Men holding official positions were often irritated at what seemed to them an interference with matters that should not concern him at all; they liked to remind him of the opinion of Malherbe: "A passenger should never interfere with the management of a boat."—To that the Abbé used to reply: "However, the poor passenger whose warnings the pilot disregards, yet whose life is in the pilot's hands and who will drown if the ship sinks, should at least be allowed to treat the pilot as he deserves." In a society in which the accident of birth either doomed a man to a life of starvation and half-slavery or guaranteed him the benefits of personal freedom, wealth, exemption from taxation, and power over others, one was surprised to find a man devoid of egotism, and to hear him say: "I think the only difference God instituted between his children is that between crime and virtue," [1] or a statement like this: "It seems to me that theological disputes are at the same time the most ridiculous farce and the most horrible scourge next to war, pestilence, famine, and smallpox," [2] and this in the early eighteenth century, when the controversy over the doctrine of quietism, the struggle between Catholics and Protestants, the disputes between the Jesuits and the Jansenists were extremely acute.

The splendor and glory of the reign of Louis XIV did not

[1] See Voltaire, *Oeuvres,* éd. Moland, XX, 466, "Symbole ou Credo."
[2] See M. Roustan, *The Pioneers of the French Revolution,* transl. from French by F. Whyte, p. 274.

hold any fascination for him.   In the wars made by the King and in the magnificence of court life he saw the source of the economic misery of the population crushed under an exorbitant and arbitrary system of taxation; he denied the King the right to be called Louis the Great, an opinion he upheld at the cost of his membership in the French Academy.   He blamed the wars of the King, declaring them to have been waged for the sake of glory and made often in breach of a treaty.   Personal considerations or the pursuit of personal advantage were alien to the Abbé; he invariably met with good humor all the jokes people made when they heard about some new reform he was trying to have adopted.   Expelled from the French Academy, he never held a grudge against those who had voted his expulsion and he continued, as Voltaire put it jestingly, "to enlighten the world and to govern it." [3]

The idea to the promotion of which the Abbé had devoted his life was that of perpetual peace.   He foresaw that the future would justify his hope.   In vain did people call him "the famous Abbé with his hobby of perpetual peace," he did not allow himself to be disturbed.   If he failed in his effort to persuade sovereigns and statesmen to try out his plan for the abolition of war, he had the satisfaction of seeing his ideas widely known.   The interest they had aroused in the whole of Europe grew steadily after the death of the author (1743).

It is in the first five "discourses" of the *Projet de paix perpétuelle,* vol. I, that we find the fundamental ideas of the Abbé's work.[4]   Three-fourths of the second volume are taken up by the sixth discourse, in which the author answers possible criticisms, and by the seventh discourse containing the eight "useful articles" which regulate details of procedure and

[3] Cf. Voltaire, *Oeuvres,* éd. Moland, XXIX, 267, "Fragments sur l'histoire générale."

[4] L'Abbé de Saint-Pierre, *Projet de paix perpétuelle,* vol. I & II, Utrecht, 1713; vol. III, Lyon, 1717. *L'Abrégé du Projet de paix perpétuelle,* Rotterdam, 1729.

matters of secondary importance. The third volume sums up the contents of the first two; in its first part one finds, however, some new objections anticipated by the author, and their refutation; and in the second part the statement of the advantages which European sovereigns might derive from the adoption of the plan. *L'Abrégé du projet de paix perpétuelle,* written also by the Abbé, gives in an abridged form the first five discourses (they are called here "fundamental articles"), then again a series of probable objections with their refutation. Some new considerations are found in this work, the revised edition of which appeared in 1738.

In his "first discourse" the author stresses the futility of the efforts to secure a lasting peace either by treaties or the system of the balance of power. Treaties are promises not backed by any kind of guarantee. As for political equilibrium, he compares it to good scales: the slightest weight put on one of the scales turns it. A similar thing takes place in the relations between political bodies: the rulers of nations differ so much in mental ability, force of ambition, and intensity of warlike spirit that the balance of power is indeed a very unsteady balance.

In accordance with this conviction, in his "second discourse" the author invites the sovereigns to delegate representatives who, assembling in one of the free cities of Europe, would declare the establishment of a Permanent League of European States. The declaration would be made after the delegates of some fourteen states have given their signatures. The remaining ten states may declare their adherence to the League at different times, but they would have to join the League since membership would be compulsory and armed force would be at any time at the disposal of the Union in order to guarantee submission.

The author would not permit any one to say that the establishment of the Federal States of Europe which he was proposing was nothing but a figment of his imagination; the Confederations of German and of Helvetian States, the Corps of the United Provinces, by their very existence, testified to the contrary.[5] The advantages that the Union would be in a position to secure for its members would be so great that all Christian nations outside Europe would be eager to join.[6] All member states would provide for the maintenance of the Union through contributions proportionate to their wealth.

The "third discourse" states that the Union will guarantee to every member state the territory it possesses by virtue of the last treaties; the basis of the new order of things will be, thus, the *status quo*. The recognition of this principle places the *Projet de paix perpétuelle* closer to the *Nouveau Cynée* than to the *Grand Dessein de Henri IV* whose main point was the altering of the map of Europe. Inspired partly by the Abbé's modesty and partly by his hope of seeing his proposals more readily put into action, he backed them by the prestige of a great name and assured his readers that he was simply commenting on the peace plan of Henry IV. It is, however, evident that the principles underlying these two plans are different, and the Abbé's scheme is, therefore, original.

Three reasons induce the author to build his plan on the *status quo:* a) he sees in it a good starting point; b) he finds that history justifies the principle; he points to the German Confederation which, built on the basis of the validity of the last treaties, could boast of centuries of lasting peace; c) he thinks also that a Union of peace should start with peace,

---

[5] Seroux d'Agincourt does not share this opinion: "Ce qui est possible sur une petite échelle est souvent impraticable sur une échelle plus vaste, et il importe de tenir compte des dissemblances des peuples dans leur caractère, leur langage, leurs traditions; et puis les confédérations mentionnées offraient les éléments de même nature, avaient le même esprit patriotique, ce qui ne sera pas le cas dans l'Union de l'Europe." He finds also that one who struggles for peace should condemn recourse to arms under any condition, even in case of non-submission to the decision of the Union: "La paix s'enfuit à la faveur de l'instrument destiné à l'établir." *Exposé des projets de paix perpétuelle de l'Abbé de Saint-Pierre et de Henri IV, de Bentham et de Kant,* Paris, 1905, p. 151.

[6] At the moment of its establishment the Union was meant to be a league of Christian nations; however, the non-Christian peoples were expected to become Associates of the Union, to sign treaties of offensive and defensive war, to have Residents in the city chosen as the Seat of the Union and pay contributions for its maintenance. As in the scheme of Cruce, the organization was expected to assume a more and more universal character. [Cf. First and tenth "fundamental articles" of the "fourth discourse."]

not with war. He does not share Sully's opinion that a last great war must precede the establishment of peace. He cites the advantages to be gained by the recognition of the principle of the *status quo* as real advantages to each member state. There would be no hope for enlarging the territory of a state, it is true, but, on the other hand, there would be no risk of losing even the smallest part of it. There would be no war in the future except in case of non-submission to the decisions of the Senate acting as a Court of Arbitration. There would be no danger of any biased decisions, each one being a precedent and as such a foundation for future decisions. Each member of the Senate would be aware that a biased judgment would hit him in his turn if his case were presented for arbitration. Appeal to the Court established as a compulsory measure would lead towards disarmament. The enormous sums of money thus saved and used for the development of industry, commerce, and education would contribute to the prosperity of a country much more than the most successful war. Through his suggestion to give half of this money to the sovereigns the Abbé hoped to secure their co-operation.

The "fourth discourse" is the most important part of the plan; it contains the twelve "fundamental" and the eight "important" articles. Unanimous vote is required for the amendment of the "fundamental articles" while a majority of three-fourths is sufficient for the amendment of the "important" ones (fund. article XII).

"Fundamental Articles"[7]

The present Sovereigns, by their under-written Deputies, have agreed to the following articles:

1. There shall be, from this day on, a Society, a permanent and perpetual Union between the Sovereigns subscribed and, if possible, among all Christian Sovereigns in order to make peace unalterable in Europe; and in that view the Union shall make, if possible, with its neighbors, the Mahometan Sovereigns, treaties of league offensive and defensive to keep each of them in peace within the bounds of his territory, by taking from them and giving them all possible reciprocal securities.

[7] The reader is referred to the English abridged edition of the *Projet de paix perpétuelle,* London, 1714.

The Sovereigns shall be perpetually represented by their Deputies in a perpetual Congress or Senate in a free city.

The author stresses the necessity of inviting non-Christian nations to become allies of the Union. So long as those peoples remained in arms or a possibility existed of their arming, the Union would naturally have to be on its guard.

2. The European Society shall not at all concern itself about the Government of any state, unless it be to preserve the fundamental form of it and give speedy and sufficient assistance to the Princes in Monarchies and to the Magistrates in Republics against any that are seditious and rebellious. Thus it will be a guaranty that the Hereditary Sovereignties shall remain hereditary, according to the manner and custom of each nation; that those that are elective shall remain elective in the countries where election is usual; that among the nations where there are Capitulations or Conventions which are called *Pacta Conventa,* those sorts of treaties shall be exactly observed, and that those who in Monarchies should have taken up arms against the Prince, or in Republics against some of the chief Magistrates, shall be punished with death and confiscation of goods.

3. The Union shall employ its whole strength and care to hinder during the Regencies, the Minorities, the weak Reigns of each state any prejudice from being done to the Sovereign . . . and if any sedition, revolt, conspiracy . . . or any other violence should happen to the Prince or to the Royal Family, the Union, as its Guardian and Protectress born, shall send Commissioners into that State to look into the truth of the facts and shall at the same time send troops to punish the guilty according to the rigor of the laws.

4. All the Sovereignties of Europe shall always remain in the condition they are in and shall always have the same limits they have now. No territory shall be dismembered nor shall any be added to it by succession, agreement between different Houses, election, donation, cession, sale, conquest, voluntary submission of the subjects, or otherwise. . . . The Sovereigns shall not be suffered to make an exchange of any territory nor to sign a treaty among themselves but with the consent and under the guarantee of the Union by the three-fourths of the twenty-four voices, and the Union shall remain guarantor for the execution of reciprocal promises.

The second, third, and fourth "fundamental articles" are those that were violently attacked by Rousseau [8] and by many political writers after him. In 1919 Lucien Lacroix, professor at the Ecole des Hautes Etudes, published an article under the title *Un Apôtre de la paix perpétuelle*.[9] He finds that the Abbé regards the subjects of a sovereign as not entitled to consideration; that his Union seems to be an alliance of rulers directed against their peoples who will have to abandon all hope for self-government. He reproaches him for his disregard of the principle of nationalities: the Abbé, says Lacroix, would find it quite natural to see Poland become a part of Prussia, Alsace-Lorraine a province of Germany, inasmuch as he absolutely refuses the people the right of self-determination. The principle of the *status quo* so fervently advocated by the Abbé is opposed by all those who assert that before declaring the permanence, the irremovability of a possession one should be assured of its compliance with the principle of justice.

The leading idea of the last four lines of the fourth article is the repudiation of secret diplomacy, which would prevent treaties from having clauses on which future claims might be based.

5. No Sovereign shall henceforth possess two sovereignties either hereditary or elective. . . . If, by right of succession, there should fall to a Sovereign a State more considerable than that which he possesses, he may leave that he possesses and settle himself in that which is fallen to him.

6. The Kingdom of Spain shall not go out of the House of Bourbon or now the House of France so long as there shall be two males of that family of the Eldest Branches or of the Youngest Branches on condition that the Elder shall be always preferred to the Younger and the Elder Branch to the Younger Branch.

This paragraph is probably meant to be a strong incentive for inducing the House of France to establish the League and to make it solid and lasting.

[8] Rousseau's comments on the *Projet de paix perpétuelle* will be found in ch. VII.

[9] See *La Grande Revue*, 1919.

7. The Deputies shall incessantly labor to digest all the articles of commerce in general and in different commerces between particular nations, but in such a manner as that the laws may be equal and reciprocal towards all the nations, and founded upon equity. The Union shall establish in different towns Chambers for the maintaining of commerce, consisting of Deputies authorized to reconcile and to judge without appeal the disputes that shall arise between the subjects of different Sovereigns, in value above ten thousand livres; the other suits of less consequence shall be decided as usual by the judges of the place where the defendant lives. Each Sovereign shall lend his hand to the execution of the judgments of the Chambers of Commerce as if they were his own judgments.

Each Sovereign shall at his own charge exterminate his inland robbers and bandits and the pirates on his coasts on pain of making reparation, and if he has need of help, the Union shall assist him.

The point stressed in this article is that no one nation should be preferred to another, that every possible means be used to facilitate commercial relations, and the subjects of one nation be prevented from wrongdoing those of a neighboring nation.

8. No Sovereign shall take up arms but against him who shall be declared an enemy to the European society. But if he has any cause to complain of any of the Members or any demand to make upon them, he shall order his Deputy to give a memorial to the Senate in the City of Peace, and the Senate shall take care to reconcile the differences by its mediating Commissioners; or, if they cannot be reconciled, the Senate shall judge them by arbitral judgment by plurality of voices provisionally, and by the three-fourths of the voices definitively. . . . The Sovereign who shall take up arms before the Union has declared war or who shall refuse to execute a regulation of the Society or a judgment of the Senate shall be declared an enemy to the Society and it shall make war upon him; he shall even pay the charges of the war, and the country that shall be conquered by him, at the time of the suspension of arms, shall be for ever separated from his dominions. . . . If, after the Society is formed to the number of fourteen voices, a Sovereign should refuse to enter into it, it shall declare him an enemy to the repose of Europe and shall make war upon him till he enter into it or till he be entirely dispossessed.

Compulsory and irrevocable membership in the League of Nations is thus one of the essential features of the Abbé's plan. To allow a state to remain outside the League is to give up every hope for permanent peace and to favor aggression. The Abbé does not feel that obligatory recourse to arbitration undermines the principle of the sovereignty of the state. Owing to the support guaranteed to the rulers by articles 2, 3, and 4, their sovereignty over their subjects becomes more absolute than ever; they can henceforth be sure of the integrity of the territories of their states, they will never know the horrors of a revolution nor the terrible disasters of war. In comparison with all they gain how small and easy is the sacrifice they are asked to make; namely, to recognize the authority of the Senate of which they themselves are members and of which each one is chief in his turn. Gaining everything, they lose but their imaginary right to attack, destroy, and conquer a neighboring state, a right which has never been theirs.

9. There shall be in the Senate of Europe twenty-four Senators or Deputies, representing the following countries:

1. France	14. Denmark
2. Spain	15. Poland
3. England	16. The States of the Pope
4. Holland	17. Muscovy
5. Savoy	18. Austria
6. Portugal	19. Courland and Associates
7. Bavaria and Associates	(Danzig, Hamburg, Lübeck, Rostock)
8. Venice	
9. Genoa and Associates	20. Prussia
10. Florence and Associates	21. Saxony
11. Switzerland and Associates	22. Palatine and Associates
	23. Hanover and Associates
12. Lorraine and Associates	24. Ecclesiastical Electors and Associates
13. Sweden	

The author has definite arguments in favor of twenty-four deputies; he regards this number as high enough to prevent plots and petty intrigues and, on the other hand, low enough to secure the efficient and speedy work of the Congress.

10. The Members and Associates of the Union shall contribute to the expenses of the Society and to the subsidies for its security, each in proportion to his revenues and to the riches of his people.

The author stipulates that the burdens and responsibilities arising from the new order of things should be equitably shared by all members. In the "Explanation" following the tenth article the Abbé states that each member of the Union shall have to send the same number of soldiers to the international army, but the smaller the state, the larger the sum of money it shall receive from the Union for the equipment of the armed force.

11. When the Senate shall deliberate upon any thing pressing . . . the question may be decided by plurality of voices provisionally, and before it is deliberated, they shall begin by deciding, by plurality, whether the matter is provisionable. [A majority of three-fourths is required for a final decision.] [10]

12. None of the eleven "fundamental articles" above-named shall be in any point altered without the *unanimous* consent of all the Members ; but, as for the other articles, the Society may always by the three-fourths of the voices add or diminish, for the common good, whatever it shall think fit.

In addition to those twelve articles which lay the foundation of the Union, there are eight others to which the author gives the name of

"Important Articles"

1. Utrecht is suggested as the seat of the Congress.[11]

2. The Senate shall always maintain an Ambassador with each of the member states and a Resident in each Province of two million people. They will be chosen among the native or naturalized residents of the City of Peace.

3. In time of peace each Sovereign shall not keep more than six thousand soldiers of his own nation, but he may, with the consent of the Union, maintain foreign soldiers and officers.

[10] Cf. "fundam. art." 12 and "useful art." 5.

[11] This city, situated in Holland, a country essentially commercial and, as such, appreciating the advantages of peace, was already chosen several times for peace conferences.

4. After the Congress shall have declared war against a Sovereign, those of his subjects who side with him against the Common Country shall be punished with death or imprisonment for life, while great reward awaits those who will support the Union.

5. Every year, on the same day, the Sovereigns, the Princes of the Blood, and fifty of the principal officials shall renew in their capital city in the presence of the ambassadors and residents of the Union their oaths of fidelity to the Common Country.

6. The Union shall give great and honorable reward to him who shall discover a conspiracy against the Union.

7. The Union shall appoint Commissioners to the settlements the Sovereigns have in countries which are outside Europe; on their report, the Congress shall give decision by three-fourths of the voices.

8. When in any one of the states of the Union there shall be no person capable of succeeding the reigning Sovereign, the Union shall regulate, if possible in concert with the Sovereign, the person who shall succeed him, or turn the Government into a Republic.

Those eight "important articles" are designed to give strength to the Federation and to make it easier at the same time to put the forces of the new State into action. They have a practical character; however, the third one seems to broach the subject of disarmament and the fourth one raises, unintentionally, it is true, an ethical problem: political dissensions among the subjects of a monarch outlawed by the Union are, no doubt, of great advantage to the latter; seeing in the Union the common fatherland of all the peoples who have joined it, the author promises support to all those who will break allegiance to their Sovereign and take sides with the Union, while a severe penalty, even death, awaits those who remain faithful to the oath of allegiance; the Abbé seems to disregard the difficulty of the problem from the ethical point of view.

In his "fifth discourse" the author tries to prove that his plan, if adopted in time of war, would lead to the cessation of hostilities; if adopted after the conclusion of a peace treaty, would help to make the agreement lasting.

The "sixth discourse" contains seventy possible objections to the plan and their refutation.

The eight "useful articles" of the "seventh discourse" refer mainly to details of organization and procedure; if we compare the "fundamental articles" to a constitution, we may compare the "useful articles" to by-laws.

"USEFUL ARTICLES"

1. To assure the safety of the City of Peace, the seat of the Federal Government, and to secure the independence of the Congress, there shall be in the City all things necessary for the sustaining of a long siege or blockade. The soldiers and officers of the garrison shall be, as nearly as possible, natives of the territory.

2. In order to prevent any danger of dictatorship, the commander-in-chief of the Federal army, appointed by the Senate in case of war, shall not belong to any sovereign family and shall not enjoy the right of nominating officers, but he may arraign them before the Council of War if they fail to perform their duty. If he has achieved success, the Senate may give him the sovereignty over a part or the whole of the conquered country in case there be no legitimate heir to the monarch who has been deprived of his state for non-submission to the Federal Government.

3. Appointments to high positions in Government should be made on the basis of merit, moral dignity, aptitude for work, and knowledge of political science.[12] The same Deputy shall not be employed above four years.

4. Each of the Senators shall, in his turn, week by week, be Prince of the Senate and Governor of the City of Peace; he shall preside in the general assemblies and in the Council of Five appointed to govern daily affairs; the Prince may not give any order without consent of the Council after a decision

[12] Since France had no school of political science, the Abbé suggested that the French Academy publish every year a definite number of political works. Cf. *Oeuvres,* éd. 1729-41, tome XVI, pp. 96-104, "Discours sur le plan de l'Académie Française."

is made by a majority of votes. This decision must be made in writing. The Senators shall place themselves in the Chamber of the Senate according to the priority of admittance to membership in the Council. The sitting of the Senators in private Committees and in public assemblies shall be regulated by their sitting in the Senate.[13]

5. Besides the four standing Committees (political, diplomatic, financial, and war) there shall be temporary Committees formed expressly to reconcile sovereigns. These *Committees of Reconciliation* shall consist of members nominated by Letters Patent of the Senate by a majority of votes. If a Committee of Reconciliation does not succeed in adjusting the difficulty, the Chairman shall give the opinion of the Committee to the Secretary, who shall distribute printed copies thereof to all the Senators that they give their opinions in writing, in full Assembly, to the Secretary; and if after the law is made by the Senate for all such cases, the sovereign who is in the wrong should not obey the law, then the Prince of the Senate shall pronounce a judgment nominally against this sovereign. This arbitral judgment shall be pronounced provisionally by plurality of votes, and six months afterwards definitively by a majority of three-fourths.

This fifth "useful article" is rich in ideas of great value which are largely applied in our time: it suggests that all deliberations be based upon printed memorials; that the Senate should examine no memorial till it is signed by three Senators stating that it is worth-while to bring it under deliberation; that in case it be resolved to have the memorial examined, it should be first studied by a Committee; that copies of the opinions of the members with their comments should be distributed to all Senators; that on an appointed day each Senator should write and sign his opinion at the bottom of the copy before handing it over to the Secretary. The author finds that condemning a sovereign by name in any decision is of less

[13] The Abbé gave definite rules which promised to guarantee peace during the sessions of the Senate. In his capacity as secretary to the Abbé de Polignac, one of the plenipotentiaries at the Treaty of Utrecht (1712-13), he was aware of all the disturbances and disputes which the question of precedence and formality could cause.

importance than the making of a general law upon a particular fact.[14]

Free exercise of any religion shall be allowed.

The Union shall endeavor to agree upon astronomical calculation, weights, measures, and coins.

6.　For the security of the Union, the Tzar will be requested to fortify all the frontiers which separate his territory from that of non-members of the Union; the Federation shall keep considerable garrisons there. In case of war between the non-members, the Senate shall offer them the means of mediation, its Court of Arbitration, and shall side with the sovereign who will accept its offer.

7.　This article determines the amount of the contribution to be paid into the common treasury by each of the European states as well as by each of the Associates (Turkey, Morocco, Algeria . . .).

8.　The European Union shall endeavor to establish in Asia a permanent Society like that of Europe that peace may be maintained there also.[15]

Summarized more briefly, the proposals forming the basis of the political scheme of the Abbé de Saint-Pierre were the following: 1) The juridical organization of a League of Nations, 2) The contribution to be made by the Allied nations for the maintenance of the Union, 3) The establishment of a permanent World Tribunal to which all differences between nations should be referred, 4) The creation of an international army which would be at the disposal of the League to support the decisions of the Tribunal, 5) The amendment of the twelve fundamental articles through unanimous vote of the Assembly and of the articles of secondary importance through a majority of votes.

[14] In his pamphlet *Règle pour discerner le droit du tort entre nation et nation* the Abbé tries to compose a kind of code which would guide the Court of Arbitration in its decisions. Divine law, moral law, and natural law, he thinks, command us that we do not do to others what we should not like them to do to us. This principle put into practice would inaugurate an era of order, justice, and peace among nations. Cf. *Oeuvres* éd. 1729-41, tome XV, pp. 5-13.

[15] Thus, peace among nations becomes in the mind of the Abbé a universal principle.

These basic ideas have found their place in our time in the Covenant of the League of Nations. It is true that, contrary to the contents of the sixteenth article of the Covenant, no kind of armed force has been placed at the disposal of the League, no attempt has been made to create an international army, such as had been planned by the author of the *Projet de paix perpétuelle;* yet the need for this kind of army was strongly felt: it found its expression in the outline of a project issued by President Theodore Roosevelt,[16] it was discussed by President Wilson [17] and, above all, stressed in the *Projet français pour l'organisation de la paix* of November 14, 1932.[18] This point was and is still an object of controversy as a principle to be accepted or rejected and as something that would meet with tremendous difficulties in its realization. Taken as a concrete problem, the question of the organization of an international army may give rise to the following considerations: can an armed force at the disposal of the League be inspired by the great thought that it fights for the ideal of universal peace, or will it be more likely ready to consider itself as an instrument of punitive measures decided upon by the Congress? This would not be a very inspiring idea. Can an army formed of soldiers of different nationalities and fighting for an abstract principle possess the moral force of an armed nation fighting for her concrete vital interests? The Abbé de Saint-Pierre strongly believed in the possibility of having an ideally efficient international army at the disposal of the Senate. He did not mean to see this governing body degenerate into a kind of "academic areopagus that does not go beyond studying the questions submitted to its competency," as Lucien Lacroix says.[19] The Abbé believed in a much lesser degree in sanctions of moral or economic character than Bentham did later. He had a practical turn of mind and looked for unfailing means to secure the realization of a great idea, the establishment of perpetual peace among na-

[16] See Th. Roosevelt's *Address* at Kristiania on May 5, 1910.
[17] W. Wilson, *Messages, discours, documents diplomatiques relatifs à la guerre mondiale,* I, 104-105.
[18] "The French Disarmament Plan," ch. 3, art. 2-a, *Series of League Publications,* No. 58, Nov. 14, 1932.
[19] *Op. cit.,* p. 436.

tions. He did not consider this ideal from the Christian point of view; that had been the approach of Pascal, for example. He did not consider it from the point of view of a pure philosopher; such was to be towards the end of the century the approach of Kant.[20] The Abbé took for the foundation of his structure the golden rule "Do unto others as you would that they should do unto you." This is the basis of the doctrine of utilitarianism. This golden rule, if adopted as a principle of conduct, cannot fail to lead man, in spite of the great dose of innate wickedness, toward a better understanding and a closer co-operation with his fellowmen, and this co-operation, in its turn, will hasten his steps along the road of progress. This idea of progress was as strong an inspiration for him as it was for the encyclopedists. His brain was constantly working on problems connected with improvement in various fields of human life. Each one of his works aimed at putting an end to some abuse and suggested a reform. His personal interests were so fully amalgamated with those of human society that one could be justified in saying he had no personal interests. The word *bienfaisance* (beneficence) which he created can be taken as the best expression of his moral attitude. Without idealizing man, he nevertheless admired his achievements in most fields of his activity, stating, however, that very little had been done for the betterment of the relations between the different peoples of the human race. It was toward a better future in this field that the *Projet de paix perpétuelle* of the Abbé de Saint-Pierre was directed. He brought to light and disseminated an idea which few people had in mind, but which now is regarded as the goal towards which the aspirations and efforts of men should be directed.

The influence of the *Projet de paix perpétuelle* can easily be traced in the schemes for an international organization that followed and above all in the ANONYMOUS PEACE PROJECT of 1745.[21]

[20] Cf. Kant, *Zum ewigen Frieden*, 1795.

[21] *Projet d'un nouveau système de l'Europe, préférable au Système de l'équilibre entre la Maison de France et celle d'Autriche*, 1745. MLA Rotograph, No. 471, Library of Congress.

What are the advantages, the unknown author asks, which a nation tries to secure in waging war against another nation? —The aggrandizement of her territory, the liberty of her commerce which is usually the main source of her revenues. Let us admit that those advantages have indeed been secured through a successful war. Is there any guarantee that he who proved to be the stronger will not in time become the weaker and be defeated in case of aggression? There are only two ways to prevent a conflict: the one is, to break up the power of the stronger; the other is to strengthen the weaker, a principle underlying all federations and leagues of states. This is precisely the system recommended by the unknown author.

Like the Abbé de Saint-Pierre, he finds that the three federations of his time—Germany, Switzerland, and the Netherlands—have sufficiently proved the vitality of the principle underlying their organization.[22] The other European nations should tread in their footsteps without allowing any state to remain outside the Union, a condition which would eliminate every possibility of war.

Passing from abstract considerations to the formulation of concrete rules which would govern the Union, the author, in nine fundamental articles, gives the essentials of his scheme. All European states would be bound to accept them and have them signed by their plenipotentiaries (Art. VII).

The starting point of this plan is the recognition of the principle of the *status quo* (Art. I). The Union shall guarantee to the sovereigns their actual possessions; only some recent unjustified acquisitions of territory will be returned to the former owners. No annexation of new territory will be authorized under any pretext (Art. II).

The author believes as much as did the Abbé de Saint-Pierre in the necessity of having an institution placed above the states. His Senate or Congress, the assembly of plenipotentiaries of all sovereigns, is such an institution. With an armed force at its disposal, it has the power to enforce its decisions and to compel those monarchs who did not voluntarily join the Union to become its members (Art. VI). The upkeep of the army as well as all other expenses of the Federa-

[22] With regard to this statement, the reader is referred to p. 95, note 1.

tion are covered by the contributions of the member states
(Art. III). The Union alone has the right to declare war and
will make it against any member who does not submit to the
decisions of the Senate in whom the legislative, executive, and
judicial powers of the Federation are vested (Art. VI). Separate treaties between the member states must be authorized by
a majority of three-fourths of the votes of the Senators. The
Union, in return, will be responsible for the execution of the
treaties (Art. IV).

In its internal affairs a state is independent unless a rebellion
against the established government takes place, in which case
the Senate will send troops to restore order (Art. I). The
rights of the subjects seem to be neglected in this plan as much
as they were in that of the Abbé de Saint-Pierre, but civil war
which is, in the opinion of the author, the most terrible of all
calamities is prevented since the first who takes up arms
against the government will be declared the enemy of the
Union. With regard to commercial relations between states,
it is asserted that no preference will ever be given to any nation. Equality of rights, freedom of commerce, the establishment of border tribunals (Chambres-frontières) for the
settlement of disputes between the subjects of different sovereigns are among the essential features of the plan of 1745
(Arts. V and VIII).

The Senate will be a permanent institution. The Delegates
will meet in some free neutral city such as Utrecht, Geneva,
Cologne, Aix-la-Chapelle and examine the complaints brought
for consideration in a written memorandum. If the Mediators
appointed by the Senate fail to settle the dispute, the Senate
will assume the rôle of a Court of Arbitration. The provisional decision based on the plurality of votes will be followed
by a final one requiring a majority of three-fourths (Art. VI).
It will be the duty of the Congress to make the Union powerful
and indissoluble in order to maintain peace among the European nations (Art. IX). Only the main features of the organization are given in the plan. The details are left to be worked
out by the Delegates whose unanimous vote is required for the
amendment of the fundamental articles.

The author thinks that his scheme is more likely to prevent

war than the unsteady system of the balance of power. The latter presupposes allies of equal force, allies upon whom one may rely, who would not be led astray by jealousy, ambition, and the thirst for vengeance:

Balance is by its very nature a state where that which is in equilibrium can be easily put and maintained in motion; the least internal or external cause is sufficient to impart a new kind of motion or to preserve the original one. . . . Balance can well permit an interruption of movement, a suspense; but far from securing stability and inalterable peace, it allows the slightest foreign influence to upset it and start war again.[23]

The system of the balance of power has protected small states against powerful neighbors in the past, but it has no future, while an organization based upon the federative principle is full of promise and cannot fail to win the adherence of one nation after the other.

Twelve years after the publication of the *Projet d'un nouveau système de l'Europe* . . . of which the author is unknown, appeared a work [24] which proposed a new method of abolishing war: a twenty-year truce which, according to the author, ANGE GOUDAR (1720-1791), would develop in nations the "habit of living in peace with each other." [25] Goudar seems to think that political, economic, and moral considerations to which we usually look in trying to establish the causes for a war do not furnish, as a rule, sufficient explanation for its outbreak. War and peace, he asserts, are to a certain extent matters of habit.[26] Is he right in transferring some deductions made in the field of psychology into the sphere of international relations? The years which elapsed since the armistice day of November 11, 1918—the day which marked

[23] *Op. cit.*, p. 24.
[24] Ange Goudar, *La Paix de l'Europe ne peut s'établir qu'à la suite d'une longue trêve* ou *Projet de pacification générale combinée par une suspension d'armes de vingt ans entre toutes les Puissances politiques,* par M. le Chevalier G——, 1757.
[25] *Op. cit.*, p. 207.
[26] *Op. cit.*, p. 207.

the end of the World War (1914-1918)—offer precisely the
length of time sufficient, in the opinion of the author, for developing in nations that have not been waging war the habit
of living in peace with each other. This habit should have
become second nature to them, and yet current events do not
confirm this.

Goudar is far from sharing the opinion of those who, draw-
ing a parallel between the animal kingdom and the human
race, assert that war is an unavoidable evil. It might be true,
he says, in regard to animals which are led by instinct, but men
are guided by their intellect.[27] War will disappear with the
advance of civilization like such scourges of mankind as
leprosy, plague, and famine. To declare that war is an unavoidable evil is to assert that "plague, famine as well as all
other scourges are likewise necessary; it is to maintain, only in
other words, that the preservation of peoples depends on their
ultimate extermination." [28]

His own plan appears to Goudar more practical than the
"dreams" of his predecessors. They saw in treaties, in the
balance of power, in political organizations, effective means of
establishing perpetual peace; they did not take enough into
consideration the instability of the conditions of human life
and, consequently, the instability of human agreements. Personal interests were usually behind these. The length of time
a truce was supposed to last was never stipulated; this allowed
governments to have recourse to arms whenever they found it
necessary. Treaties were, as a rule, concluded only among a
few parties; they failed to unite all of Europe; they divided it
into hostile camps and fostered war rather than peace. Instead of being the first cause of events, they were, on the contrary, brought up and molded by events.[29] As for the balance
of power, there cannot be any doubt that this system cannot
be established otherwise than through war; besides, it is like
a game of chance where fortune favors now one, now the
other:

[27] *Ibid.*, p. 135.
[28] *Ibid.*, p. 17.
[29] *Ibid.*, pp. 116, 208.

The system of the balance of power falls continuously back on itself: one state wins what another loses, thus the general balance is always the same. The pendulum alone changes its position and, as an author has expressed it so well: "Whatever the motion of the wheel, it does but one thing—it displaces name for name." [30]

Goudar is not interested in presenting a scheme for a "permanent" political organization. His plan is simply as follows: The Mandataries of all the states of Europe will meet for the sole purpose of guaranteeing by their signatures that for twenty years from that day their states shall not have recourse to arms under any pretext whatsoever, and that all shall be ready in case of a breach of promise by any one of those who signed the agreement to take action against him conjointly with all the others. They shall promise to force him to disarm, to oblige him to pay the war expenses and, in addition, a heavy fine if he is a recidivist. The Representatives shall agree that no state shall ever merge with another and that a territory which at the time of the meeting of the Congress is the subject of some dispute can be disputed by war at the close of the twenty-year truce. Passing from abstract considerations to their immediate realization, Goudar gives eleven articles which read as follows:

1. All European Sovereigns (inclusive of the Heads of the small Italian Principalities and those of the Republics) would have to sign through their Ambassadors their agreement to the cessation of hostilities.

2. All Princes shall have to declare themselves the warrantors of this treaty.

3. No other subject shall be discussed by the Congress.

4. The treaty stipulates for twenty years of peace.

5. During the above-mentioned twenty years no state shall be allowed to take up arms against another state under any pretext whatsoever.

6. In case of the breach of the treaty the whole Republic shall declare itself the enemy of the disturber of peace.

7. All the expenses of the war waged against him shall have to be paid by him.

8. In case of recidivism, the offender shall be forced to pay a

[30] *Ibid.*, p. 102.

certain sum to each state besides the sum of money owed by him to the Universal Republic.

9. A sovereign who would persist in disturbing peace shall be outlawed until the time when the agreement is over.

10. The domain of the outlawed Prince shall not become a part of any other state; it will be considered, however, as one that has lost its active political power.

11. It will be positively declared in the treaty that no state will lose its claims and its rights on the territory of another state. After the expiration of the time of the treaty, every state shall have the right to support its claims through recourse to arms.[31]

We see that Goudar's plan is based on his belief in the influence that our habits have on all the course of our lives. He feels that what is true and right in regard to the lives of men as individuals, must be true and right when applied to the larger sphere of social and international relations. This explains why he takes for a starting point the immediate unconditional suspension of international disputes for a well-defined period of time (twenty years):

If we want to repair a machine the mainsprings of which have been out of order for a long time, we have first of all to stop its movement, otherwise it will continue to function irregularly. Likewise, in order to put an end to the disturbances in Europe, it is necessary to stop them for a time.[32]

After Goudar had his work published, he did not try to further the propagation of his ideas. He was well aware that statesmen, as a rule, consider state affairs as matters exclusively their concern and dislike any suggestions from outsiders. Besides, their personal interests are so closely interwoven with political conditions that they cannot possibly be impartial judges of a cause that should be a common cause.[33] So much for those who play a leading part in politics or hold high positions in the army and navy. As for the rank and file, the victims of this policy, Goudar calls their heroism "the heroism of slaves." He writes mainly in their behalf. They do not gain anything by the victories they win; therefore,

---

[31] *Ibid.*, p. 238.
[32] *Ibid.*, "Préface de l'éditeur."
[33] *Ibid.*

when they march against the enemy, they are seldom determined "to conquer or to die," as were the old Romans.[34]

Goudar is neither a statesman nor a plenipotentiary; he cannot have a direct influence on the destinies of Europe; he feels that the only way in which he may be of service to the "Universal Republic," as he calls Europe, is to publish his notes:

The only purpose of this work is the political tranquillity of Europe; I have but one goal: the preservation of mankind; I am writing for the benefit of our Universal Republic and I am making stipulations for Mankind.[35]

The driving power behind the French peace plans of the first part of the eighteenth century was quite different from that which had moved the political writers of the seventeenth century. For Dubois and Sully the thing that really mattered was the power and greatness of France. Cruce's source of inspiration was purely ethical. But the Abbé and his followers wrote from more purely humanitarian motives during a period when the greatest part of the population of France lived under very hard economic conditions. These conditions were brought about mainly by war. To work toward its abolition became the great goal of the Abbé de Saint-Pierre. His carefully elaborated project was realistic and utilitarian, and his devotion to his ideal inspired his followers.

[34] *Ibid.*, p. 80.
[35] *Ibid.*, "Préface," p. XXXIII.

CHAPTER VI

PHILOSOPHERS AND ENCYCLOPEDISTS

THE leading thoughts of the *Projet de paix perpétuelle* did not stir great response among the French philosophers of the eighteenth century. To share the aspirations of the Abbé de Saint-Pierre—and they certainly shared them—was a thing too intangible; the main point was to find the right path towards their realization. The means proposed by the Abbé seemed to them impractical; they knew too well the political and social conditions prevailing in Europe to find his plan anything but a utopia. In their opinion, the establishment of peace would take place in a very distant future as a result of the progress of civilization. The efforts of their group were accordingly directed toward the enlightenment of the masses. The philosophers taught them to question the reasonableness of tradition, the foundation of authority, the principles underlying religious intolerance, the legal processes of the courts in the administration of justice, and they attacked the cruelty of criminal law. With the same acute analysis they approached the issue of civil and foreign wars. The most revealing passages on this subject are found in the works of Montesquieu, Voltaire, Diderot, Holbach, and Condorcet; however, by way of introduction, I am going to speak very briefly of one almost unknown writer of this same eighteenth century—Dom Deschamps. His *Observations métaphysiques* and *Observations morales* appeared for the first time in print in 1939.[1] MM. Jean Thomas and Franco Venturi published them under the general title of *Le Vrai Système* (the author used to give this

[1] L. M. Deschamps, *Le Vrai Système* ou *Le Mot de l'énigme métaphysique et morale,* 1939.

definition to his doctrine) ou *Le Mot de l'énigme métaphysique et morale.*

The "riddle" to which Dom Deschamps (1716-1774) tries to find an answer (*le mot de l'énigme*) is the same over which many an altruist has already puzzled his brains—the happiness of mankind. Each of us, he says, would gladly welcome an order of things in which no one is more happy or less happy, more favored or less favored than his fellowmen; and this applies alike to groups of individuals and nations. Equality becomes thus the principle on which human society must be organized. Although absolute equality is not found in nature, it is, he asserts, nevertheless, a law of nature.[2] The tendency toward living in harmony with others is innate in man and leads toward common good. He who wants to enjoy the blessings of this life with impunity and without fear must see to it that no one be less fortunate than he, for unhappy people are prone to become his enemies. If no man ever tried to raise himself above the average human type or to acquire property, men and women, shepherds and kings would be very much alike, more alike, as a matter of fact, than animals of the same species. Passion, competition, envy, ambition, vice, crime, and wars would be unknown. Moral poise, mental composure, a quiet serene bearing that knows neither laughter nor tears would lead man not to regret the intense joys which occasionally fall to his share in the present organization of the human society. Gone without regret would be the joys of a happy lover, an acknowledged artist, a great conqueror, a successful statesman, a rich business man, or a nobleman puffed up with pride over his lineage and his titles. Charity whose sole purpose is to prevent the poor from trampling the rich under foot would have no place in the new order of things. Like Rousseau, Deschamps considers the life of man in a state

[2] A. Cloots, whose political plan is being discussed in chapter IX, was of the same opinion: "C'est précisément parce que l'inégalité physique et morale est une condition de la nature que les lois sociales doivent niveler les forces et contrebalancer le poids." (*L'Orateur du genre humain, pp.* 93, 94.)

of nature as a happy one. Except for the moments when instinct brought men together, they lived apart, and fighting
among them was not of usual occurrence. Deschamps considers the present state of human society, the reign of laws
(*état des lois*), as a state of utter disunion under the mislead-
ing semblance of union. To the perfect organization of the
future, his utopia, he gives the name of the reign of manners
(*état des moeurs*), a state of perfect union based on the principle of equality. There are to be no laws : regulation of man's
conduct becomes purposeless as soon as he understands that
individual happiness is unthinkable without the happiness of
all.

What steps should be taken to bring about this ideal of
life? The first step is the return to simple primitive ways
without personal property and family life, with women and
children belonging to the whole community. No reading, no
writing ; Deschamps's book is meant to put an end to all books.
Discoveries and achievements of science are either useless or
harmful ; works of art ought to be reduced to ashes. Only
people unable to set gain against loss would call this "a great
sacrifice." Work will be easy, overstrain unknown in a world
where neither honor nor profit reward even the greatest services rendered to society. Rewards breed envy and are incompatible with the spirit of equality, Deschamps thinks.

With a better balance in his moral life, man will be insured
against the fear of death : why should he worry over his non-
existence as a human being in the future since he does not
shudder at the idea of not having existed in the past? This
thought inclines Deschamps less to mourn the sacrifice of life
involved in war than to feel indignation at the wickedness of
those holding sovereign power. The main preoccupation of
a prince, he writes, is to have his troops well trained through
their participation in foreign wars. The experience his men
acquire will enable him to use them for settling internal
disorders. Universal peace could be easily established and
maintained had the sovereign only his neighbors to fear. Unfortunately, in building up military force, a ruler has in view
either his safety, should his subjects turn against him, or his
glory as a conqueror. In the "state of laws" the origin of

government is not the so-called "social compact," the decrees of government are in no way expressions of the general will; force alone has created the "state of laws," force alone can maintain it. The sovereign finds supporters in lawyers, judges, financiers, and above all in the army and the clergy: the priests preach submission in the name of the so-called divine laws which, according to Deschamps, are mere products of the human brain, since even the belief in God has its origin in the fear of the unknown.

Asserting the necessity for passing from the "state of laws" into the "state of manners," Deschamps devises the method of action: he would like to found an order of seers (*l'ordre des voyants*) who will make his vision a reality. Thus even his ideal state of absolute equality presupposes leaders—"shepherds who alone can find good pastures and can protect their flocks of sheep against wolves."

The extremism of Deschamps's doctrine prevented him from being on friendly terms with Rousseau and even with the encyclopedists. He had, however, a group of disciples whom he used to meet, under the assumed name of M. du Parc, in the castle of his friend and benefactor the Marquis de Voyer. He lived and died a good Catholic in a small Benedictine monastery, near Saumur, where no one had ever questioned the orthodoxy of his beliefs.

Less extreme, but more revealing are the passages on war and peace we find in the writings of MONTESQUIEU (1689-1755) who approaches these important issues partly from a juridical, partly from an essentially practical point of view:

A new sickness has spread itself over Europe [he writes]; it has infected our princes and has induced them to keep up an inordinate number of troops . . . of course, it becomes contagious: for, as soon as one prince augments his military forces, the others do the same, so that nothing is gained thereby but the public ruin. And they give the name of peace to this general effort of all against all.[3]

---

[3] Ch. de Montesquieu, *Oeuvres*, éd. Lefèvre, 1826, "De l'Esprit des lois," L. XIII, ch. 17.

The futility of competition in armaments had already been emphasized by Fénelon in his *Dialogues des Morts*.[4] Since every nation does its best to render its means of defense conformable to the means of attack of prospective enemies, the world at the moment of the invention of gunpowder is, on the whole, not more advanced than at the time of the battle-axe and the battering-ram.

Such problems as war and peace could not fail to be on Montesquieu's mind, for they affect the welfare of numberless people, and Montesquieu wrote for the benefit of the human race. He was a citizen of the world, in the best meaning of those words. His deep love for France did not prevent him from conceiving a real affection for other countries. He had traveled a great deal and in his relations with foreigners he was as congenial as with fellow-countrymen. His principle was to put his own interest and, in general, the interests of individuals beneath those of groups of people:

> If I knew of anything advantageous to my family, but not to my country, I should try to forget it. If I knew of anything advantageous to my country which was prejudicial to Europe and to the human race, I should look upon it as a crime.[5]

He thought that political liberty is essential for human happiness. Nothing could endanger it more than war, hence his hatred of it and, above all, of the spirit of conquest so inherent in European sovereigns prone to see in public law a science teaching them how to violate every principle of justice without harming their own personal interests. They are convinced that there are two kinds of justice entirely different: one which regulates the affairs of private persons and controls civil law; another which regulates the differences that arise between people and people; they do not see that the law of nations should control the whole world in the same way as civil law controls a nation.[6]

The mistake of Montesquieu, according to Helvétius, was

---

[4] Fénelon, *Oeuvres*, éd. Lefèvre, 1835, II, 572, "Dialogues des Morts: Confucius et Socrate."

[5] Cf. A. Sorel, *Montesquieu*, transl. by M. and E. Anderson, 1892, p. 58. [Cf. Fénelon, p. 45, note 35.]

[6] *Oeuvres*, "Lettres persanes," L. XCIV.

that he did not establish the principles to which individuals and nations could refer in order to be able to judge rightly of the merit of a law. For Helvétius, as well as for the Abbé de Saint-Pierre, the greatest happiness of the greatest number is the criterion; but, since happiness is a personal thing, freedom must be guaranteed to every man and every nation. Despotism exercised by one man over another or by one nation over another can never be justified since intelligence, talent, power of will are not inherited, but are the results of conditions in which a man or a nation has grown up.[7]

Montesquieu has no admiration for Roman conquests; he sees in them the "longest conspiracy ever plotted against the universe." [8] He finds that the annexation of boundless territories made the final downfall unavoidable. Even the lasting peace (pax romana) given by Rome to the tired world could not incline him to bow before the grandeur of the roman world domination:

It is the fate of heroes [he writes] to ruin themselves by conquering countries which they suddenly lose again or by subduing nations which they themselves are obliged to destroy; they are like that maniac who ruined himself by buying statues which he threw into the sea and mirrors which he broke as soon as he had bought them.[9]

There are, however, circumstances, Montesquieu thinks, when a people is not guilty of waging war: war against an aggressor, support given to an ally forced to repulse an attack are just wars. Another case in which Montesquieu is prone to consider war if not precisely just, but excusable, is that of a steady growth of the territory of a neighboring people and of its menacing power and wealth, an opinion violently attacked by Voltaire.[10]

Montesquieu thought that the monarchical form of government prevailing in Europe was greatly responsible for the frequency of war on that continent: "The spirit of monarchies

[7] See Helvétius, *Oeuvres* (éd. Didot, 1795), XIV, 63 ff.
[8] Cf. M. Lipschütz, *Montesquieu*, p. 64.
[9] *Oeuvres*, "Lettres persanes," L. CXXII.
[10] *Oeuvres*, "De l'Esprit des lois," L. X, ch. 2. See also Voltaire, *Dictionnaire philosophique*, "Guerre," and *infra*, pp. 117-118.

is war and aggrandizement, the spirit of republics is peace and moderation." [11]   Besides the changes that might occur in the form of government of the European states, wars would occur less frequently in the future, he thought, owing to the power of assimilation with which most peoples are endowed to a greater or lesser degree; he expected also great changes from international commercial relations.

In trying to combat the spirit of conquest, he analyzed the so-called "right of conquest." He wonders what people mean precisely by those words. For him, conquest is always a deed of violence; as such it cannot create a right; on the contrary, it is something which needs to be atoned for; the duty of the conqueror is to repair the evil he has done:

Conquest is an acquisition and carries with it the spirit of preservation and use, not of destruction. . . . The authors of our public law . . . have adopted tyrannical and arbitrary principles by supposing the conquerors to be invested with I know not what right to kill. . . . It is a plain case that when the conquest is completed, the conqueror has no longer the plea of natural defense and self-preservation. . . . From the destruction of the state it does not at all follow that the people who compose it ought to be destroyed. The state is the association of men, and not the men themselves; the citizen may perish, and the man remain.[12]

Montesquieu emphasizes the importance of the recognition of this principle, since from the right of taking the life of a prisoner statesmen deduced the right of reducing prisoners to slavery. Slavery can be admitted, according to him, only as a provisional order of things by which prisoners would be deprived of the possibility of doing any harm to the conqueror; but the people enslaved ought to be made capable of becoming subjects:

When, after the expiration of a certain space of time, all the parts of the conquering state are connected with the conquered nation by customs, marriages, laws, associations, and by a certain conformity of disposition, there ought to be an end to slavery.[13]

11 *Ibid.*, L. IX, ch. 2.
12 *Ibid.*, L. X, ch. 3. [The translation of the passages quoted from Montesquieu has been taken from the *Complete Works of M. de Montesquieu*, London, 1777.]
13 *Ibid.*, L. X, ch. 3.

In the sixteenth century Jean Bodin had raised his voice against this institution, but his protest evidently remained unnoticed since in the second half of the seventeenth century a man as prominent as Bossuet could speak of slavery as of something inherent in the natural order of things.[14] The abstract idea of the dignity of man that Montesquieu has succeeded in establishing as an immutable principle as well as the stinging irony of the pages in which he attacked slavery, has dealt this institution a deadly blow. Montesquieu explains the existence of slavery mainly by the contempt which one nation feels for another on account of differences in customs:

Lopès de Gomara tells us that the Spaniards found near St. Martha some baskets of food; there were crabs, snails, grasshoppers, and locusts which proved to be the ordinary food of the natives. This the conquerors turned to a heavy charge against the conquered. The author assures that this, together with their smoking and trimming their beards not in the same manner as the Spaniards did, gave rise to the law by which the Americans became slaves to the Spaniards.[15]

Racial differences and varieties of ethnographical types have contributed very much to the spreading of slavery:

The natives are all over black; their nose is so flat that they can scarcely be pitied.

It is impossible to believe that God, who is a wise being, should place a soul, especially a good soul, in a black body.

The best proof that the Negroes are wanting common sense is the fact that they prefer a glass necklace to that gold which polite nations value so highly.

The color of the skin may be determined by that of the hair which among the Egyptians (the best philosophers in the world) was of such importance that they put to death all the red-haired men who fell into their hands.[16]

The strongest arguments, however, were dictated by economic considerations which, unfortunately, inclined people to lose all conception of the dignity of man as human being:

[14] Cf. *supra,* pp. 61-62.
[15] Montesquieu, *De l'Esprit des lois,* L. XV, ch. 3.
[16] *Ibid.,* L. XV, ch. 5.

Were I to prove our right to make slaves of the Negroes, I should say as follows: "The Europeans, having exterminated the Americans, were bound to make slaves of the Africans in order to make them clear vast tracks of land. . . . Sugar would be too expensive if the plant which produces it were cultivated by any others than slaves." [17]

Montesquieu repeats again and again that men are equal by birth and that, consequently, slavery is contrary to natural law. To those who affirm that slavery always existed and is a useful institution, he answers: Let us not take into consideration that it would be profitable to rich idle persons to possess slaves. No doubt, it would. The question is to know whether their claim is legitimate. Let us then suggest that both, masters and slaves, draw lots; these will indicate the people who will have the status of slaves and do their work.[18] Well aware, however, that there are people prone to turn a deaf ear to arguments of moral or philosophical character, he takes up the subject from a purely economic point of view and proves that slave labor is less effective and more expensive than free labor.

Slavery and war have been closely connected since the dawn of human history. With the establishment of the Christian religion, the Church directed its influence toward making the life of the slaves less hard, but it did not withhold recognition of the institution itself. It is mainly to Montesquieu's deep thought and bold word that humanity owes the abolition of an institution which degraded her.

There was no place for religious wars in eighteenth-century Europe, but the relations between various Churches were still full of warlike spirit. Now and then cruel persecutions took place and torture was regularly applied to those who were being tried. Freedom of conscience was not guaranteed. Montesquieu recognized that in a state a citizen is not permitted to cause trouble either to the political body itself or to any fellow-citizen, and he thought this principle should be strictly observed in mutual relations between members of various denominations. The least desirable of the denominations are those which are most anxious to have proselytes; in

[17] *Ibid.,* L. XV, ch. 5.
[18] *Ibid.,* L. XV, ch. 9 (éd. posthume, 1757).

this desire Montesquieu sees a proof of intolerance. A new denomination which establishes itself in a state is likely to eliminate some abuses of the old ones; however, the government should not favor the introduction of new forms of religious worship, but never take action against those which had been established before. "This indirect and imperfect toleration," A. Sorel says, "is very far removed from the liberty of conscience, yet great merit was shown in proposing it, and great courage in sustaining it openly." [19] Montesquieu asserts his belief in the necessity of tolerance both by the means of philosophical argumentation and by the power of his wit:

In things that prejudice the tranquillity or security of the state, secret actions are subject to human jurisdiction; but in those which offend the Deity, where there is no public act, there can be no criminal matter; the whole passes between man and God who knows the measure and time of his vengeance. . . .[20]

It is an important maxim that we ought to be very circumspect in the prosecution of witchcraft and heresy. The accusation of these two crimes may be vastly injurious to liberty and productive of infinite oppression. . . . For, as it does not directly point at a person's actions, but at his character, it grows dangerous in proportion to the ignorance of the people; and then a man is sure to be always in danger because the most unexceptionable conduct, the purest morals, and the constant practice of every duty in life are not a sufficient security against the suspicions of his being guilty of the like crime.[21]

Montesquieu's struggle against fanaticism does him the highest honor, since in the eighteenth century intolerance was still observable both in law and custom. He pretended that a Jew of Lisbon had written a letter to the Inquisitors of Spain and Portugal as follows:

You complain that the emperor of Japan caused all the Christians in his dominions to be burnt by a slow fire. But he will answer: "We treat you, who do not believe like us, as you yourselves treat those who do not believe like you. But it must be confessed that you are much more cruel than this emperor. You put

[19] A. Sorel, *op. cit.*, p. 44.
[20] *De l'Esprit des lois*, L. XII, ch. 4.
[21] *Ibid.*, L. XII, ch. 5.

us to death, us who believe only what you believe, because we do not believe *all* that you believe. We follow a religion which you yourselves know to have been formerly dear to God. We think that God loves it still, and you think that He loves it no more. . . . If you have the truth, hide it not from us by the manner in which you propose it. The characteristic of truth is its triumph over hearts and minds, and not that impotency which you confess when you would force us to receive it by tortures. . . . If you were wise, you would not put us to death for no other reason but because we are unwilling to deceive you.[22]

In his *Lettres persanes* Montesquieu assumes another tone, that of sharp irony:

I have heard that in Spain and Portugal the dervishes do not relish jesting and will burn a man as readily as they would straw. When a man comes into the hands of these people . . . though he should swear like a pagan that he is orthodox, it is possible they may not admit his plea and may burn him for a heretic . . . he shall be in ashes before they even think of hearing him. The judges here commonly presume upon the innocence of the accused; there they always suppose the party culpable. . . . In their sentence [they] pay a slight compliment to those whom they dress up in a shirt painted with flames of fire and assure them that they are extremely concerned to see them so badly habited; that their own disposition is to mercy; that they abhor blood, and that they are grieved at having condemned them. But for their own consolation, they confiscate to their own emolument all the effects of the miserable sufferers.[23]

Montesquieu's works show that he has directed many a witty attack against fanaticism, slavery, the spirit of conquest, and that he has also given a thorough analysis of these evils. He saw in them the greatest obstacles towards a peaceful and happy coexistence of human societies. He did not consider this ideal unattainable: man's life begins in a family; social instincts are noticeable in a child right from the first days of his life. As years go by, reflection and experience strengthen in man those natural dispositions and prepare him to give his full co-operation in every field of human activity. Prejudice,

22 *Ibid.,* L. XXV, ch. 13.
23 *Lettres persanes,* "Lettre XXIX."

intolerance, and, above all, the spirit of conquest are disruptive influences. The formation of federative states might prove a remedy against the evils brought about by the spirit of conquest; however, Montesquieu admits it only to a certain extent; this prevents him from showing enthusiasm over the peace plan of the Abbé de Saint-Pierre.

VOLTAIRE (1694-1778) did not endorse the Abbé's plan either and allowed himself many jokes at its expense. When Rousseau's *Extrait du Projet de paix perpétuelle de M. l'Abbé de Saint-Pierre* appeared in print, Voltaire said that "the citizen of Geneva" Jean-Jacques had borrowed his peace plan from the "bonze" Saint-Pierre, and the "bonze" Saint-Pierre, in his turn, had borrowed his scheme from the "mandarin" Sully.[24] Voltaire called the Abbé's *Projet de paix perpétuelle* a "chimera." Although war belies human nature and is inconsistent with the teachings of most religions, it is as ancient as human nature and more ancient than any religion. To prevent princes from waging war on each other is as difficult as to prevent fights between elephants and rhinoceroses, between wolves and dogs: "Bloodthirsty animals always tear each other under the same circumstances." [25]

If we pay attention to the word "princes" mentioned by Voltaire, we shall be ready to agree that he did not really mean to say that the hope for seeing peace reign in the relations between peoples is absolutely futile. He rather objected to the means advocated by the author for establishing peace. The book of the Abbé de Saint-Pierre was mainly intended for sovereigns and was expected to become in their hands an instrument in achieving the abolition of war. Voltaire knew of the steps the Abbé was untiringly taking in order to interest people in his plan; he knew of his letters addressed to sov-

[24] F. M. A. de Voltaire, *Oeuvres*, éd. Moland, 1877-85, XXIV, 231, "Rescrit de l'Empereur de Chine à l'occasion du Projet de paix perpétuelle." [In any case it does not seem likely that Voltaire could have admired Sully's plan either, since the latter was drawn for Europe alone. Voltaire already foresaw the rôle Japan, for example, would play in the future destinies of the world.]

[25] *Ibid.*, XXVIII, 103, "De la paix perpétuelle."

ereigns and their ministers.   The Abbé's optimism amused
Voltaire.   For his part, he thought of the princes as being the
last persons on whom those who try to promote the peace ideal
may depend.   Their indifference to the welfare of their
peoples, their senseless passion for military glory, their greed
for new territories, the futility of the results they usually attain through war, and the worthlessness of the reasons that
lead them to bloodshed, all this was well known to Voltaire.
The following passages chosen from his different works give
an account of his scepticism:

A genealogist proves to a prince that he descends in a right line
from a count whose parents made a family compact, three or four
hundred years ago, with a house the recollection of which does not
even exist. . . . The prince and his council see his right at once.
This province, which is some hundred leagues distant from him,
in vain protests that it knows him not, that it has no desire to be
governed by him, that to give laws to its people, he must at
least have their consent; these discourses only reach as far as
the ears of the prince whose right is incontestable.   He immediately assembles a great number of men who have nothing to lose,
dresses them in coarse blue cloth, borders their hats with broad
white binding, makes them turn to the right and left, and marches
to glory.[26]

The amazed Babouc introduced himself to the generals and became familiar with them.   One of them finally said to him: "The
cause of this war which ruined Asia for twenty years was orig-
inally a quarrel between a eunuch of a wife of the great King of
Persia and a clerk of an office of the great King of India.   It was
a question of a right which was worth about the thirtieth part of
a piece of gold.   The Prime Minister of India and our own worth-
ily supported the rights of their masters.   The quarrel waxed hot.
On either side a million soldiers were brought into the field.
Every year four hundred thousand men are needed as recruits
for the army.   Murders, fires, ruins, devastations are multiplied,
the whole world suffers, and the animosity continues.   Our Prime
Minister and the Indian Minister often protest that they are only

26 *Ibid.*, XIX, 316-319, "Dictionnaire philosophique: Guerre."   [The
quotations from Voltaire's *Philosophical Dictionary* are given in the
translation into English made in 1824.]

acting for the good of the human race; and at each protestation there are always towns destroyed and provinces ravaged." [27]

"You must know, for example, that this very moment while I am speaking, there are some hundred thousand animals of our own species, covered with hats, slaying an equal number of fellow-creatures who wear turbans; they are either slaying or slain; and this has been nearly the case all over the earth from time immemorial." The Syrian, shuddering at this information, begged to know the cause of those horrible quarrels. . . . He was given to understand that the subject of the dispute was some pitiful mole-hill, no bigger than his heel; not that any one of those millions who cut one another's throats pretends to have the least claim to the smallest particle of that clod . . . the question is to know whether it shall belong to a certain person who is known by the name of Sultan or to another whom they dignify (for what reason I know not) with the appellation of Caesar. . . . The punishment should not be inflicted upon them [the soldiers], but upon those sedentary and slothful barbarians . . . who give orders for murdering a million men and then solemnly thank God for their success. [28]

In another short story, *La Princesse de Babylone,* Voltaire tells us how the happiest country in the world, that of the Gangarids, was once invaded by a King of India, one of those sovereigns whose rage seems to consist in laying waste their neighbors' lands, in shedding the blood of their fellowmen, and in fixing their thrones on hillocks of the slain. The King advances with a million warriors, but is taken prisoner and is bathed in the salutary waters of the Ganges which cures his thirst for conquest. [29]

Voltaire was on friendly terms with some of the European sovereigns; faithful to his convictions, he tried many a time to use his prestige in the interest of peace. During the Seven Years' War he even assumed the rôle of a negotiator for peace, but, in spite of all his energy, of all the tact he had shown by always remaining in the background, he could not prevent his efforts from being vain. This experience accounts partly for

[27] *Ibid.,* XXI, 2, "Vision de Babouc," transl. by R. Aldington.
[28] *Ibid.,* XXI, 119, "Micromégas," transl. taken from *The Works of M. de Voltaire,* London, 1742.
[29] *Ibid.,* XXI, 384-385, "La Princesse de Babylone."

the fact that he had no high esteem for the political scheme of the Abbé de Saint-Pierre; it seemed to him that other kinds of arms should be used in the fight for peace. He saw the source of the evil in the ignorance of the masses who did not realize that they had not only duties to perform, but rights to uphold. People were wrong in blindly submitting to those above them, in allowing themselves to be treated like slaves; as a result, theirs was a life of great suffering. They pillaged, killed, marched to death without even knowing what they were fighting for; they often took part in a war which started for one reason, continued for another, and sometimes ended suddenly for no reason at all.

Babouc, the hero of the story *Le Monde comme il va,* asks a soldier the destination of the march of his division and receives the answer: "I swear by all that is sacred that I do not know; it is not my business; my profession is to kill or to be killed and to earn thereby my livelihood." [30] In *Candide* Voltaire describes the usual destination of the march of a division—a battlefield:

Never were two armies better arranged or more brilliantly accoutered; never did men appear more fiercely martial; the fifes, hautboys, drums, trumpets, and cannon formed a pandemonium concert.

A grand discharge of cannon overthrew nearly six thousand men on either side, then volleys of musket balls exterminated from the best of terrestrial worlds ten thousand *villains* who disgraced its surface; next, several thousand were cut down by swords and bayonets; the whole number of warriors slain might be thirty thousand.

Candide, who trembled like a philosopher, concealed himself as well as he could during this heroic carnage; and while the two kings were singing *Te Deum* in their separate camps, he resolved to depart and reason in some quieter situation upon causes and effects. He passed unobserved among heaps of dead and dying warriors and soon arrived at an Abarian village which he found had been burnt, according to the rights of war, by the Bulgarians.

Here, by their once happy homes, now fallen in a little heap of smoking ruins, lay the peaceful owners pierced with many wounds. Some had still the agonizing power of fixing their dying eyes upon

[30] *Ibid.,* XXI, 2, "Vision de Babouc."

their murdered wives who clasped their infants to their bleeding bosoms. There expired youth and beauty, violated and destroyed. Half burned amidst the ruins groaned many a hoary sire and feeble matron, soliciting a final blow to end their misery.[31]

In his *Eloge des officiers morts dans la Guerre de 1741* Voltaire expresses the thought that the sole aim of war (if war cannot be avoided) should be a lasting peace. The more we appreciate peace, the more grateful should we be to those who suffered and perished while fighting for it:

Live eternally, you warriors who died in our behalf ; we owe you the glorious peace treaty bought at the price of your life. The more dreadful the scourge of war is which focuses in it all calamities and all crimes the greater should be our gratitude to our courageous fellow-countrymen who died in order to give us this blessed peace. Peace, indeed, should be the only aim of war and the sole object of the ambition of a true monarch.[32]

War makes our earthly dwelling a vast cemetery. Voltaire wonders what leads people to inveigh in eloquent, thunderous speeches against harmless irregularities in the conduct of men and to remain so astonishingly silent in regard to war, this greatest scourge of human life:

Weak and silly creatures as we are, we anathematize the slightest irregularities of conduct, the most secret weaknesses of hearts ; we thunder against vices and faults which, while deserving blame, hardly disturb the life of men. Yet what voice whose duty it is to preach virtue has ever been raised against war, this great universal crime, this destructive fury that changes men, born to live like brothers, into wild beasts, against this atrocious depredation and cruel deeds which make of earth a place of brigandage, a vast and horrible sepulchre ? [33]

The ceremonial blessings given by priests to "the standards of murder (the flags of regiments)" make him indignant. War, for him, is always "robbery, harvesting the grain that others have sown. A hero . . . always begins by ordering

[31] *Ibid.*, XXI, 141-142, "Candide," transl. by M. J. Young.
[32] *Ibid.*, XXIII, 250, "Eloge des officiers morts dans la guerre de 1741."
[33] *Ibid.*, XXIII, 250.

the population to furnish bulls, cows, sheep as well as hay, bread, wine, wool, linen, and blankets." [34]

Voltaire's general point of view in regard to war is also very clear from his historical works, *Histoire de Charles XII* and *Siècle de Louis XIV*. As historian, he is very objective; he neither praises nor blames his heroes; yet those who read those works cannot help condemning in both kings vain aspirations for glory and irrational passion for conquest. Voltaire writes about Louis XIV : the King was young, rich, blindly obeyed by his subjects, yet he did not seem happy : he longed for the glory of a conqueror. A pretext is soon found by those who seek it. In breach of the agreement signed at the time of his marriage (1659), Louis pretended that Flanders, which was then a province of Spain, should be inherited by his wife, Marie-Thérèse, daughter of the deceased king of Spain, Philip IV, who had been married to the sister of Louis XIII. This was the beginning of an interminable series of wars, many of which seemed to be aimless, while millions of men perished and many parts of France were laid waste. Toward the end of his life, Louis realized, while comparing the gain to the loss, that the brilliant genius of his generals, the courage of his officers and soldiers, the sacrifice of so many lives, owing to his wrong policy, had brought few real advantages.[35]

In his *Histoire de Charles XII* (1748) Voltaire speaks of the outstanding traits of character of the young king, of his stoicism, aversion to pomp or display, absence of greed, his readiness to share with the army all the privations of a soldier's life . . . yet, with all these remarkable qualities, he brought nothing but great misery to Sweden, and was a cause of unceasing trouble for the whole of Europe. The King's greatest ambition was to dictate his will to other sovereigns and to cover his name with the glory of a conqueror. It is impossible not to see mere folly in his desire to conquer at any price, since sometimes he had previously made up his mind to give away the territory he was preparing to seize. Voltaire refuses to see in those generous gifts any greatness of soul :

[34] *Ibid.*, XXVIII, 130, "Dieu et les Hommes."
[35] *Ibid.*, XIV, 481, *"Siècle de Louis XIV,"* [1752].

people who knew Charles XII testify that human suffering left him indifferent, that he considered human labor and the sacrifice of life by his subjects as something due him, and of little value. When defeated, he breathed forth vengeance. After the battle of Poltava in 1709, his desire to take revenge on Peter the Great was so overwhelming that it made him lose even his personal dignity. He remained for five years at Benders with the remnants of his army, taking advantage of the hospitality of the Turkish Sultan and trying in vain to incite him against the Czar. When forced at last to return to Sweden, he engaged once more in an aimless war; this time against Norway.

Voltaire shows in this work to what extent the passion for conquest can pervert a character. The blind love of the subjects for Charles XII arouses pity rather than admiration in the author. Yet one should not think that he did not admit war at all. His ideas are far from any doctrine of non-resistance or even non-violent resistance. According to him, an individual has the right of self-defense, and so has a nation; self-defense in both cases is just; only it is wrong to call the resistance which a nation opposes to "armed thieves" [such is the name which Voltaire gives to an invading foreign army] a "defensive war"; this only leads to many a misunderstanding:

C. You do not admit that war can be just?
A. I have never known one of this kind; the very idea seems contradictory and impossible. . . . There are only offensive wars; a defensive war is merely resistance against armed thieves.[36]

Voltaire was puzzled by the fact that Montesquieu was ready to admit the existence of "just" offensive wars. He violently criticized the following statement of Montesquieu:

Between societies, the right of natural defense sometimes induces the necessity of attacking, when one people sees that a longer peace puts another in a situation to destroy it and that attack at the given moment is the only way of preventing this destruction.[37]

[36] Ibid., XXVII, 372, "Dialogues entre A, B, C, (onzième entretien)."
[37] Ibid., XIX, 322, "Dict. philos.: Guerre."

Voltaire replies:

How can attack in peace be the only means of preventing this destruction? You must be sure that this neighbor will destroy you if he becomes powerful; to be sure of it, he must already have made preparations for your overthrow. In this case it is he who commences the war; it is not you; your supposition is false and contradictory. If ever war is evidently unjust, it is that which you propose: it is going to kill your neighbor who does not attack you, lest he should ever be in a state to do so. To hazard the ruin of your own country in the hope of ruining without reason that of another is assuredly neither honest nor useful, for we are never sure of success.[38]

Conscious of her right of self-defense, a nation should be conscious of her duty not to be weaker than her prospective enemies in the means of defense. To stand upon one's guard is the surest way to avoid war: "dogs of equal strength show each other their teeth, but do not lash each other to pieces." [39] Let a prince disband his troops, allow his fortifications to fall to ruins, and you will see whether in two or three years he has not lost his kingdom.[40] Thus, while Voltaire absolutely rejects offensive war, he does advocate preparedness to meet aggression. He realizes that the abolition of war is a matter of the distant future; he believes in the realization of this ideal since the urge for war is not something innate in man. If such were the case, three-fourths of our earth would be nothing but a desert covered with the bones of the dead. Born to kill his neighbor, man would necessarily fulfill his destiny:

Man is not born wicked . . . why . . . are several infected with the plague of wickedness? It is that those who are at their head, being taken with the malady, communicate it to the rest of men. . . . The first ambitious man corrupted the earth . . . this first monster has sown the seed of pride, rapine, fraud, and cruelty. . . . I confess that, in general, most of our brethren can acquire these qualities; but has everybody the putrid fever, the stone and gravel because everybody is exposed to it. . . .? [41]

[38] *Ibid.*
[39] *Ibid.*, XXVII, 370, "A, B, C."
[40] *Ibid.*, XXVII, 371.
[41] *Ibid.*, XX, 54-55, "Dict. philos.: Méchant."

Since man is not born wicked, as time goes on, mankind will understand more and more fully that war is the destroyer of all those values material, intellectual, and spiritual the creation of which forms the goal of life:

What becomes of and what signifies to me humanity, beneficence, modesty, temperance, mildness, wisdom, and piety while half a pound of lead sent from the distance of a hundred steps pierces my body and I die at twenty years of age in inexpressible torments in the midst of five or six thousand dying men, while my eyes, which open for the last time, see the town in which I was born destroyed by fire and sword, and the last sounds that reach my ears are the cries of women and children expiring under the ruins, all for the pretended interests of a man whom I know not.[42]

While passing a judgment on kings and statesmen of France, Voltaire gives the first place to those who followed a pacifist policy and centered their attention upon a just administration of the state. Such was Henry IV, the hero of Voltaire's epic poem *La Henriade;* such was the first minister of the King, Sully, in whose praise he wrote some magnificent lines in the same poem.[43]

In his *Lettres philosophiques* a whole chapter is devoted to the Society of Friends (the Quakers) who, claiming that they follow the teachings of Christ, profess absolute pacifism:

We never war or fight in any case; but 'tis not that we are afraid, for so far from shuddering at the thoughts of death, we, on the contrary, bless the moment which unites us with the Being of beings; but the reason of our not using the outward sword is that we are neither wolves, tigers, nor mastiffs, but men and Christians. Our God, who has commanded us to love our enemies and to suffer without repining, would certainly not permit us to cross the seas because murtherers clothed in scarlet and wearing caps two foot high enlist citizens by a noise made with two little sticks on an ass's skin extended. And when, after a victory is gained, the whole city of London is illuminated, when the sky is in a blaze with fireworks, and a noise is heard in the air of thanksgivings, of bells, of organs, and of the cannon, we groan in silence and are deeply affected with sadness of spirit and brokenness of

[42] *Ibid.,* XIX, 321, "Dict. philos.: Guerre."
[43] *Ibid.,* VIII, 62, "La Ligue," éd. 1723.

heart for the sad havoc which is the occasion of those public rejoicings.[44]

In his correspondence with the King of Prussia and Catherine the Great we find lines like the following: "Are you and the kings, your colleagues, never going to stop devastating this planet which, according to your own words, you are so anxious to make happy?"[45] Voltaire had no admiration for military spirit:

Philosophers, moralists; burn all your books. While the caprice of a few men makes that part of mankind consecrated to heroism, to murder loyally millions of our brethren, can there be anything more horrible throughout nature?[46]

A very considerable part of Voltaire's work aimed at the promotion of tolerance. He began where Bayle, his "spiritual father," as he called him, left off. Their methods had much in common, but the genius of Voltaire was more versatile; he could take advantage of his brilliant poetical talent, his sharp mind imparted a great strength to his dialectical arguments, while his ability at detecting the ridiculous side of things and to emphasize it in a most striking manner filled his adversaries with terror and paralyzed the power of the Court, the aristocracy, the Church, and the parliaments. At the time when Voltaire began his struggle against superstition and fanaticism the acute period of religious wars was over, but about one hundred thousand Huguenots were in exile; France was more or less "all Catholic," incarnating thus the ideal of Louis XIV. Intolerance had triumphed, and the absence of freedom of thought, speech, and written word was strangling progress. There was no fuel to kindle another religious war, but there was every evidence that neither the attitude of the Church nor that of the Court and the parliaments had changed: in 1762 Calas was sentenced to be broken on the wheel; in 1766 the eighteen-year-old La Barre died under horrible torture; Sirven would have met the same fate

[44] *Ibid.*, XXII, 86, "Lettres philosophiques," Lettre I, transl. by N. L. Torrey.
[45] *Ibid.*, éd. Beuchot, LIV, 430, "Lettre à Frédéric II (1747).
[46] *Ibid.*, éd. Moland, XIX, 321, "Dict. philos.: Guerre."

had he not escaped abroad. All three men were victims of superstition. Voltaire felt that the Catholic Church was responsible for the death of millions; its conviction that the Father of all men has chosen a small number of His children to have the others exterminated in His name seemed to him absurd and impious. "This rage for making proselytes, this intensely mad desire to bring others over to partake of their own peculiar cup or communion" [47] has been the cause of infinite misery. Religious fanatics feel their duty to avenge offenses against God; how can such offenses be under human jurisdiction, Voltaire wonders, and how can it fail to be clear to any one that a man's creed depends on the accident of birth: time and place determine whether he will be Christian, Mahometan, or Buddhist. The heroine of his tragedy *Zaïre* gives the following expression to this conviction:

> I see too plainly, custom forms us all;
> Our thoughts, our morals, our most fix'd belief
> Are consequences of our place of birth!
> Born beyond Ganges, I had been a Pagan;
> In France, a Christian; I am here a Saracen.
> 'Tis but instruction all! Our parents' hand
> Writes on our heart the first faint characters
> Which time, retracing, deepens into strength
> That nothing can efface, but death or Heaven!
>
> . . .
>
> I honor from my soul the Christian laws,
> Those laws which, softening nature by humanity,
> Melt nations into brotherhood. . . .[48]

Voltaire could never forget that Henry IV whom he considered as the first tolerant ruler and the first king-pacifist, had perished at the hand of a Catholic fanatic who up to the moment of his death was proud of his bloody deed:

> Soon as they saw the crimson torrents flow,
> A thousand hands revenged the fatal blow.
> The zealot wished not for a happier time,
> But stood unmoved and triumphed in his crime.

[47] *Ibid.*, XIX, 84, "Dict. philos.: Fanatisme."
[48] *Ibid.*, II, 560, "Zaïre," transl. by Aaron Hill, 1776.

> Through opening skies he saw the heavenly dome,
> And endless glories in the world to come;
> Claimed the bright wreath of martyrdom from God,
> And, falling, blessed the hand that shed his blood.[49]

What can be said, Voltaire wonders, in answer to a man who says he will rather obey God than men and who, consequently, feels certain of meriting heaven by cutting the throats of his fellowmen? When fanaticism has taken such a hold upon the brain of a man, it becomes almost ineradicable.[50] The wise policy should be to get rid of such a man without doing him, however, any harm. The following passage seems, at least, to recommend this policy:

> He [the Emperor of China] has just banished from his dominions a society of foreign Bonzes who had come from the distant parts of the West with the frantic idea of compelling all the inhabitants of China to think as they did; and they had not only acquired large sums of the ignorant, but kindled the flames of persecution in their weak minds under the pretense of teaching the only true religion. The Emperor, when he expelled these religious incendiaries, addressed them in these words: "Strangers, you are come to preach your dogmas of intolerance in China, the most tolerant Empire upon earth; therefore, that you may not do as much harm here as you have done in other countries, I expel you from the walls of China for ever, that I may not be obliged to punish you. I have given orders for you to be conducted honorably to the frontiers. Depart in peace, if peace can ever dwell in such contracted minds, and never return to these dominions.[51]

In the same novel, speaking of the demoralizing influence of the Inquisition, Voltaire gives the following description of Spain at the time when this tribunal was all powerful there:

> Tracing the route which the Princess of Babylon had taken, Amazan passed the Pyrenees. Nothing appeared like joy and gaiety in this country; if here or there a peasant was heard to sing, it was some doleful ditty; the people were all habited in black; each of them had a rosary and a poniard pendant from his

49 *Ibid.*, VIII, 143, "La Henriade," transl. by W. F. Fleming.
50 *Ibid.*, XIX, 80, "Dict. philos.: Fanatisme."
51 *Ibid.*, XXI, 399, "La Princesse de Babylone," tr. by M. J. Young.

belt. If the servants of Amazan asked these grave personages any questions, they answered by signs. . . . Amazan moved forward toward the province of Betica. The Tyrians cultivated the land. They had brought with them some Palestines, who at that time wandered through every count.y where money was to be got; and in Betica, by usury of fifty per cent, they had possessed themselves of nearly all the riches of the country. This made the inhabitants imagine that they were sorcerers and accuse them as such to the Antropocaies or Inquisitors who, without hesitation, took hold of their property, dressed them in frightful masquerade habits, and then roasted them by a slow fire, *por l'amor de Dios*.[52]

How strongly Voltaire blamed intolerance and theological disputes is clear also from the following lines:

. . . one of those spirits which fill the intermundane spaces came down near me. . . . He carried me into a desert all covered with piles of bones. . . . "These," he said, ". . . are the bones of the Christians who have cut one another's throats over metaphysical disputes. They are divided into several mounds of four centuries each. A single mound would have reached way up to heaven; it was necessary to divide them."—"What?" I cried, "brothers have treated their brothers thus, and I have the misfortune to belong to this brotherhood?"—"Here," said the spirit, "are the twelve million Americans killed in their native land because they had not been baptized." [53]

Voltaire loved mankind and could be profoundly affected by the misery of man's life:

I saw in the distance [he writes] some half-naked spectres who, with oxen as gaunt as themselves, were scraping the soil which was even more exhausted and meager.[54]

More than half the habitable earth is still populated by two-legged animals who live under terrible conditions not far removed from those of a pure state of nature. They have scarcely any food or clothing, they are almost deprived of the gift of

[52] *Ibid.,* XXI, 424.
[53] Quoted from N. L. Torrey, *Voltaire and the Enlightenment*, pp. 76-77. See also Voltaire, *Oeuvres*, éd. Moland, XX, 342-343, "Questions sur l'Encyclopédie: art. Religion."
[54] Voltaire, *Oeuvres,* XIX, 113-114, "Dict. philosophique: art. Fertilisation."

speech, they hardly notice that they are miserable, they live and die almost without realizing it.[55]

The selfishness of those who are at the head of a state, the superstition systematically developed in people by their religious and political leaders have been, in no little degree, responsible for this state of things. Narrow fanatical nationalism which creates a military spirit rouses individuals and nations against each other. It stands in the way of the legitimate desire of man for happiness and checks his attempts at creating for himself a happy life based on good will toward his fellowmen and co-operation with them.

Voltaire's special task, particularly during the last twenty years of his life, was the enlightenment of men. He shook the foundation of the prevailing social and religious systems; he replaced the old ideals by new ones. Only a man of his intellect, his heart, and his will could undertake a task of this kind. That the eighteenth century is often called "the century of Voltaire," is the best proof that his efforts were not lost. The biting irony, the sarcastic laughter of this "solicitor general of mankind," as Catherine the Great was wont to call him, proved to be of immense value to the cause of reason, justice, tolerance, and peace.

Whereas in the life of Voltaire there were moments in which he felt impressed by military glory and by the whole atmosphere surrounding a nation preparing for war or already waging it, it does not seem that there were similar moments in the life of DIDEROT (1713-1784). His disregard of external evidences does not imply, however, that the subject of war left him indifferent. The work connected with the production of the *Encyclopedia*, the great task of his life, had compelled him to meditate about the matter. In one of his letters written to the Empress of Russia we find the following passage:

I eagerly wish to see Your Majesty direct her efforts towards the duration of peace rather than any other advantage. . . . The

[55] Quoted from G. R. Havens, *Voltaire's Marginalia on the pages of Rousseau,* 1933, p. 11.

blood of one thousand enemies must have less value in Your Majesty's eyes than a drop of Russian blood. It is evident that triumphs succeeding one another give glamour to a reign; but do they make it happy? As a result of the progress of reason, our admiration is aroused by virtues other than those of a Caesar or Alexander.[56]

The glamor of the reign of Catherine the Great, the annexation of new territories to the already vast Russian Empire failed to exercise any fascination on Diderot as we can judge from the above-quoted passage; he frankly tells the Empress his opinion; the worship of conquerors, characteristic of all epochs of history, is on the decline in his time. The idea of the brotherhood of man begins to gain ground. Nations are considered by all leading philosophers of the eighteenth century as members of one human family; war as something abnormal.

Diderot rejects Hobbes' statements that primitive humanity offered a picture of perpetual war of all against all. According to Diderot, war is as little a natural feature in the life of human society as are pain and illness in the life of an individual. War is the violent convulsive illness of a political body whose natural condition is peace. The reigning princes are in most cases responsible for the breaking out of war. Some of them are personalities so insignificant that they cannot have any influence on the course of the world events and cannot therefore prevent the breaking out of war. The author describes the type in the following passage:

Jupiter sits down to dinner. He jollies his wife, he addresses ambiguous compliments to Venus, he looks with tenderness at Hébé . . . he has his glass filled with wine. While he drinks he hears clamorings coming from all parts of the world. . . . He opens the trap-door of the canopy of heaven and says: "There is plague in Asia, war in Europe, famine in Africa, hail here, storm elsewhere, an eruption of a volcano . . . then he drops the trap-door, sits down, and continues his meal. He drinks to excess, then goes to bed, falls asleep, and . . . he calls this governing the world.[57]

[56] Cf. M. Tourneux, *Diderot et Catherine II*, 1899, pp. 251-252.
[57] D. Diderot, *Oeuvres*, éd. Assézat & Tourneux, 1875-79, II, 449, "Réfutation de l'ouvrage d'Helvétius intitulé *De l'Homme*."

The opposite type is represented by the honor-seeking monarchs. These share the old tradition which links the greatness of a reign to military glory; their ambitious ministers as well as all those who are materially interested in war do their part in making every effort to maintain peace appear ridiculous. Fortunately, as time goes on, a more sound judgment of things emerges, and the personality and deeds of the so-called hero are carefully examined and weighed:

In an enlightened century the number of heroes is not great; good judges are very discriminating in granting this title; they divest Alexander of it. . . . No prince who has only victories and trophies to offer can lay claim to it. Most heroes, La Rochefoucauld says, are like certain paintings: if they are to obtain appreciation, they must be looked at from a distance. But masses are always masses and, since they have no idea of real greatness, they often see a hero in some one who, reduced to his true value, is the shame and the scourge of mankind.[58]

An even more sweeping condemnation of war one finds in Diderot's pamphlet written under the impression of the *Examen de l'Essai sur les préjugés* in which the author, Frederick the Great, had bitterly attacked D'Holbach:

In his *Examen de l'Essai* the author speaks in praise of warriors. All we have to say in regard to this passage is as follows: one does not fight alone; there are usually two, three, four master-butchers involved in those terrible massacres in which millions of men lose their lives. . . . It is easy for us to cite wars in which justice was on neither side; woe then to men of genius who had the misfortune to sacrifice their sublime talents to diabolical and murderous leaders who placed them at the head of armies. If they were not utterly devoid of humanity, they must have bewailed their forced submission; they must have hated both the frivolous or iniquitous cause of war and the monsters who had compelled them to lead the armies; they must have wept over their trophies. . . . I should hate to have been the ferocious beast who ordered the devastation of The Palatinate or the highly honored servant who carried out the order.[59]

58 Diderot, *Encyclopédie*, "Héroïsme."
59 Diderot, *Pages inédites contre un tyran*, 1937.

One easily understands why the dethronement of military glory is so common to the eighteenth century. The spirit of the time is the spirit of liberty. This spirit is incompatible with the demands of war which give the conqueror the power to force the defeated enemy to submit to any clauses of the peace treaty. The principle of liberty is sacrificed even more when war takes place outside Europe, and the conquered people are forced to bear the most cruel treatment or even be reduced to slavery. In his article, *L'Education d'un prince,* Diderot wants the future ruler not to forget that the wickedness of one man in power can cause one hundred thousand other men to curse their lives; that it is not nature, but war that creates slaves; that a moral philosophy and a political organization which have the tendency to estrange man from man should be rejected. As slavery is precisely an order of things which engenders profound hostility among men, there cannot exist any reasons which might excuse it; neither conquest, purchase, nor contract can give any rights to the person of man; therefore, any means that allows a slave to recover his freedom is a legitimate means.

In religious matters Diderot is a champion of tolerance as much as most of his great contemporaries. He sees in our conscience a law-giver on whom our actions are dependent:

It is impious to prescribe laws for the conscience, the universal ruler of action. It must be enlightened, not constrained. If one is allowed to pull a hair from the head of anyone who thinks otherwise than he does, he will be prone to dispose of his head, for injustice has no limits.[60]

He thinks that if the Christian religion would have kept its primitive simplicity, if the dogmas men are invited to accept and the form of worship they are urged to adopt could always find their foundations in the human soul, men would never reject them or have disputes after they have accepted them.[61] In the *Encyclopédie* Diderot defines "tolerance" as the virtue of a weak being doomed to live among other similar beings. He urges everyone to keep in mind that what seems evident to

[60] *Oeuvres,* I, 183, "La Promenade du sceptique."
[61] *Ibid.,* I, 183.

one is obscure or quite ununderstandable to another, that our thoughts and feelings depend very little on our will which, in its turn, is a resultant of all which took place between the moment of our birth and that in which it makes itself known. He insists upon the necessity of separating the Church, whose object is to prepare men for the life to come, from the State, whose object is our present, terrestrial life. Unless the great principle of tolerance gains recognition, nothing is left to a man than to be "Catholic under Mary and Protestant under Elizabeth." [62]

Diderot was one of the great philosophers of the eighteenth century who were striving for a better future for mankind. Their common work, the *Encyclopédie,* which would never have seen the light but for Diderot, was the powerful means of spreading the ideas of liberty, freedom of conscience, and humanity.

Besides a great power of mind, Diderot had a great heart. Realizing the immense importance of the *Encyclopédie* not only for his contemporaries, but also for future generations, he sacrificed everything to the completion of his great task; he consoled himself and his collaborators for all the disillusionments, afflictions, and hardships which the publication of their work inevitably brought with it by the idea that men would remember them when they will be no more.[63] He had an unshaken faith in the human mind and in its future achievements, but he considered the moral aspects of the life of man as even more important:

The charms of virtue affect me more than the ugliness of vice; I turn away from the wicked, and I fly towards the good.[64]

May he [man] above all be good; he may then be great if he can. For himself, for me, for those about him I wish him to have a great soul rather than a fine genius.[65]

[62] *Encyclopédie.* "Tolérance."
[63] *Oeuvres,* XVIII, 101, and *Encyclopédie,* art. "Encyclopédie."
[64] *Ibid.,* XVIII, 260, "Lettre à S. Volland."
[65] *Ibid.,* III, 540, "Lettre sur l'éducation des enfants."

And he desired that kindness, good-will, and above all peace might prevail not only among individuals and citizens, but also in the stormy sea of international relations.

The interest one naturally feels in the opinions of D'HolBACH (1723-1789) in regard to the issues of war and peace lies in the fact that this prominent thinker of the eighteenth century was one of the acknowledged leaders of a school of philosophy and played an important rôle in the social, political, and literary movement of his time. An essentially materialistic outlook on life was united in him with a real devotion to the highest ideals of thought; his interests, far from being sensual in nature, as some people wrongly felt, were of a spiritual character. Men of high intellectuality had a great appeal for him, especially those whose materialistic convictions were in accord with his own, and he was ready to be of service to them not only through his influential friends but also by means of his wealth. He was not of an emotional character; while thinking of all the miseries of human life, and above all of those which war leaves in its wake, he never lost his habitual serenity. His deeply deterministic outlook on life did not interfere with his faith in progress or his activity; it merely gave him great poise. Since everything in man and life is determined, that which happens is unavoidable, consequently, there cannot be any place for regret or complaint.

Looking from this point of vantage on the lives of so many peoples whose history consists mainly of the history of war, D'Holbach thinks that nothing else could be expected. The heads of nations are usually men of average mental ability; their decisions are motivated by greed, caprice, a false *point d'honneur,* a desire to play an important rôle among nations and make their neighbors tremble before them, and, finally, by a mad thirst for conquest. The example of those so-called heroes encourages the rise of demagogues who impart their fury to their naïve, imprudent followers. Encouraged by panegyric songs of poets, by the sheepish submission of the common people, by the support of those who profit by war, men holding sovereign power move on unchecked, blind to the evil they are doing. Unfortunately, those who suffer most from wars are frequently proud of being the chosen instruments that fulfill the ambitious ends of the leaders. More often they obey merely because of fear for their lives. The gain achieved through wars of conquest is negligible when compared to the loss:

Nations are ready to cut each other's throat for possession of "some heaps of sand" where greed already imagines treasures. Entire nations are the dupes of the avarice of hungry businessmen who beguile them with the hope of wealth the fruit of which they gather for themselves alone . . .[66]

The welfare and happiness of the people, the only *raison d'être* of all government, are forgotten, yet only a government pursuing these ends has the right to claim submission.

D'Holbach attaches great importance to the personality of the head of a state, since the stability of international friendships depends greatly thereon. He admits that order in international life is a goal most difficult of attainment: there is no world tribunal, no codified law, no executive power upon submission to which the peaceful co-existence of peoples may rest. Everything depends on the ability to conciliate opposing interests through negotiations; and yet D'Holbach does not mean to say that, even if none of these desiderata exists, the world would necessarily be in a state of perpetual anarchy: there is a natural law of which every human creature is conscious. Reason and experience, man's universal guides, may be regarded as a kind of ultimate source of reference which ought to command the attention of every thinking man and every nation.[67] Sovereigns should obey this natural law and rely on it much more than on the balance of power, a system by which each state tries to seize power by force or fraud.

D'Holbach finds that the "war of all against all," of which Hobbes speaks, takes place among individuals to a lesser degree than among nations. Likewise he calls our attention to the fact that in every country it is the military caste which

[66] P. H. D. d'Holbach, *La Politique naturelle,* éd. 1773, II, 154.
[67] *La Morale universelle,* éd. 1820, II, 1-4.

plays the foremost rôle; that a military career is everywhere the surest path to honor.[68]

War waged by a people is always declared to be a just war, while the study of history proves that a "just war" is a great rarity. Even a purely defensive war against an enemy guilty of breaking an agreement cannot always be considered a just war. D'Holbach feels as strongly as Rousseau that treaties, in most cases, represent the triumph of force over right. If one cannot blame a people for getting rid of a sovereign whose rule proves to be disastrous for his subjects, how can one blame a nation for rising in arms in protest against an unjust treaty imposed on her by a stronger adversary? Justice, says D'Holbach, is above the sanctity of an agreement.[69] The right to insist on the enforcement of the clauses of a treaty depends upon their justice.[70] "We must be careful not to prescribe in politics those superstitious and romantic virtues the vigorous application of which would sometimes be the ruin of a society: virtues that harm mankind are false virtues." [71] Furthermore, if we admit the right of self-defense for an individual, we are bound to acknowledge it for a people. It is thus clear that D'Holbach does not declare any and every war unlawful, but he condemns a war of conquest. The extent of territory, the number, size, and natural resources of colonies, the plenitude of the national treasury are of little value unless they give security and happiness to the majority of the citizens.[72] In order to be able to achieve this end, the state must be self-sufficient. D'Holbach does not favor the tendency toward acquiring colonies; he admits that they may be useful in case of the over-population of the mother-country and that they can serve as markets; but free trade can secure the same advantage. One should not forget, he remarks, that all colonies are bound, in due time, to become independent states and that, even during their subjection to the homeland, their inhabitants should be under the same

[68] *Ibid.*, II, 6.
[69] *La Politique naturelle*, éd. 1773, II, 216-217.
[70] *Ibid.*, II, 207-208.
[71] *Ibid.*, II, 208.
[72] *Le Système social*, éd. 1822, II, ch. X, XI.

laws and enjoy the same advantages as the citizens of the mother-country. D'Holbach does not consider worth while the struggle to secure temporary advantages like those mentioned above. The most successful war leaves in its wake a national debt. An active, industrious man has to work doubly hard while the bondholders enjoy an idle life: "Every *rentier* is a charge on the man who works." [73] Wealth which is not the fruit of labor is a source of corruption. We see that D'Holbach's determinism is perfectly compatible with the recognition of the value and the need of effort and knowledge. Nature has endowed man with an invincible desire for happiness; in order to be happy he must learn to take reason for his guide, to be active, industrious, full of courage and tenacity. D'Holbach's ethics, based on the nature of man, is utilitarian in character and offers a system applicable to any man in any country. He defines it as a science the principles of which can be demonstrated as clearly and logically as those of arithmetic or geometry, a science the essentials of which can be brought within the comprehension of the most simpleminded men and even children.[74] He finds that nature is a better guide than religion: the latter, in directing the aspirations of man toward the world beyond the grave, makes him unapt to perform his duties as a member of human society and, consequently, contribute to the preservation of a community; it is this reason which compels D'Holbach to declare himself in favor of the separation of Church and State. If man concentrates all his efforts upon the study of nature, of which he is a part, and arrives at the understanding of its laws, he will attain not only his personal well-being, but the happiness of mankind.

The assurance of this unfailing happiness of future generations lies, according to CONDORCET (1743-1794), in the absolute perfectibility of the human race:

The organic perfectibility or deterioration of the classes of the vegetable or species of the animal kingdom may be regarded as

[73] *La Politique naturelle,* II, pp. 137-140.
[74] *Eléments de la morale universelle,* éd. 1790, Avertissement.

one of the general laws of nature. This law extends itself to the human race. . . . Would it be absurd to suppose the quality of melioration in the human species as susceptible of an indefinite advancement; to suppose that . . . the interval between the birth of màn and the decay will itself have no assignable limit . . . ? If we cannot fix the term, it may for ever approach, but can never surpass. . . . We cannot even tell whether there be any circumstance in the laws of nature which has determined and laid down its limit.[75]

In Condorcet's opinion, progress is to be achieved mainly through the improvement of human institutions; this explains the fervent co-operation he gave to the leaders of the Revolution as a member of the Municipality of Paris, of the Legislative Assembly, and of the National Convention. His *Esquisse du tableau des progrès de l'esprit humain* gives the full measure of his boundless faith in progress as well as a detailed exposition of its theory. Anticipating the disappearance of the darker aspects of human life such as inequality of fortune, education, social standing, he imparts to the reader a vision that seems to border almost upon a utopia. He foresees the advent of an era when there will be no competition, no struggle between men and nations, no war. War and civilization are, in his opinion, things irreconcilable, for one excludes the other. It is not the time of war, but the time of peace that requires of man the greatest effort of mind and will for the everyday struggle for existence in a world of intense competition, and it is precisely on this struggle that the development of his personality rests. Since peace is essential for progress, steps should be taken toward lessening in men ideas and feelings that favor a military spirit, hatred for foreigners, patriotism: the military spirit, Condorcet says,

"is not a passion to defend unto death our friends and our fatherland; it is rather a science to destroy men. It inspires slaves to kill anyone when commanded, at the first sound of the drum; it destroys all moral sentiments and substitutes in their place mechanical obedience."[76]

[75] *Outlines of an Historical View of the Progress of the Human Mind*, ed. 1795, pp. 367-370.
[76] Quoted from Salwyn Schapiro, *Condorcet and the Rise of Liberalism*, 1934, p. 145.

Condorcet has no admiration for patriotism; he sees it mainly as the love for old customs, standing in the way of useful reforms, and as a national outlook mingled with national pride that fosters hostile feelings, dissensions, and conflicts.[77]

Like Amos Komensky in the seventeenth century, Condorcet thought that the creation of a universal language would bring the different nations of our world into closer relationship. The use of a common language would help to give a more perfect form to ideas, and this would prove a great step forward on the way of progress and lead to a better understanding between individuals and nations.[78]

Like most French thinkers of the eighteenth century, Condorcet was cosmopolitan in his outlook. Centering his thoughts on plans and measures which were likely to assure a rapid improvement in various spheres of human life, he seldom spoke in terms of the French nation; he rather had in view the future happiness of the human race. In his opinion, the three basic principles proclaimed by the French Revolution, "Liberty, Equality, Fraternity," besides being used to determine the relationships of citizens within a nation, were to become in the future powerful mottoes in the sphere of international life. The universal acceptance of those principles would eliminate war and would lead to the abolition of slavery, that barbarous institution which had gained fresh strength from the discovery of the New World. Condorcet fought many a fierce battle against slavery as the President of the French Anti-slavery Association and as the author of the pamphlet *Reflexions sur l'esclavage des Nègres* (1781), in which he advanced invincible arguments in favor of the abolition of this remainder of a barbarous epoch. When a measure was dictated by reason and a sense of humanity, he never questioned the possibility of making it practical. In accord with Rousseau, Condorcet asserted that man is morally good by nature. He drew this conclusion from the fact that a nor-

[77] A. N. C. de Condorcet, *Oeuvres,* éd. 1847-49, V, 372, "Dissertation politique et philosophique."

[78] *Outlines of an Historical View of the Progress of the Human Mind,* 1795, pp. 363-364.

mal individual is affected in a greater or lesser degree by the suffering of his fellowmen; this innate feeling is susceptible of development and promises to become the most powerful weapon against war. Condorcet's firm belief in its abolition in the future rested also on the conviction that the autocratic form of government was bound to disappear. Since the "popular" government would not be blinded by age-old traditions, it would be more apt to realize that there is more advantage in sharing, under reciprocal arrangement, the gifts which have fallen to the lot of another nation by reason of her geographical position, her trade, or her industries than in extorting these advantages by force, which would impose great sacrifices on citizens and put the very existence of a nation at stake. In the international society, as well as in the civil society, the superiority of mind, of talent, of wealth of some members are a real benefit to all; therefore, instead of erecting barriers between states, governments should favor close intercourse, co-operation, free industry, and free trade. Freedom of industry and commerce would broaden the outlook and the interests of men and favor the distribution of wealth, preventing its concentration in the hands of a few individuals.

Condorcet was deeply interested in all that was going on in the new-born Republic across the ocean. Many aspects of American life aroused his admiration, above all the attitude of American people towards religious issues. While Europe, even in the eighteenth century, had to struggle over questions of religious tolerance in order to prevent the return of religious wars and the terrors of the Inquisition, full freedom of conscience, which is more than tolerance, characterized the American religious outlook; the Constitution of the United States had completed the separation of the Church from the State and prevented forever the possibility of the establishment of a national governing Church in the Republic.

Since plans for international organization reached their fullest and most ingenious development during the eighteenth century, one is not astonished at Condorcet's admiration for the new American Republic which had just accomplished the federation of the member states. The young Republic had adopted a system of militia in the place of a permanent professional army, showing thus that the idea of any war of conquest was alien to her mind. Condorcet wanted France to proclaim the same principle; it was he who drafted the decree of the Legislative Assembly addressed to the peoples of Europe:

> The French nation, faithful to the principle not to wage wars of conquest or use her power to the prejudice of the freedom of other nations, takes up arms only for the defense of her liberty and independence.[79]

In the same effort to give dynamic force to his theories in his struggle against wars of conquest, he later urged the Convention, of which he was a member, to take steps toward the establishment of a World Court which would have the right to examine and judge international disputes. He foresaw the usefulness of this kind of institution even in time of peace. The delegates, permanently assembled, would learn to cooperate and would accustom the nations to the idea of the necessity of common action in many circumstances of international life.

The rationalism of Montesquieu, Voltaire and the Encyclopedists, far from drying up their hearts, made them very human. Humanitarian feelings, transformed by the intellect, found clear expression in their writings. None of them could be enthusiastic about such peace plans as that proposed by the Abbé de Saint-Pierre because it was based on the political *status quo* of Europe and depended for its execution on the good will of sovereign Princes. All of them believed that social changes were first necessary. Montesquieu, advocating a constitutional monarchy, was the most conservative. Diderot saw most clearly the need for social upheaval before desirable political reforms could be hoped for. Voltaire, D'Holbach, and Condorcet were less explicit but all felt that progress, however slow, should be made in men's habits of thinking before any such scheme as the Abbé's could be put

[79] Quoted from E. Garcin, *J. J. Rousseau dans la Révolution*, p. 275 [transl. into English].

into effect. All were united in their hostility to the political power of the Church and believed that the subordination of Church to State, or at least the separation of the two powers, should be the first consideration in the fight for tolerance and peace. They thus built no peace projects, but they laid the foundations for the democratic way of life and on that they pinned their hopes for world peace.

CHAPTER VII

ROUSSEAU AND THE MORALISTS

THE advent of the new era was foreseen by Rousseau more clearly than by any one else. It was he who gave to many of the most cherished ideas of the eighteenth century a tremendous dynamic force. Rousseau and the group of writers who shared his philosophical outlook approached the issue of war from a moralistic point of view. They felt themselves citizens of one vast universe. This did not prevent them from being at the same time faithful and devoted citizens of their native countries. There was nothing contradictory in this attitude. It made their patriotism free from the desire to see their own country larger, richer, and more powerful than the others. To be a good citizen was, in their opinion, to work for the welfare of one's fatherland without wishing to dominate other peoples. Aggressive military spirit was alien to them.

In his *Jugement sur le Projet de p. p. de M. l'Abbé de Saint-Pierre* ROUSSEAU (1712-1778) mentions that the author, in trying to interest the sovereigns and statesmen of his time in his plan for perpetual peace, had shown "the zeal of a missionary," [1] but that, in spite of his untiring efforts, his ideas had not been gaining ground. Soon after the death of the Abbé (1743), his nephew collected the manuscripts left by his uncle and handed them over to Rousseau whom Mme Dupin, Mably, and Saint-Lambert had asked to further the spread of the Abbé's ideas by couching them in a more

[1] See *The Political Writings of Rousseau,* ed. by C. E. Vaughan, 1915, I, 388.

138

concise and attractive form. In deciphering those manuscripts which were often scarcely legible, Rousseau found that they contained ideas of great value. In his *Extrait du Projet de paix perpétuelle de M. l'Abbé de Saint-Pierre, Jugement sur le Projet de p. p., Extrait de la Polysynodie, Jugement sur la Polysynodie,* Rousseau analyzed the ideas of the Abbé and, if later they became widely known throughout the world, it was due in a large measure to his criticism.

The Powers of Europe [the Abbé wrote] constitute a kind of a whole united by identity of religion, moral standards, international law, by letters, commerce . . .[2]

The European nations should, therefore, be closely united, Rousseau says, but they are not:

To behold the continual dissensions, depredations, usurpations, revolts, wars, and murders, which daily ravage this respectable abode of sages, this brilliant system of arts and sciences; to consider our sublime conversations and our horrible proceedings, so much humanity in our discourses and such cruelty in our actions, a religion so humane, and an intolerance so sanguinary . . . governments so moderate, and wars so cruel, one knows not how to reconcile such strange contradictions, and this fraternity of European nations seems to be a term of derision, ironically to express their mutual enmity.[3]

But was it not the great goal of the Abbé de Saint-Pierre's life to find a remedy against the great evil of war? And, once his *Projet de paix perpétuelle* was published, was he not right in thinking that he had found the infallible remedy? If it could be accepted and put to the test, his plan—he was sure of that—would open a new era in the history of Europe.

Rousseau was unable to share the Abbé's faith in the possibility of the immediate realization of his ideals; for, although he found his plan for perpetual peace "beautiful, constructive, sound"[4] from the theoretical point of view, he

[2] J. J. Rousseau, *Oeuvres,* éd. Furne, 1835-39, I, 607, "Extrait du Projet de paix perpétuelle. . . ."

[3] *Ibid.,* I, 608, transl. from the French with a Preface by the translator, London, 1761.

[4] *Oeuvres,* éd. Volland, 1790, XIII, 525, "Jugement sur le Projet de p. p."

did not think it practical, because men are senseless, unfair, greedy, and prone to place their personal interests above everything else.[5] The Abbé places all his hope in statesmen and sovereigns. Rousseau finds this hope foolish:

> Ministers are in perpetual need of war, as a means of making themselves indispensable to their master, of throwing him into difficulties from which he cannot escape without their aid, of ruining the state, if things come to the worst, as the price of keeping their own office. They are in need of it as a means . . . of finding places for their creatures, of rigging the market and setting up a thousand odious monopolies. . . . With a lasting peace, all those resources would be gone. . . . Is it not obvious that there is nothing impracticable about it [the plan] except its adoption by these men? What then will they do to oppose it? What they have always done: they will turn it into ridicule.[6]

> You are taking from sovereigns the right of doing themselves justice. . . . You are taking from them the power of making themselves great at the expense of their neighbours. You are forcing them to renounce those antiquated claims whose value depends on their obscurity . . . that parade of might and terror with which they love to awe the world, that pride of conquest which is the chief source of their glory. In one word, you are forcing them to be equitable and peaceful. What amends do you propose to make them for all these cruel privations?[7]

> The whole life of kings is devoted solely to two objects: to extend their rule beyond their frontiers and to make it more absolute within them. Any other purpose they may have . . . is merely a pretext for attaining them; such pretexts are: the good of the community, the happiness of their subjects, or the glory of the nation . . . therefore, the people groan with apprehension when their masters speak to them of their "fatherly solicitude."[8]

In full accord with these pronouncements of Rousseau was the opinion of Cardinal de Fleury, who, upon receiving,

---

[5] Cf. Vaughan, *op. cit.,* I, 387, "Jugement sur le Projet de p. p."

[6] *Ibid.,* I, 391, transl. by C. E. Vaughan.

[7] *Ibid.,* I, 379, "Extrait du Projet de paix perpétuelle," transl. by C. E. Vaughan.

[8] *Ibid.,* I, 389, "Jugement sur le Projet de p. p.," transl. by C. E. Vaughan.

enclosed in the Abbé's letter, a copy of the five "fundamental articles" of the *Abrégé du Projet de paix perpétuelle,* advised the author not to forget a very essential point: namely, to send missionaries to sovereigns in order that they may try to touch their hearts and win them to his cause.[9]

Rousseau had, moreover, another reason for not sharing the Abbé's enthusiastic hope: he wondered whether there would be any possibility of maintaining a fair degree of equality among the member states if, in spite of all difficulties, the Union of the European nations were finally established. Since the rich and the mighty take the lead in civil society and are the oppressors of the humble and the poor, shall we not see the same order of things in the new political body? In planning for men, one should have men, not imaginary beings, in view and raise the structure of a new society on a sound and real foundation:

> Planning for his contemporaries, the Abbé, if we speak frankly, was working for imaginary beings and designing the top of a building the foundation of which was still to be laid.[10]

To judge of what kind of stones Rousseau, in his turn, would lay the foundation of the great building of an international body, one ought to consider the works of Rousseau as a whole. Only sovereign peoples, full masters of their destinies, he believes, are in a position to make a reality of a dream of perpetual peace; only democracies whose principle it is to put the welfare of the masses above the benefit of the individuals are likely to be ready to apply that principle when they will have to consider matters regarding a great number of nations; and in the critical moment when the peace of the world is at stake only they are likely to oppose the will of the mighty and of all who might derive a profit from general suffering. It is obvious that Rousseau's thoughts move in just the opposite direction to those of the Abbé de Saint-Pierre. The latter puts his hopes in sovereigns; Rousseau,

<hr />

[9] L'Abbé de Saint-Pierre, *Oeuvres,* 1729-41, tome XVI, pp. 117-125.
[10] Quoted from Lassudrie-Duchêne, *Rousseau et le droit des gens,* 1906, p. 172. See also Sreckeisen-Moultou, *Oeuvres inédites de Rousseau,* p. 310.

on the contrary, does not believe that one could expect to
see a pacified Europe until the downfall of the European
monarchies has come to pass. He does not believe in the
divine right of anointed heads; he does not see in them the
proprietors of their states; he wonders how the Congress
planned by the Abbé could be given the right to guarantee
the sovereigns against the revolt of their subjects without
assuming the duty of guaranteeing the subjects against the
tyranny of the Princes. According to Rousseau, there are
instances in which revolt is legitimate and even sacred.

The principle of the *status quo,* which is the cornerstone of
the Abbé's plan, does not find a supporter in Rousseau. The
political organization of a given moment can be the result of
violence, fraud, usurpation, or violation of right, and to this
we should not give our acknowledgment. Under certain circumstances, revenge might be the duty of a people, as when
it is a victim of conquest, for example:

All efforts of a conquered people should be directed towards
freeing itself of the yoke which force has laid upon it. It has no
duties in respect to its new master; it has but to submit to force
as long as no other course is possible.[11]

The political map of Europe seemed a puzzle to Rousseau;
he had the foreboding of the coming storms: "We are rapidly approaching a state of crisis and a century of revolutions. . . . It seems to me impossible that the great European monarchies can last any length of time." [12]

Rousseau's point of departure is the idea that the society
of European nations, in their relations to each other, in the
eighteenth century as well as through the whole time of their
political existence from the dawn of their history, has been in
a state of nature. Primitive men, capable as they were of
development, had discovered, after ages of solitary existence,
the advantages of co-operation and had entered the stage of
social life in which they formed families and tribes. As
time went on, those elementary social groups passed by means
of contracts concluded among them to a more perfect social

[11] *Oeuvres,* éd. Volland, VI, 5, 16, "Confessions."
[12] See M. Markovitch, *J. J. Rousseau et Tolstoï,* p. 242.

form called the state. The next step of development, the formation of a union of states, unfortunately has not taken place and therein is the root of the evil which is tearing Europe to pieces.

Man in the state of nature, Rousseau says—and in this he is in full accordance with Puffendorf and Montesquieu against Hobbes—is a peaceful, timid being;[13] competition, anger, jealousy, strenuous activity are unknown to him; since he has no property of any kind, a conflict with another man can be only accidental and transitory. In the main, the primitive man is an animal, but an animal capable of pity, the source of moral life. The stages of social conditions through which he passes—family, tribe, state—presuppose some kind of ownership, and this invariably leads to conflicts. The "social contract" gives a means for settling these conflicts and makes possible the existence of man in those more advanced stages of his development. Each member surrenders willingly his individual rights to the community at large in exchange for the protection the latter gives him:

Each of us puts in common his person and his whole power under the supreme direction of the general will, and in return we receive every member as an indivisible part of the whole.

Since each one gives himself up entirely, the conditions are equal for all; and, the conditions being equal for all, no one has any interest in making them burdensome to others.

In short, each giving himself to all, gives himself to nobody; and as there is not one associate over whom we do not acquire the same rights which we concede to him over ourselves, we gain the equivalent of all that we lose, and more power to preserve what we have.

Forthwith, instead of the individual personalities of all the contracting parties, this act of association produces a moral and collective body which is composed of as many members as the assembly has voices and which receives from this same act its unity, its common self (*moi*), its life, and its will.[14]

[13] Cf. C. E. Vaughan, *op. cit.*, I, 293, "L'Etat de guerre."
[14] Cf. Vaughan, *op. cit.*, II, 33, "Du Contrat social" (version définitive). [The passages from the *Contrat social* are quoted in the translation of Henry Tozer.]

The social contract has solved the problem of the mutual relations between the members of a state, but obviously it cannot solve the problem of the co-existence of a number of states. The nature of a state is different from that of man: the state is an artificial body and, according to Rousseau, "all things are good coming from God's hand; they all degenerate in the hands of man." [15] Unlike man, the state is not a moral being, it is not capable of pity, it is warlike (belliqueux), "a state grows powerful or feeble according to what its neighbor becomes, strong or weak." [16] If the territory is extensive in proportion to the population, it is likely to be invaded; but if, on the other hand, the population is too dense, the state will try, probably, to tear a piece of land from some neighbor, to acquire colonies, and to secure by force markets for its products. It is driven to those actions partly by the instinct of self-preservation, but mainly by greed, which in most cases gives to war the character of common burglary and brigandage. What makes things even worse is that in order to attain its ends, the state usually allows its sovereign's power to degenerate into tyranny. Where men, trying to be lawful and loyal to their leader, blindly agree to have their rights, goods, security, and even lives sacrificed to assure the triumph of their ruler over other rulers, there the hope for peace and justice must be given up. [17]

Rousseau seems at times to wonder whether the establishment of more normal relations among the European states and the abolition of war could not be expected as a result of the influence of the Christian Church? The Abbé de Saint-Pierre in his *Projet de paix perpétuelle* speaks of a "Christian" republic. Rousseau, under his influence, begins to use this term, but he promptly corrects himself:

I should not say "Christian Republic," each of these two words excludes the other. Christian religion preaches servitude and dependence. Its spirit strongly favors tyranny and allows tyrants

[15] Rousseau, *Émile* (the opening lines).
[16] Vaughan, *op. cit.,* I, 297, "L'Etat de guerre."
[17] *Ibid.,* pp. 299-300.

to domineer over the weak. True Christians are made for the rôle of slaves.[18]

He reverts to history, but can it lead anywhere? "Let us not look for what was done, but for what should be done.[19] And in order to learn what should be done for the abolition of the greatest scourge of mankind, he decides that he must thoroughly study the nature of war:

I call war the consequence of a natural, constant, and evident tendency to destroy a hostile state or at least to weaken it by all means at one's disposal. This tendency expressed in action is actual war; while in latent form, it is the state of war.[20]

War is not at all a relation of man to man, but that of state to state, a relation in which men become enemies only accidentally, not as individuals or citizens, but as soldiers; not as members of the fatherland, but as its defenders.[21]

A people takes arms to contend for power, wealth, or honor; the object of the dispute is so remote from the personal interests of the citizens that they are neither better nor worse whether they have vanquished or have been vanquished.[22]

The statement that war is not a relation of man to man, but that of state to state has been of tremendous importance on account of the inferences drawn from it by Rousseau and other writers after him. It cannot be said that the thought was quite new: in Saintard's *Roman politique sur l'état présent des affaires de l'Amérique* (1756) we find the following lines:

In Europe war is waged against political bodies, not against men. The practice of sparing the blood and property of citizens at the risk of sparing thereby the states they form . . . has even become a sacred maxim.[23]

In principle, war should not be made against merchants, but against soldiers. Nations formed of men act among themselves

---

[18] *Ibid.*, I, 504, "Du Contrat social" (prem. version).
[19] *Ibid.*, I, 300, "L'Etat de guerre."
[20] *Ibid.*, I, 300.
[21] *Ibid.*, II, 29, "Du Contrat social" (version défin.).
[22] *Ibid.*, I, 313, "Fragments relating to the earliest chapters of the "Contrat social."
[23] P. 263.

as men act among themselves. Only armies, fortresses, warships should become the objects of attack—things which can defend themselves.[24]

In his work *J. J. Rousseau et le droit des gens* Lassudrie-Duchêne mentions Bynkershoeck as the first who expressed this thought.[25] If the important statement had been made, it did not go beyond the realm of books and it remained to Rousseau to make of it a living force, a principle universally accepted. Was not Mme de Staël right in saying: "Rousseau did not discover anything new, but he set everything on fire." [26]

From his main principle that war is essentially a relation between political bodies, Rousseau draws the conclusion that the expression "civil war" contains a contradiction in terms. In war not individuals, but states are enemies; not citizens, but soldiers as instruments or officers of the state; therefore, no harm ought ever to be done to the peaceful population; between armies, the mandataries of the states, the struggle should proceed with the least shedding of blood, the least cruelty, since "war confers no right except what is necessary to its end." [27] "One kills in order to defeat; as soon as the vanquished yields, the victor takes possession of the object of dispute, and the war is over." [28] The prisoners do not belong to the fighting force of the enemy; they might be kept until the end of the war in order to weaken the army of the adversary; as citizens of their country, they should never be compelled to fight against it or to be employed as guides.[29] Since war is a relation of state to state, only property belonging to the state should pass to the conqueror; private property as well as buildings devoted to educational or cultural interests such as schools, museums, and churches should be spared; their destruction, not furthering the operations of war, would be mere vandalism. The peaceful population

[24] P. 270.

[25] See Bynkershoeck, *Questiones juris publici*, L. I. ch. X.

[26] See E. Garcin, *J. J. Rousseau dans la Révolution*, p. 31.

[27] Vaughan, *op. cit.*, I, 511, "Du Contrat social" (prem. version).

[28] *Ibid.*, I, 312, "Fragm. relating to the earl. chapters of the *Contrat social.*"

[29] *Ibid.*, I, 310-311.

should be—in principle at least—spared the suffering being brought about by war. Citizens cannot avoid sharing in the expenses for military operations; they suffer from the high cost of living; no harm, however, should be done to them directly. That appropriate measures might be taken for the protection of the non-combatants, war should be declared: "The foreigner, whether king or private person or nation who robs, slays, or detains subjects without declaring war is not an enemy, but a brigand." [30]

The importance of Rousseau's doctrine becomes evident when we compare the wars waged by France against the European coalition at the time of the French Revolution with all the preceding wars known to history. From the remotest times, war had meant extermination and vandalism. There was nothing that could safeguard the rights of neutral nations, citizens, women and children, sick and wounded soldiers, and, above all, of prisoners against the violence of the conqueror. To sack towns and villages, to make a desert of a flourishing country, to reduce to ashes the monuments of human genius was, in time of war, an everyday occurrence which could not always be excused by *force majeure* or *raison d'état*. Prisoners were killed or reduced to slavery; they were ransomed or exchanged for prisoners of the enemy only in exceptional cases. Rousseau could not think of all this suffering without being deeply moved; in the MS. Neuchâtel, 7856 one finds the following passage:

I open the books on law and morals; I listen to savants and jurisconsults and penetrated by their beguiling words . . . I bless the wisdom of public institutions. . . . I close the book . . . and look about me: I see unhappy peoples groaning under a yoke of iron, the human race crushed by a handful of oppressors, everywhere the strong armed with the redoubtable power of the laws against the weak. All these things take place peaceably and without resistance. It is the tranquillity of the companions of Ulysses shut up in the cave of Cyclops, waiting to be devoured. One must groan and be silent. . . . I lift my eyes and look afar. I perceive fires and flames, the country-side deserted, the towns being pillaged. Savage fellows, whither are you dragging these

[30] *Ibid.*, II, 30, "Du Contrat social" (version défin.).

unfortunates? I hear a frightful sound; what tumult, what cries! I draw nearer; I see a theater of murders, ten thousand men massacred, the dead piled high, the dying trampled under the feet of horses, everywhere the image of death and agony. . . . Pity, indignation rise up in the bottom of my heart. . . . But it is no longer permitted one to be simply a man and to plead the cause of humanity. . . . Alas, I must be silent; but the voice of my heart, would it not still know how to pierce so sad a silence? [31]

The changes Rousseau succeeded in bringing into the sphere of war are obvious from the instructions given by Lazare Carnot, commander-in-chief of the French army, to the commanders of different corps during the Revolutionary wars:

Do not allow an army . . . to bring shame upon its triumphs through plunder and cruelty. . . . Take care of objects of worship; see that the wretched population, homes, women, children, old people are treated with respect. Be the benefactors of nations. . . . The name of the French people should inspire awe, not hatred.[32]

Carnot was a fervent disciple of Rousseau as was another member of the National Convention, l'Abbé Grégoire, who in his *Projet de code en vingt et un articles* demanded the recognition of the following principles:

Nations are naturally linked together by a universal moral law. —They are independent and sovereign.—One nation owes to another everything a man owes to a man.—The sea belongs to all men and cannot be the property of any particular people.—Defensive war is sacred.—All offensive war is an attempt against the human family.[33]

This project, acclaimed by the National Convention, is, according to Eugène Garcin, the first legislative monument of international law, the first step taken by a great legislative assembly toward the establishment of universal peace.

Rousseau's influence can easily be traced in all those tre-

31 *Ibid.*, I, 302-303. [The English version is from Ch. W. Hendel's *J. J. Rousseau moralist*, p. 89.]
32 Cf. E. Garcin, *op. cit.*, p. 313.
33 *Ibid.*, p. 278.

mendous changes in thought and deed. In particular, it is to be noticed that his point of view in regard to the upkeep of standing armies became a matter of great discussion. Disavowing a war of conquest, Rousseau speaks of a defensive war as a just war and feels that it is every citizen's sacred duty to take arms for the defense of his country: "War is sometimes a duty; it must never be a profession; every man should become a soldier in case circumstances require him to defend his liberty; no one should become a soldier with the idea of depriving some one else of his freedom.[34] We see that Rousseau is not in favor of standing armies and is strongly opposed to militarism. A national guard or a militia, he feels, should be able to protect a state against aggression. Small states should form confederated republics in order to counterbalance the power of large political bodies. He does not reject the possibility of the abolition of war in times to come, for he feels that "war is not something inherent in the nature of man; its source lies in the absence of social order."[35] To obtain its abolition, the nations should follow the same path which was followed by individuals; from the primitive state they should try to pass to the next stage of civilization and establish by means of an international contract a union of peoples "which would defend and protect with all its force the person and property of every member, and by means of which every one, coalescing with all, may nevertheless obey only himself and remain as free as before,"[36] "for there is a great difference between being subservient to individuals or to a group, because, if one is a member of a group, there is a possibility that he may become its leader and have others under his command."[37] In an international organization the individual will of the state, in matters concerning the whole Union, would be subjected to the general will of the Congress of Nations; the reign of positive international law would be brought about, but the prerequisite for the establishment of this new order of things

[34] Rousseau, *Oeuvres,* éd. 1835-39, I, 500, "Réponse à M. Bordes."
[35] Vaughan, *op. cit.,* II, 32, "Du Contrat social" (version déf.).
[36] *Ibid.*
[37] *Ibid.,* I, 383, "Extrait du Projet de paix perp."

is, as it was stated before, the downfall of monarchies; they will have to give way to the democratic form of government based on the principle of the sovereignty of the people. The subjection of every state to common law would bring about the triumph of right over might, of the general will of nations over the arbitrary will of particular rulers.

The nearest approach to the outlook of Rousseau is found in the works of MABLY (1709-1785); it is sufficient to read the following passages:

As soon as I see landed property established, I see unequal fortunes and from these unequal fortunes must necessarily result different and opposed interests, all the vices of the rich, all the vices of the poor, the brutalization of the intelligence, the corruption of civil manners.[38]

It is property that divides us into two classes, the rich and the poor; the first will always prefer their fortune to that of the state, while the second will never love a government or laws that leave them in misery.[39]

The civic functions of a citizen should never be set apart from his military functions; let every citizen be a soldier.[40]

Thinking of a social order under which there would be no landed property, neither rich nor poor, no privileged classes in a position to enslave the others, he has the vision of a state where every citizen would be entitled to make laws (since only infants and insane persons, he adds, are doomed to be guided by the reason of others), where every citizen would be conscious of his right to resist by violence any excess of power. A nation should be as jealous of her independence as is an individual; the greatest circumspection should characterize her intercourse with other nations. States having common boundaries are natural enemies; they are always in-

[38] G. B. de Mably, *Oeuvres*, éd. 1796, XI, 10, "Doutes proposés aux philosophes économistes sur l'ordre naturel et essentiel des sociétés politiques."

[39] *Ibid.*, IX, 75, "De la Législation."

[40] *Ibid.*, X, 152-153, "Entretiens de Phocion."

clined to increase their respective territories at the expense
of their neighbors. Geographical position is usually the key
for the solution of the problem of friendship or animosity
between two states. An alliance must have for its foundation natural conditions and the services one can render to
the other; this condition failing, the alliance will be sterile
and ephemeral. The ally who does not need you will become
rude and hard to please. The more exacting he becomes, the
more thoughtful and cautious should be your course of action; there is no place for optimistic confidence in the thorny
field of foreign relations; it should be continuously kept in
mind that "to trust an enemy is to encourage him to set a
snare for us." [41] In the world as it is, virtue not backed by
force does not inspire respect and cannot even be called virtue
since it tempts the stronger to take advantage of his strength.
These considerations incline Mably to think of "prudence"
as one of the three cardinal virtues: justice, prudence, courage,[42] and to assert that "the prosperity of a state is a reward
for its virtues, and adversity, a chastisement for its vices."[43]

Seeing in war the greatest of all calamities that can affect
a people, Mably feels inclined to meditate on the possibility
of its prevention. The stumbling block against which the
efforts of the peacemakers break is the individualism of the
states. The whole trend of Mably's thought is strongly opposed to it. He would like to see the ideas and feelings
which one usually connects with the word "patriotism" be
consistent with the ideal of justice and brought down to a
level acceptable to reason. He does not feel that "patriotism"
could be put on the same level with justice, prudence, and
courage. These three virtues, in harmony with each other,
never fail to bring forth good. The other virtues are dependent on each other; the higher is to direct its subordinate.
In regard to patriotism, the higher virtue to which it must be
subordinated is the love of mankind.[44] Mably puts virtue
above happiness or rather he affirms their identity; therefore,

[41] *Ibid.*, V, 45, 78-80, 84, "Des Principes des négotiations."
[42] *Ibid.*, X, 90, "Entretiens de Phocion."
[43] *Ibid.*, X, 52.
[44] *Ibid.*, X, 129-130.

any attempt to reach happiness through greed and injustice is considered by him as a wrong policy for an individual as well as for a political body.   Insisting on the full harmony of personal and common interests, of the interests of a state and those of other states, he goes so far as to make Plato's disciple Phocion speak as follows:

Let us do away with frontiers, with borders which separate Attica from Greece, and Greece from barbarian countries; this thought broadens my reason, exalts my mind; my whole being feels enriched and uplifted.   If it is pleasant to see my fellow-citizens take care of my security, will it not be still more pleasant to think that the whole world is working towards my happiness? [45]

He tries to wake in other people the faith and hope that animate his soul and persuades them not to allow themselves to be discouraged in their struggle toward a better future: "Amidst a stormy sea full of rocks, let us hope against hope and never cowardly forsake our ship." [46]

In regard to war, statements similar to those with which we met above are disseminated in the writings of CONDILLAC (1715-1780); his works are, however, pre-eminently metaphysical in character.   In his hatred of violence, moral as well as physical, he refuses to share the opinions of his brother, the Abbé de Mably, who asserted that a people is entitled to resort to acts of violence in order to get rid of a despotic government.   Every *coup d'état,* every revolution is, according to him, a step backward, an impediment in the possibly slow, but continuous trend toward a better order of things.[47]

Religious wars arouse his indignation.   Devotion to one's faith is not an excuse for injustice, cruelty, or crime.   He characterizes the Crusaders as men who "with religion constantly on their lips, had none in their hearts." [48]   He condemns Pope Innocent III who in the name of Christ "seemed

[45] *Ibid.,* X, 135-137.
[46] *Ibid.,* X, 27.
[47] E. B. de Condillac, *Oeuvres,* éd. 1798, X, 399.
[48] *Ibid.,* XV, 564.

to wish the extermination of all Christians." [49] With regard to religious wars he seems to doubt, as much as Helvétius, the sincerity of the motives alleged by those who wage them. "Religious intolerance," says the latter, "is the most dangerous form of intolerance. What is it that they punish in a heretic or an ungodly man? His insolence in daring to think for himself, to trust his own reason more than that of the clergy, and to consider himself their equal. Those who presume to act as God's avengers, avenge in fact nothing but their own humiliated pride." [50] Between nation and nation resort to force is permissible only in case of aggression, self-defense being the only form of legitimate war.

In his *Cours d'études pour l'instruction du Prince de Parme,* which pretends to make a survey of all the wars known to history, he draws the attention of his pupil to the fact that, with few exceptions, all wars had for their motives erroneous ideas of glory, court intrigues, jealousy between two nations, and sometimes nothing but a kind of restlessness seizing a people after a long period of peace.[51] All those wars were illegitimate notwithstanding the praise lavished on the victors, the worship of conquerors being, at the bottom, the survival of the awe inspired in our ancestors by pirates and brigands. Conquest is plunder unless it is a compensation for the wrongs and damages suffered. A nation, like a man, has a right to the fruit of her work. It is the cultivation of land, it is labor, in general, which establishes the right of a nation to the territory she occupies. A conqueror has no more right to the land belonging to a people than he has to the inhabitants or the community they form. All sovereign states are *de jure* equal and independent. Condillac protests against the "right of the mighty," pointing to the contradiction in terms comprised in this statement: "If force compels one to obey from prudence, it can never make obedience a duty. It would, on the contrary, destroy every obligation in transferring the power to the weaker at the moment when he becomes strong enough to be

[49] *Ibid.,* XVII, 43.
[50] C. A. Helvétius, "De l'Homme," *Collection des plus belles pages,* 1909, p. 213.
[51] Condillac, *Oeuvres,* 1798, X, 399.

able to disobey with impunity." [52]   If those obvious principles have not won recognition, it only proves that passions rule the world and form its soul.

One of the great miseries brought about by war is the interruption of regular commercial relations.   In time of peace free exchange of commodities smooths the disproportion existing in the distribution of wealth.   Commerce cannot establish economic equality, since the services rendered to the community by different persons are not of the same value; the important objective reached is, however, that every one's immediate needs are satisfied.   With the breaking out of war, land is laid waste, wealth is destroyed, profiteers build up their fortunes with the spoils of war, and the very existence of a state is exposed to peril.

The assertion that, after having passed through the usual phases of childhood, youth, and maturity, a state is bound to die, like an individual, is wrong, in Condillac's opinion.   A state perishes through its own fault, not like an organism the death of which is due to the wearing out of separate parts. In a political body new generations come in place of the old ones, and this permanent inflow of new energy is a source of life whose end is not predetermined by natural causes. [53]

Whereas Condillac's thoughts on war and peace are scattered through a great number of volumes of his writings, the ideas of LA HARPE (1739-1803) are found concentrated in one short work.   This work, *Des Malheurs de la guerre et des Avantages de la paix*, [54] won for him in 1766 the honor of the prize offered by an unknown donor for the best article on war and peace.   According to the will of the donor, the French Academy assumed the rôle of adjudicator.

In the above-mentioned essay La Harpe challenges those who assert that moral diseases—among which it may not be amiss to place the urge to fight—are incurable, that progress may be achieved only in man's struggle against the sickness of

[52] *Ibid.*, X, 513.
[53] *Ibid.*, XXI, 87.
[54] J. F. de La Harpe, *Oeuvres*, 1778, IV, 6.

the body. A typical author of the eighteenth century, he shared the belief in the possibility of limitless progress in all aspects of human life:

It is the task of philosophy to prepare and hasten the coming of the change. . . . Its innermost meditations have for their objective the happiness of man. It ceaselessly sows precious seeds which, though often trampled upon, do not perish, but ripen in darkness for future generations to harvest.[55]

The best remedy against war is the moral improvement of man, the widening of his understanding. This will prevent him from becoming a victim of those in whose hands power rests and will prevent nations from becoming mere playthings in the hands of their masters. Peoples will realize that "the shepherd is for the flock, not the flock for the shepherd," [56] that the sole *raison d'être* of government is that of securing the welfare of the majority of the population. To indulge in war is the greatest sin of any government: war destroys the well-being of the masses, takes the means of livelihood from the husbandman who feeds the nation, ruins the merchant, the artist, and the scientist, to whom we owe all that art and science contribute to the comfort and happiness of life. The argument that military training develops in man a readiness to obey and a sense of discipline is, according to him, of no force. To bring forth an argument like this is to flatter those who are in command and to insult those who suffer. Some advocates of war considered it a good way to free a country from dangerous, vicious elements and from those who threaten to become a public charge. Instead of thinking how to get rid of them, the state should find a way to make of them worthy men and useful citizens. The opinions of La Harpe in matters of war and peace become especially clear from what he writes under the impression of Voltaire's *Histoire de Charles XII*:

Europe still speaks of this famous Swede who was suited to astonish his contemporaries rather than to arouse the admiration of posterity; who knew neither the compass of virtue nor that of success; who made more than one man king and knew not

[55] *Ibid.*, IV, 8.
[56] *Ibid.*, IV, 18.

how to be a king himself; who had delusions in regard to glory which he worshiped as well as in regard to the strength of the enemy he scorned; who, while invading so many countries, did greater harm to his own than to any one of them; whose heroism was but excess and whose run of good luck—a mere delusion; who, after a vain effort to dominate nature and events, went at last to hide his eclipsed fame, his precarious life, and his captive and insulted kingship among a barbarian people and finally met the death of a simple soldier to enjoy thereafter nothing more than the fame of a mere adventurer.[57]

Refusing to see any greatness in Charles XII, La Harpe looks on Louis XIV as a king deserving to be called Louis the Great (on this point he disagrees completely with the Abbé de Saint-Pierre). He admits that Louis XIV craved glory at least as much as the King of Sweden, but his personal glory was closely bound with that of France whose greatness was so much enhanced during his reign. Furthermore, the dignity he showed under misfortune and the final acknowledgment of his mistakes atoned for the arrogance of his conquests.[58]

The craving for military glory, the spirit of conquest were as much hated by La Harpe as by the Abbé de Saint-Pierre. From La Harpe's point of view, every conquest strengthens absolutism in government and deprives the subjects of certain rights. Instead of contributing to their happiness, the acquisition of new territories by way of conquest impairs their lives. To those who pretend to be tired of the subject, La Harpe answers: "We do not feel bound to stop our complaints until everything is done to put a limit to our suffering and to hasten the advent of the day when moral law will count for something in the political administration of states." [59]

A short time after La Harpe had become the recipient of the prize offered by an anonymous donor for the best work on

[57] La Harpe, "Eloge de Voltaire." See Voltaire, *Oeuvres,* éd. Moland, I, 163.
[58] *Ibid.*
[59] La Harpe, *Oeuvres,* 1778, t. IV, "Des Malheurs de la guerre et des Avantages de la paix."

the subject of peace, it became widely known that the French Academy, acting as adjudicator, had hesitated between two articles: one had for motto "Humanum paucis vivit genus" which identified La Harpe's work, the other—"Pax omni anteferenda bono, quae scilicet omnem exuperat sensum, et grato sale condit amara" which identified Gaillard's article. One can easily understand the joy of the members of the jury when another prize was offered, again anonymously, and they could award it to Gaillard (January, 1767).

In the opening lines of his article GAILLARD (1726-1806) pays tribute to the Abbé de Saint-Pierre; he admires the courage the Abbé had shown in raising his voice against "those despoilers of the world who boast everywhere of their infamous, arrogant triumphs.[60] The subject on which he writes is not new and he knows it. "Love one another, for you are brothers" is an old maxim; unfortunately, it is old only as principle; it is very new, if we consider that this principle has not yet become a living force, especially in the sphere of international relations. The history of mankind is to a great extent the history of wars; as centuries go by, cruelty does not decrease:

Oh! under how many horrible and new forms destruction shows itself again! Foreign wars waged near at hand or far away, wars on land, on sea, beyond the mountains, across the ocean; wars of succession, of commerce, of honor, of vanity, of intrigues, civil wars. . . . I see nothing but a chaos of crimes and a sea of blood![61]

The means of destruction are being studied and perfected, even looked upon as works of art. Potentates declare war, flatterers glorify it. Christianity has added to wars which were already devastating the world the so-called "sacred" wars. It brought about the night of Saint-Bartholomew.

[60] G. H. Gaillard, *Mélanges académiques, poétiques, littéraires, philosophiques, critiques et historiques*, 1806, I, 51, "Des Malheurs de la guerre et des Avantages de la paix."
[61] *Ibid.*, I, 55.

War can never be "sacred" nor can it ever be called "just" because, logically, there cannot be a war that is "just" in respect to both fighting parties. War does not choose its victims; it defeats the arguments of those of its defenders who are prone to see in it a means of freeing the country of men whose life is a danger or a burden to society. Great minds and talents, men whose life and work would benefit humanity run the same risk of perishing as the others. Besides, do only exceptionally gifted individuals deserve to be spared? Is it possible to feel reconciled to those numberless deaths especially for one on whom the teachings of history have not been lost, who realizes that a state that indulges in the policy of conquest invariably ends in being conquered? All known attempts at establishing a universal monarchy have failed: the well-being of the whole country ceases to be of interest to its separate parts, and a government cannot adequately "carry blood and life to the extremities of so vast a body."

Like many other thinkers, Gaillard accuses the sovereigns of being the instigators of war; however, the names of Elizabeth of England and Henry IV of France prevent him from despairing in the cause of peace. He expects that the eighteenth century will be a turning point in the history of nations. It is the time when people begin to talk more seriously than ever before of international law, begin to realize that its aim is developing a maximum of friendly feelings and actions between nations in time of peace and allowing a minimum of harm in time of war. One ought, nevertheless, to keep in mind that the ultimate end of international law is the abolition of war, because war and international law are conceptions that mutually exclude each other.

Stressing the need for the establishment of an international tribunal, Gaillard asserts his belief that sovereigns, as a rule, would accept its verdicts. They are accustomed to submit to "force," so why should they not be ready to submit to a decree inspired by reason and equity?

At the end of his article Gaillard expresses the wish that those on whom depend the destinies of millions of people take for the motto of their lives and activities not the word "glory," but the word "beneficence" (bienfaisance) coined by the Abbé de Saint-Pierre.

How small was the part the idea of "beneficence" had played in the relations between the natives and the European conquerors of America is emphasized in the famous work of RAYNAL (1713-1796).[62]

World history, says Raynal, offers the amazing picture of a large number of political bodies whose steadiest, though unreasonable, tendency is to expand. Most rulers are unable to realize that a vast territory and a large population are often great evils: "Let there be few men, but let them be happy; let the empire be small, but well governed," [63] are watchwords which, if adopted by sovereigns, would spare the world streams of blood.

What idea [Raynal asks] is it proper to entertain of settlements established at so much expense and with so much labor by the governments of Europe in the New World? Does our real happiness require the enjoyment of the things which we go in search of at such a distance . . . ? Is man born eternally to wander between the sky and the waters . . . ? Can the articles of commerce we derive from thence be an adequate compensation for the loss of citizens . . . ? How will their obedience to the laws of the mother-country be enforced? By what firm tie shall we secure a possession from which we are separated by an immense interval . . . ? Can colonies interest themselves . . . in the misfortunes or prosperity of the mother-country? Or can the mother-country be very sincerely rejoiced or afflicted by the fate of the colonies . . . ? This is the decree pronounced by fate upon your colonies: you must either renounce them or they will renounce you.[64]

Raynal refuses to admire those men who, instead of in-

[62] G. Raynal, *Histoire philosophique et politique des Isles françaises dans les Indes Occidentales,* éd. 1784.
[63] *Ibid.,* I, 1-2.
[64] Raynal, *A Philosophical and Political History of the Settlements and Trade of the Europeans in the East and West Indies,* transl. from French. Dublin, 1784, IV, 312-314.

creasing the prosperity of the land on which they are placed, spend their lives traveling, thus losing every idea of patriotism.

His sympathy goes above all to the farmers on whose work the very existence of a state rests and who during the unjustifiable wars made by the government "will be led like their cattle or transported like their corn . . . will be collected and dispersed at the nod of a tyrant to be slaughtered in the carnage of war or to perish to no purpose in naval engagements or in different colonies." [65]

Refusing to take into consideration that property, by its very nature, is based either on work or on long uncontested possession, European states, not satisfied with tearing away territories from one another on their own continent, vie with each other in seizing lands of other continents and have, in particular, succeeded in setting the New World afire.

Raynal's attacks—not sparing France—were mainly directed against the Spanish conquerors who, after they had stripped the Indians of every piece of land, reduced them to slavery and forced those unfortunate beings, accustomed to freedom and life in the open, to work in mines.   To safeguard themselves against the victims of their plunder, they extirpated tribes wholesale.   Their contempt for the native and their cruelty were equaled only by their greed for gold and their fanaticism.   The teaching of Christ does not give to its followers any rights over vanquished enemies through the mere assumption that the latter are not Christians.   The Spanish conquerors transgressed every commandment of their religion in their treatment of the native; there were, however, exceptions and Raynal points to the Jesuits of Paraguay.

The eleventh book of his work is devoted to the issue of slavery.   In the chapter *Origin and Progress of Slavery* we find his pathetic address on behalf of the Negroes:

Sovereigns of the earth . . . refuse the sanction of your authority to the infamous and criminal traffic of men turned into so many herds of cattle, and this trade will cease.   For once

[65] *Ibid.*, VI, 450.

unite, for the happiness of the world, those powers and designs which have been so often exerted for its ruin. . . . Your armies will soon be inspired with the sacred enthusiasm of humanity. But . . . if interest alone can exert its influence over you, listen to me once more, ye nations of Europe! Your slaves stand in no need either of your generosity or your counsel in order to break the sacrilegious yoke of their oppression . . . there are so many indications of the impending storm; the Negroes only want a chief sufficiently courageous to lead them on to vengeance and slaughter. . . . The plains of America will suck up . . . the blood which they have so long expected, and the bones of so many wretches heaped upon one another during the course of so many centuries will bound for joy! [66]

The opinions of Raynal in regard to wars between Catholics and Protestants on the continent of Europe are quite consistent with his other statements. His trend of thought is typical of that of the eighteenth century. Tolerance, he says, is the only acceptable attitude in matters of religion. The interdiction and persecution of every denomination but that of the sovereign is "a tyranny over man's thought and conscience; it is a cruel kind of piety which for the sake of religious ceremonial destroys multitudes of worshippers and exacts oaths contrary to one's conscience." [67]

Raynal's thoughts center on this issue—how to eliminate violence from the sphere of national and international life. This partly explains why he is so strongly opposed to acquiring colonies. Life in the midst of peoples whom the Europeans have to fear because of their number, whom they despise as men belonging to a different race, creed, and civilization exerts a demoralizing effect on the conquerors. Never being at peace amidst those whom they have every reason to think hostile to their rule, they cannot be at peace with themselves.

This dependence of individual happiness on the happiness of others is stressed in the works of LOUIS-SÉBASTIEN MER-

[66] *Ibid.,* IV, 147.
[67] *Ibid.,* VI, 475.

CIER (1740-1814). "A virtuous man [he says] does not care
for happiness unless the whole world can enjoy it with him." [68]
Diderot expresses a thought corresponding to this feeling when
he writes: "I want to be happy, and those I live among want
to be happy too. Let us therefore look for means of securing
our happiness, not forgetting to secure theirs at the same
time. At least, let us never stand in the way of their well-
being." [69] "What are in your opinion [he says in another
work] the duties of man? To make himself happy, where-
from derives the necessity of contributing to other people's
happiness; in other words, to be virtuous." [70] Diderot holds
to the utilitarian point of view in a greater degree than Mercier, but both believe in the possibility of making this world
a better dwelling place for man than it has been; both hope
for more social justice, for more friendly relations among
individuals, citizens, and nations.

Mercier, like Rousseau, with whom he was on friendly
terms, is convinced that man is thoroughly good by nature;
the elimination of evils which mar human life and above all
of war is therefore simply a question of time; the duty of
every one is to hasten it. This explains why Mercier devotes
so many chapters of his work to war.

In one of his "philosophical dreams" which has for title
War the author sees himself as a skeleton lying on a boundless plain among numberless skeletons of those who killed
their fellowmen. The blood shed by murderers since the
world began is falling on them in a ceaseless shower of rain;
the sky is black with clouds. Century passes after century;
time is like a frightful torrent tearing its way along with a
deafening roar. All of a sudden bright sun pierces the clouds,
and Justice appears in rays of light. With terror the guilty
recollect every moment of their past lives, every bloody deed
for which they have now to account. In the miserable desti-
tute beings, pale and shaking with fear, one can hardly recognize those proud, mighty conquerors whose glory was once
ringing all over the world. Thousands of men for whom

68 L.-S. Mercier, Songes et Visions, 1789, p. 8.
69 Diderot, Encyclopédie, éd. 1780-82, "Programme."
70 Diderot, Oeuvres, éd. 1875-79, II, 85, "Aux Grands Principes."

their word had been equivalent to law charge them now with the slaughter they had committed while executing their orders. And the voice of Justice is heard: "You sovereigns, conquerors, field-marshals, soldiers, you have taught men to commit the unjustifiable sin of murder; you have allowed war to become an occurrence of everyday life; your sin is unredeemable; you shall suffer until the time comes when the enlightened nations will have learned how to execrate war and those who kindle it." [71] Hardly was the sentence pronounced, when another skeleton knelt before Justice. "You are right in saying that you have never killed any one," she said to him, "yet you deserve the same punishment as the others because you have dared to immortalize in your works the names of those murderers." Then Justice calls forth all those who had fought against slavery, despotism, and war. Beside Henry IV of France, the author sees the Abbé de Saint-Pierre. He yearns to meet him but, at this moment, a discharge of guns announcing a new victory wakens him from his beautiful dream.[72]

In *Mon Bonnet de nuit* [73] we find chapters entitled: *Oiseaux de proie, Batailles, Officiers, Poudre à canon,* in which he discusses some particular aspects of war, and he does likewise in his *L'An deux mille quatre cent quarante,* the year when he pretends to wake to a new life after six hundred and seventy-two years of sleep. He finds the world much changed and yet, if we judge from the chapter in which the author describes a certain room in the King's palace, called "The Hell," there still seem to be plenty of men of belligerent spirit. What makes the difference, however, is the common attitude toward this particular spirit regarded now as something to be suppressed. When a young prince shows an undue enthusiasm for arms and combats, he is taken to "The Hell." The artist immediately puts the springs in motion and treats his eyes and ears to all the horrors of a battle: the prince sees dying men and hears their groans. Those who have visited this room of terror are cured of their belligerent

[71] Mercier, *Nachtmütze*, "Der Krieg," Berlin, 1784, pp. 72-96.
[72] *Ibid.*, pp. 72-96.
[73] *Mon Bonnet de nuit*, éd. 1784.

spirit forever. In the year 2440, though there are sporadic cases of the disease that had afflicted the human race for thousands of years, this folly can no longer take the form of an epidemic. Things have changed and are more conformable to the exigencies of reason than before. Armaments have been considerably reduced in every country.

In the chapter entitled *Armées* Mercier draws the picture of what preparedness for war will be like in the twenty-fifth century: his imaginary ideal state has but a small army (40,000 soldiers), the number of men being less important than the training of each individual. The army will be composed of the *élite* of the nation for whom courage and the sense of honor and duty are the essential qualities in man. They fight with side-arms but, since the aim of war is the establishment of peace in the shortest delay of time, any means, even the most terrible ones, are legitimate.[74] On the whole, Mercier's ideas of what an army and the technical preparedness for war may be like in the future are in evident contradiction with the direction the military sciences and the military art have taken in our time.

Judged by his opinions stated above, Mercier was not at all optimistic as to the possibility of a prompt establishment of peace among nations. Even a period of time as long as six hundred and seventy-two years is not sufficient to bring about all necessary changes. He is at variance with Rousseau when he declares that, since the aim of war is to force the enemy to lay down arms and sign any clauses of the peace treaty set before him by the successful adversary, all means which answer the purpose are legitimate. He is thus far from the ideas of Rousseau that have led to the humanization of war.

There is, however, another point on which their opinions are in accord: both accuse the rulers of being the instigators of international conflicts and express the conviction that the adoption of the republican form of government can alone lead to a better understanding among peoples.

---

[74] *L'An deux mille quatre cent quarante,* éd. 1791, pp. 106-108, "Armées."

The writer with whom Mercier seems to have much affinity is Fénelon; it is sufficient to compare, for example, the passage in which Fénelon speaks of the invention of gunpowder [75] with the following lines of Mercier:

How imperceptible to the human foresight is the coherency of events! A monk, in search of medicaments, happens to discover this fatal powder. . . . What an endless chain of public and private calamities has its beginning in this fortuitous cause! When man fought with side-arms, daring, courage, strength, love of freedom could perform miracles; but what can be done against a cannon pointed by a geometrician! [76]

Mercier was a man whose mind was incessantly occupied with thoughts, or more often with dreams, about a better future for mankind:

Let us always keep in mind [he says] that it is possible to reach beyond the things we can see; this will give our thoughts more daring and allow us to rise to higher regions of achievable things.[77]

If we try to sum up the feelings of this group of moralists in regard to war, we find them ready to say with Fontenelle:

Why, after we have indulged in all those absurdities, should we not partake of reason and wisdom? Is it not a real pleasure to raise ourselves morally in our own eyes, to cherish order and harmony and, by improving our mind, by taking care of this divine attribute, to clothe ourselves in human dignity? Let us then partake of that luxury before our great-grandchildren do so, and let us not give them the sorrow of weeping at our misfortunes or the satisfaction of laughing at our foolishness.[78]

[75] Fénelon, *Oeuvres,* éd. 1835, II, 572, "Confucius et Socrate."
[76] Mercier, *Mon Bonnet de nuit,* éd. 1784?, II, 41-42, "Poudre à canon."
[77] *L'An 2440,* éd. 1791, I, 150.
[78] *Ibid.,* III, 119.

CHAPTER VIII

PHYSIOCRATS AND FINANCIERS

THE rôle of economists such as Boisguillebert, Boulainvilliers, Vauban, in the seventeenth century, Saintard, Turgot, Necker, Vergennes, in the eighteenth century, should not be overlooked or minimized by those who are investigating the development of the peace idea in France. The economic doctrine of the time was that of free trade. Such eminent economists as the physiocrats Quesnay and Gournay saw the only remedy against a life of privation, which is the lot of the greatest part of mankind, in the abolition of trade barriers between states. The system of *laisser faire, laisser passer* would allow the commodities produced in abundance in one country to be directed into lands which are in need of them. The economic causes of war would thus be eliminated, the standard of living raised everywhere. The economists stressed the idea that a policy of laying waste a neighbor's land in order to make one's own country prosperous is a wrong policy. The wealth of your neighbor furthers your own prosperity, they claimed. Far from aspiring to any expansion of her territory, France should definitely renounce any new territorial acquisition, Vergennes asserted.

One of the most earnest and sincere champions of free trade as a means of abolition of war was SAINTARD. (No data are obtainable concerning his birth and death.) His work [1]

---

[1] *Roman politique sur l'état présent des affaires de l'Amérique*, ou *Lettres de M——— à M——— sur les moyens d'établir une Paix solide et durable dans les Colonies et la Liberté générale du Commerce extérieur.* . . . , 1756.

was published at the time when England was directing all her efforts towards taking from France her Canadian possessions. Observing the struggle for economic advantages which was taking place on the continent of America and studying the history of wars which had incessantly disturbed the life of nations, Saintard came to the conclusion that the primary cause of any war is economic in character:

How can peace prevail among nations when there is abundance only for a, few of them . . . when the riches of the earth, the commodities, flow into one or two centers of Europe, leaving outlying parts in want of them?[2]

People dream and speak of peace but, in trying to make out of the ideal a reality, they set off on a wrong road. The direct path that leads towards peace is the recognition of the principle of free trade on land and sea for all countries large and small, mother-countries and colonies. This recognition should not be considered only as a temporary measure.[3] One should also not forget that freedom of commerce means freedom of competition:

Europe should allow nations to regulate their wealth according to the combined needs and industries of each country. This could be done through constant open competition brought about by freedom of trade and those means which perpetuate it.[4]

This system of general immunity of commerce and freedom of the seas would soon lead all peoples to the realization of the famous project for universal peace with which Henry IV is credited.[5]

Let us leave to her [nature] the care of concentrating men, industries, and ships in places where rich soil will insure a good livelihood and where good harvests may be reaped.[6]

Speaking of the part the freedom of commerce might play in the establishment of peaceful relations among nations, Saintard stresses, however, one point: the spirit of commerce

[2] *Ibid.*, p. 332.
[3] *Ibid.*, p. 178.
[4] *Ibid.*, p. 161.
[5] *Ibid.*, Préface, p. XXXI.
[6] *Ibid.*, p. 332.

should be a spirit of conservation, not that of acquisition which always generates a kind of fermentation incompatible with peace. Let the spirit of acquisition prevail in the world, and there will be no means which could·prevent war :

Like those poisonous germs which, floating in the air, cause epidemics, false political systems gradually infect all nations. Clouds gather ; desolation and death soon follow. War breaks up old alliances, new ones put an end to it only to be broken up in their turn. Treaties are not the product of reason free from costly errors nor are they the measure of justice since war can break them up; they are but the proof of weariness.[7]

By the last lines Saintard does not deny altogether the importance of a peace treaty; it is no more than a truce, no doubt, but a truce is preferable to war; only one should not expect that it can satisfy men or nations; they long for rest, security, for things lasting; even when they fight, they fight for safety and peace. But are those blessings attainable? Saintard thinks that they are and bases his belief on data which the observation of men and nations furnish him. He finds his time, the eighteenth century, very different from all preceding centuries. Owing to the better means of communication, the development of commerce, the spread of knowledge, many common interests are noticeable among the European nations and a kind of public spirit is born. Interest in science, art, social and political issues, a longing for the abundance and comfort of life have, as a rule, taken the place of the dreams of conquests, military glory, and domination. They cannot fail, the author thinks, to bring about in Europe an era of mutual understanding and peace. Attainments in knowledge rapidly become the property of all peoples; economic interests are common and can be easily satisfied if the principle of free trade is generally accepted. People who refuse to see that the European nations are becoming members of one family are just those who put spokes in the wheel of progress which is leading to the realization of the peace ideal. They refuse to hope for a future of international peace, forgetting that hope is a great stimulant and that we

[7] *Ibid.*, pp. 132-133.

often owe to hope the possession of things we have longed for. The establishment of peace between nations will be the noblest of all monuments which attest the greatness of man.[8] Saintard deems it possible that in the future even the names of separate European nations will be no more than recollections of prejudices which, fortunately, have been overcome. "In ceasing to be a citizen, one would become a man."[9] In this respect he seems to anticipate Anacharsis Cloots, "l'orateur du genre humain," one of the most sincere and enthusiastic leaders of the Jacobin Club in the first years of the French Revolution.

It is only too natural that the issues of war and peace should have occupied the minds of Turgot and Necker, the two famous Secretaries of the Treasury under Louis XVI; they had much to say on the subject since, as a result of so many wars, they were brought face to face with an empty Treasury and an enormous national debt.

Soon after his appointment, TURGOT (1727-1781) showed himself a man of courage in opposing the prevailing opinion that France should recover the possession of Canada ceded by Louis XV to England by the Treaty of Paris (1763). He maintained that Canada would be a heavy burden upon France and would demand enormous sacrifices only to become in the future an independent state. Pointing to the Spanish and the English colonies in America, he foretold their defection from their mother-countries. He considered the tendency of a state toward expansion as most unwise; preservation was in his eyes a continuous conquest.[10] A wise government should act as an experienced gardener who cuts off a certain number of branches in order to give strength to a tree; the leaders of a nation should realize that there are circumstances under which it is a real advantage for a state to lose a part

---

[8] *Ibid.*, pp. 349-352.
[9] *Ibid.*, pp. 3-4.
[10] A.-R.-J. Turgot, *Oeuvres*, éd. Daire, 1844, II, 616, "Géographie politique."

of its territory.[11] While holding it, a state should do everything to further its prosperity and should treat its population
as free men.   In accordance with this opinion Turgot suggested that the French Government declare the ports of the
île Bourbon and the Isle-de-France free ports.   Turgot is for
free trade and free industry; he insists on the abolition of
the "corvée" and the "jurandes" (an organization of labor
that prevented the free choice of employees by employers).
He thought that all those restrictions of freedom are the nega-
tion of natural law and are responsible, in no lesser degree
than privileges granted to men and nations, for the greatest
part of frictions and conflicts.   His conviction was that the
products of the soil and industry, no matter where they come
from, are the common goods of all men.

The dissensions between Catholics and Protestants did not
leave him indifferent.   In his *Mémoire au Roi sur la Tolérance*
(1775) Turgot begged the King not to pronounce at the
Coronation ceremony the customary formula by which the
king of France promised the extermination of heretics, a plea
which aroused against him the clergy of the royal entourage.

In judging men [Turgot wrote] God will not ask them if they
have believed and practiced the religion of their sovereign. How
could He demand this if all sovereigns are not of the true religion?   Cast your eye over the map of the world, Sire, and see
how few countries there are whose sovereigns are Catholics.
How can it be that the greater number of sovereigns in the universe being in error, they should all have received from God the
right to judge of the true religion?   If they have not this right,
if they have neither the infallibility nor the divine mission which
alone could confer it, how can they dare to take it on themselves
to decide on the fate of their subjects, on their happiness or their
misery for all eternity . . . ?   To follow his own conscience is the
right and the duty of every man, and no man has the right to
make his own a rule for another.   The opinion of the prince is
absolutely foreign to the truth of a religion and, consequently,
to the obligation to adopt it . . . his incompetence is absolute in
matters of this order . . . the conscience of each individual has
and can have no other judge but God alone.[12]

11 *Ibid.,* p. 624.
12 Quoted from W. B. Hodgson, *Turgot,* 1870.

One does not find in Turgot's writings any plan for the establishment of peace, but Condorcet, in his *Vie de Turgot,* asserts that the latter had very definite ideas with regard to the possibility of the abolition of war. The first step toward this goal should be the federation of small republics in which people speak the same language and have the same customs. Those small groups would tend to form larger associations; Europe would become finally one great Union. The body representing the whole Confederation would alone have the right to declare war (only in case of invasion) and to make peace. The representatives of the confederated groups would be responsible to their constituents for their decision. According to Condorcet, Turgot did not think it possible to have armed force placed at the disposal of the Supreme Council nor to allow any state to have its own army. It would be sufficient to have forts and arsenals built in every state following the plan approved by the Supreme Council. Local militia in command of the officers appointed by the state would form the garrisons of those fortified places. Turgot did not see any need for a regular army; the garrisons of the forts would be professionally trained soldiers. In time of war the whole power would rest with the Supreme Council.

Turgot must have believed in the future advent of an era of peace. His conception of the predominant rôle of the human will in social evolution leads to this assumption. He notices that as long as man does not try artificially to create varieties of plants, the dying specimens are replaced by similar ones; the same phenomenon is characteristic of the animal kingdom; in respect to man this is true only partly. Men consciously improve themselves and try hard to leave after them a better generation. With plants and animals physical phenomena play the determinant rôle; with man the mental factors come into the foreground: it is mainly human knowledge and human will that create historical events. At the dawn of the history of the human race their influence was hardly noticeable: mankind has been rent asunder and broken up into divergent groups in conformity with the configuration of the earth's surface. Vast bodies of water and mountain chains, standing in the way of intercourse between groups of people, gave birth to varied languages. Each group unable to understand the others became unlike them. The numerous governments, in their turn, differently directed the lives of these groups and thus strengthened dissimilarity. The advance of civilization rapidly wipes out the obstacles on the way leading towards unification; everything tends to become leveled, and the relations between peoples become more stable and calm.[13]

This statement of Turgot follows the general trend of thought of the eighteenth century summed up so well in the following words of Mirabeau pronounced from the rostrum of the Constituent Assembly on May 20, 1790: "The time will come, no doubt, when Europe will be just one big family." [14]

To this prophecy of Mirabeau NECKER (1732-1804), who succeeded Turgot as Secretary of the Treasury, might have readily agreed. The nations of the world, he thought, will make up one family when the light of reason becomes the active principle directing human life.

I repeatedly saw [Necker says] how the best institutions supported by no one but the man who had established them vanished with him. I saw how the meanest vanity was triumphing over ideals of order and improvement. The light of reason and knowledge can alone prevent this perpetual wavering and impart steadiness to public opinion.[15]

Necker approves as little as his predecessor of the tendency of a state toward expansion. According to him, expansion weakens patriotism which "becomes no more than a word in the dictionary." He sees in the ocean surrounding the British Isles the main guardian of English patriotism. The greater the part a citizen takes in the spiritual and political life of his state, the greater his love for his country. The growth of territory weakens the ties between citizen and state; he still

13 Turgot, *On the Progress of the Human Mind,* 1929.
14 *Moniteur,* No. du 21 mai 1790.
15 J. Necker, *De l'Administration des finances de la France,* 1784, vol. III, ch. 36.

has a country, but it cannot be said any more that he has a mother-country.[16] How often we hear, Necker says, the assertion that men owe themselves to their fatherland, that in giving their lives for their country they merely pay the debt of citizenship. What one is prone to forget is that it is the government which decides whether peaceful relations with other countries should be abandoned. The enthusiasm with which people usually greet the declaration of war does not necessarily prove the wisdom of the leaders' decision; in most cases it testifies solely to ignorance of the real issues. Nothing will be left of this enthusiasm either in the soldiers themselves or those who see them in a later stage of events when they are lying on battlefields or in make-shift shelters, where the wounded are usually waiting for transportation to the rear; when they defend the dugouts which the explosion of a mine can reduce to an accumulation of mud and stones; when they try to save a burning ship. There are, no doubt, people to whom war brings honor and glory, but they are few. Necker cannot think without a shudder of having once seen on a list containing the estimate of the funds needed for sending troops to the colonies a statement concerning the tremendous percentage of mortality among the soldiers:

40,000 men to be put on shipboard for the colonies....40,000
To deduct one third for the mortality of the first year..13,333
                                                          ——————
                                          Balance 26,667

Human life and suffering do not seem to count for anything, Necker thought. These men are miserable victims of a foolish government which for the sake of conquest stops the achievement of important plans, dries out the sources of prosperity, and allows hatred, the thirst for destruction, and the love of domination and oppression to take the place of justice and humanity.[17]

When Necker contemplates the bitter antagonism between Christian Churches, two main arguments in favor of religious tolerance come to his mind: every attempt at forcing

[16] Necker, *Oeuvres*, éd. de Staël, 1820-21, vol. XV, "Le Patriotisme."
[17] *Ibid.*, vol. V, ch. XLII, "De la Guerre."

people to accept one form of worship in preference to another is a repudiation of the dogma of the spirituality of the soul. To presume that violence or the infliction of suffering can make one change his opinions is to admit the identity of thought and matter and to adhere to the doctrine of materialism. In his contemplation of the infinity of time and space Necker finds another argument for tolerance. It seems hard to believe that a small group of people who occupy so infinitesimal a position in the boundless universe and whose life is no more than a moment among the countless moments of eternity claim to know the only true way in which the Creator of that universe should be adored. Is it not more likely that truth is on the side of those who believe that love is the only path leading to God, and that those who have recourse to injustice and oppression cannot hope to draw near Him? [18]

There are evidences of religious outlook and religious feeling in the writings of Necker, but the main angle from which he considers the issues of war and peace is that of gain and loss. "To make war is to sow ten grains in order to gather one." His approach to the subject, being partly that of Fénelon who appealed to the intervention of morality in politics, was mainly that of Vauban:

You enjoy immense revenues, [Necker says to the King] but war will cost from 800 to 900 million francs. . . . You will crush your people under new taxes; you will hamper the flow of commerce and industries, those precious sources of wealth; in order to furnish you with soldiers and sailors, husbandmen will

[18] *Ibid.,* vol. XII, ch. XVI.
Seraient-ce donc les habitants de ce grain de sable qu'est notre terre, serait-ce un petit nombre d'entre eux qui auraient le droit de prétendre que seuls ils connaissent la manière dont on peut adorer le souverain Maître du monde? Leur demeure est un point dans l'infinité de l'espace; la vie dont ils jouissent est un des moments innombrables qui composent l'éternité; ils vont passer comme un éclair dans cette route des siècles où les générations des générations se sont perdues et où d'autres sont prêtes à disparaître. Comment donc oseraient-ils annoncer à tous les âges présents et à venir qu'on ne peut éviter les vengeances célestes si l'on s'écarte des usages et des pratiques de leur culte? Il est plus doux et plus raisonnable de penser que tous les peuples de la terre ont accès auprès de Son trône, qu'on s'élève à Lui par un sentiment d'amour et de reconnaissance et qu'il n'est jamais permis de s'approcher de Lui par aucun moyen d'injustice et d'oppression.

be torn from the land they cultivate, and hundreds of thousands of families will lose the hands that support them. If even you achieve success, what will you gain at the price of so much suffering?—A temporary ally, an uncertain gratitude, some island two thousand miles away, or some new subjects in the other hemisphere.[19]

All economists would agree with the above. One cannot increase wealth by destroying it. The establishment of peace is possible, the economists think, even in the immediate present. The only prerequisite is the necessity that certain economic doctrines take hold of the minds of men and be put into practice.

[19] *De l'Administration des finances de la France,* vol. III, ch. 36.

CHAPTER IX

LATE EIGHTEENTH-CENTURY POLITICAL PROJECTS

DURING the seven years which immediately preceded the outbreak of the Revolution there were published in France three schemes for an international organization of Europe. It would be only natural to think that those plans were composed under the impulse given to Europe by the young American Republic that had just come into existence. The former English colonies had found a form of interstate organization which, in spite of some defects, led them to mutual understanding. This opened the way to co-operation and made possible both victory and independence. Could not the European states follow this example, come at last to an agreement and unite? What should be the character of their organization? Such were the questions discussed in the peace projects of Pierre André Gargaz, in the anonymous plan of 1782, and in that of Palier de Saint-Germain. The year 1792 saw the publication of *La République universelle*. The author, Jean Baptiste Cloots, broke away from all traditions: he proposed a union of all men as individuals, excluding altogether the idea of a league of states.

It is due to Benjamin Franklin that the work of PIERRE ANDRÉ GARGAZ (no data are obtainable with regard to his birth and death) was preserved. It was written under very unusual circumstances. A schoolmaster in Thèse near Sisteron (Provence), Gargaz was charged with murder. Arraigned before the Court of Justice at Aix, he was sentenced to the galleys for twenty years. In his letter to Franklin, written from the penitentiary of Toulon in February, 1779, he testifies that he had not committed the crime; his mistake was that, relying on his innocence, he did not try to secure a counsel who would furnish proper defense and prove the falsity of the testimony on which he was being tried.[1] With his letter to Franklin, signed P.A.G., forçat numéro 1336, he enclosed the authentic certificate of probity, good life, and morals which had been given him too late by the school where he had been teaching before the indictment and which he had failed to produce at the Court of Justice at the time of his trial. The letter of Gargaz to Franklin was accompanied by a manuscript containing a plan for the abolition of war, on which Gargaz had been working in the penitentiary during the hours in which he was free from hard labor.

If we keep in mind that this convict, a victim of judiciary error, as it seems, was able to take heart and forget his hardships while thinking about the means by which he might contribute to the happiness of mankind, we understand how right Franklin was when, some years later, he wrote in his letter to David Hartley in behalf of Gargaz: "I honor much the character of this true philosopher." In forwarding the copy of his work to Franklin, Gargaz begged him to publish his manuscript for the sake of the benefit it would give to men. If Franklin answered this letter, no copy has come to light.

In 1781 the twenty-year term of his detention came to an end, and Gargaz was given his discharge. He wrote again to Franklin, asking him to help him to secure letters of rehabilitation which would facilitate his earning a livelihood; and soon afterwards he made up his mind to walk to Paris where Franklin was residing, for he was at this time Ambassador of the United States to Louis XVI. The American statesman who saw in the manuscript a work of value, "full of common sense," anyway, as he put it in his letter to D. Hartley, had the peculiar spelling of the author revised and his work printed in 1782 at his private printing office at Passy. He could not share the hopes Gargaz pinned on his pamphlet,

[1] See G. S. Eddy, *A Project of Universal and Perpetual Peace by Pierre André Gargaz*, 1922.

but, working steadily for the establishment of friendly relations between his country and England, he was able to appreciate any effort furthering peaceful intercourse between states. He gave Gargaz the following recommendation:

Recommendation of a galley slave
Passy, May 22, 1783

Sir,

The bearer Pierre André Gargaz is Author of a very humane Project for establishing a perpetual Peace. This has interested me much in his behalf. He appears to me a very honest sensible Man and worthy of better Fortune:—For, tho' his Project may appear in some respects chimerical, there is merit in so good an intention. He has serv'd faithfully twenty Years as a Galley-Slave, and now requests Letters of Rehabilitation, that he may enjoy for the Rest of his Life the Douceurs that State would be attended with: If the Request of his is not improper, and you can assist him in procuring such Letters, you will do me a most sensible Pleasure. He will show you authentic certificates of his good Conduct. With great Esteem, I have the honor to be,

Sir,

B. Franklin

To whom it may Concern.[2]

A letter of Franklin to D. Hartley makes clear why Gargaz had sent his manuscript to no one else but to Franklin. Here is only a part of this interesting document:

Passy, July 10, 1782

. . . I do not know why thy good work of peace goes on so slowly on your side. . . . We are ready here, on the part of America, to enter into treaty with you in concurrence with our allies and are disposed to be very reasonable. . . . A vessel just arrived from Maryland brings us the unanimous resolutions of their Assembly for continuing the war at all hazards rather than violate their faith with France. . . . There is, me thinks, a point that has been too little considered in treaties, the means of making them durable. An honest peasant from the mountains of Provence brought me the other day a manuscript he had written on the subject and which he could not procure permission to print.

[2] *The Writings of B. Franklin,* ed. by A. H. Smyth, 1905-07, vol. IX, No. 1415.

It appeared to me to have much good sense in it; and therefore I got some copies to be struck off for him to distribute where he may think fit. I send you one enclosed. This man aims at no profit from his pamphlet or his project, asks for nothing, expects nothing, and does not even desire to be known. He has acquired, he tells me, a fortune of near one hundred and fifty crowns a year (about eighteen pounds sterling), with which he is content. This, you may imagine, would not afford the expense of riding to Paris, so he came on foot: such was his zeal for peace and the hope of forwarding and securing it by communicating his ideas to great men here. His rustic and poor appearance has prevented his access to them or his obtaining their attention; but he does not seem yet to be discouraged. I honor much the character of this "véritable philosophe." [3]

When Thomas Jefferson was appointed Ambassador to Louis XVI in place of Franklin, Gargaz wrote to him, requesting him to recommend his book. As before, he did not aim at any advantage for himself. In Part II of the *Calendar of the Correspondence of Thomas Jefferson*, containing letters *to* Jefferson, this letter has been registered: "1785, December 15, Garga, soliciting his recommendation of a pamphlet entitled *Union souveraine*." [4]

The title of the work of Gargaz is *Conciliateur de toutes les nations d'Europe* ou *Projet de paix perpétuelle entre les Souverains de l'Europe et leurs Voisins* par P.A.G. The plan of the work, which comprises about thirty-five pages, is as follows:

I   Definition of the word "Peace."
II Dedication of the work to Louis XVI.
III Letter to the Reader.
IV The eight infallible means for the establishment and the maintenance of peace among the European sovereigns and their neighbors.

[3] *Ibid.,* vol. VIII, No. 1338.
[4] See: *Bulletin of the Bureau of Rolls and Library of the Department of State,* vols. 6, 8, 10. (The original letter—two pages—is in the Library of Congress, Washington, D. C., in the *Collection of Thomas Jefferson Correspondence,* Series 2, vol. 35, No. 4.)

V   Some objections to the opinions of the author and his answers.

In dedicating his work to Louis XVI, Gargaz reminds him that one of his ancestors, Henry IV, cherished the hope for the establishment of perpetual peace in Europe, and expresses his readiness to welcome any amendment which the King should deem necessary to make in his plan.

The influence of the *Projet de paix perpétuelle* of the Abbé de Saint-Pierre is noticeable in his plan to a much greater extent than is that of Sully's *Great Design;* but, while the Abbé wrote a plan worked out to the last details, Gargaz, in his work, gives only the principles on which his Universal State should be built.

Art. 1 establishes in Lyons or some other city a Permanent Congress of Mediators delegated by the sovereigns ruling over European and non-European peoples, Christian and non-Christian. Membership is not compulsory. As soon as ten Delegates counting among them five representatives of hereditary sovereigns are assembled and the first deliberation takes place, the Universal Union comes into existence, and the Congress passes judgment, by a plurality of votes, upon any difference among the Member-States. If the votes divide equally, the vote of the President solves the question. Every Delegate has the right to call a meeting of the Congress, and full freedom of deliberations is guaranteed.

Art. 2 states that the oldest of the Mediators delegated by the hereditary states shall be given precedence in the mutual relations of the Representatives.

Art. 3 states that territories the possession of which has not been contested at the time when the Universal Union has been established remain for ever in the possession of their present owners; those which are the subject of some dispute at the above-mentioned time are to be assigned to sovereigns by the Congress. After the new order of things has been inaugurated, the territory of a state can never be enlarged or reduced under any pretext whatsoever.

Art. 4 places an armed force at the disposal of the Congress so that the latter may prevent or stop any invasion. Every member of the Union makes definite contributions in order that the common purpose may be achieved. A nominee of the Congress is to be the Head of the state whose sovereign has been deprived of his rights or has died, leaving no heir to the throne.

Art. 5 establishes freedom of commerce on land and sea, but allows the government to levy taxes upon imports and exports.

Art. 6 states that, in order to put a country in a position to defend itself against an invasion, every state is allowed to have at a certain well-defined distance from its frontiers an unlimited number of fortresses, war vessels, and troops.

Art. 7 guarantees to every man in the army and navy steady employment and promotion in time of peace so that no soldier or sailor might be interested in bringing about war. Gargaz thinks that there should be in a country a fixed number of men in the army and navy; they should be directed in time of peace to perform useful work for the government. Only those who can support themselves might be discharged.

Art. 8 states that in order to diminish the fascination military career exercises on so many people belonging to the higher classes of society, interest in agriculture, arts, and trade, and a good knowledge of them should be furthered among them. The enjoyment those occupations can give, together with the profits one can derive from them, is likely to teach the love of peace.

In his pamphlet Gargaz suggests to the Universal Union certain concrete problems such as the necessity of having the Atlantic Ocean united with the Pacific and points to the Isthmus of Panama as the place suitable to the purpose. He speaks also of the advantage that a canal between Port Saïd and Suez would give to trade.

Gargaz's political scheme is characterized by a broader vision than the one published anonymously during this same year (1782).

The unknown author of the PEACE PLAN OF 1782 [5] does not feel as did the Abbé de Saint-Pierre and the author of the peace project of 1745, that the establishment of a federation

[5] *Causes politiques secrètes* ou *Pensées philosophiques sur divers événements qui se sont passés depuis 1763 jusqu'en 1772, suivies d'un Projet de Haut-Pouvoir-Conservateur dirigé par les quatre grandes Puissances de l'Europe.* Londres, 1782. (MLA Microfilm, No. 420F, Library of Congress).

of states, great and small, all enjoying an equal right of self-determination and vote, would bring about the pacification of Europe. He insists, on the contrary, upon the necessity of granting all power only to those states which are strong enough to maintain it and to secure the submission of all the others. Those states, in his opinion, are France, Austria, Spain with Portugal and all their possessions, and Prussia with Poland. He thinks that if after the death of Stanislas Poniatovsky, the crown of Poland were made hereditary in the House of Saxony, Poland would be safeguarded against continuous political commotions and could be henceforth in close alliance with Prussia.

Suggesting the establishment of a union of these four Great Powers under the name of "Universal Monarchy" or "Christian Republic of Europe," he wants their delegates to form in some central European city of their choice a governing body "Le Haut-Pouvoir-Conservateur" whose aim will be: to uphold in Europe the *status quo* based on the treaty of Aix-la-Chapelle (1748),[6] to restore their rights to those states which have suffered from injustice,[7] to apportion the contribution to be made by each state for the protection of its territory, the burden of which is however to be carried mainly by the four Great Powers,[8] to be the high tribunal, the supreme court of arbitration which would settle all disputes between European peoples and guarantee to Europe a lasting peace.[9]

The "Haut-Pouvoir-Conservateur" is not to be an institution placed above the states. Its decisions are to be ratified by the governments of the Great Powers. It is only after their ratification that the decisions become decrees liable to be enforced by recourse to arms.[10] For this purpose an international army will always be at the disposal of the "Haut-Pouvoir-Conservateur." The important issue of political equilibrium would be thus put for all time to come into the hands of the Great Powers, the supreme arbiters of Europe.[11]

[6] *Ibid.*, pp. 59-61.
[7] *Ibid.*, pp. 61, 75.
[8] *Ibid.*, p. 77.
[9] *Ibid.*, p. 74.
[10] *Ibid.*, p. 75.
[11] *Ibid.*, p. 74.

The rôle of the delegates of the other European states is, as a matter of fact, of no consequence: they do not vote, they enjoy only the right of a consultative voice. But what they lose in sovereignty and dignity is compensated, according to the author, by their security.[12] No war will be possible in Europe, he thinks, once his plan is adopted. He does not believe that any sovereign will ever dare to disobey a decree of the High Tribunal; he risks to lose his state which will be given by the High Court to another prince of the same House or made into a republic, since no other state, not even the Great Powers, are allowed to profit by war.[13]

Each of the four Great Powers, at the time of the establishment of the Union, has to furnish an army of one hundred thousand men. One-fourth of this force will be stationed in the vicinity of the seat of the central government, while the main body will be on the frontiers. As for the navy, its most important task is to secure freedom of commerce on the Mediterranean, destroying the vessels, harbors, and hiding-places of the pirates of Barbary.[14]

The author hopes that since his plan answers the interests of the four Great Powers, it will be readily accepted by them. If all the other states formed an alliance, they still would be the weaker party and their decisions could therefore be set aside. A feature like this disposes one to consider the plan of 1782 as inferior to that of the Abbé de Saint-Pierre. Besides, a state of things where security is bought at the price of renouncing sovereignty and equality cannot promise a stable order. Moreover, some of the political bodies viewed by the author are so heterogeneous with regard to nationality, religion, and language that a bitter struggle seems unavoidable. One should also not overlook the fact that the Delegates of the four Great Powers might not reach a decision, the predominantly political character of the High Tribunal making such a possibility quite probable. Some of the states might also object to the payment of a contribution, however

[12] *Ibid.*, pp. 74, 75.
[13] *Ibid.*, p. 76.
[14] *Ibid.*, p. 97.

limited, for the upholding of an organization in which they have but a consultative voice.

The author was anticipating the advent of a golden age through the acceptance of his scheme. Dr. Jacob ter Meulen seems to have been nearer to its true significance when he characterized this project as a Holy Alliance.[15]

The last scheme for world peace written before the outbreak of the French Revolution is that of PALIER de SAINT-GERMAIN published anonymously, as the preceding plan had been.[16]

This author tries to understand what are the main causes of the chaotic state of Europe with its perpetual wars. Where war is, there is the reign of force, not that of right or law. People do their best to establish order within states; very little is done in that direction in the domain of international relations though lawlessness in the sphere of international life affects exceptionally large masses of people. Thousands of men who have not done any wrong, who often belong to the *élite* of a nation are doomed to be mutilated, to suffer from life-long infirmities, or to die in war. Who are those irresponsible men, he asks, who take the liberty of declaring war?

Rousseau in his *Jugement sur la paix perpétuelle de M.. l'Abbé de Saint-Pierre* throws the blame entirely on the sovereigns and their ministers. Saint-Germain feels that herein Rousseau is guilty of exaggeration characteristic of him whenever he draws a picture of human perversity.[17] There are enlightened sovereigns and honest, clear-sighted ministers. The root of the evil lies less in the personality of a ruler than in the principle according to which he is not bound to give an account to any one and is allowed to enjoy a right, denied to any one else, of being judge in his own cause. The result is that a decision affecting the lives of thousands as,

[15] *Op. cit.,* II, 271.
[16] (A. Palier de Saint-Germain), *Nouvel Essai sur le projet de paix perpétuelle,* 1788. (MLA Microfilm No. 453F, Library of Congress.)
[17] *Ibid.,* pp. 14-15, 20-21.

for example, that of war, can be a matter of little moment to him.[18]

Why should two or three irresponsible leaders decide on an issue that threatens the lives of millions? Instead of driving others to die and kill and reserving for themselves prosperity and prestige, should not those who breed wars pay for them, in their turn, with their lives and worldly goods?

The author was well acquainted with the *Projet de paix perpétuelle* of 1713. He speaks of it as a sublime book. The contemporaries of the Abbé de Saint-Pierre did not give enough consideration to his work, he remarks. They refused to believe in the possibility of forming one federative republic of so many heterogeneous bodies, of monarchies hereditary or elective, of republics aristocratic or democratic, of a multitude of rival nations foreign to each other, with conflicting commercial, agricultural, industrial, and military interests, of entirely different customs, manners, and characters, speaking different languages, belonging to different Churches, and living under different laws.[19] In tightening the bonds which link political bodies to one another, one risks changing foreign wars into civil wars which are more cruel. It is a sad truth that the closer men are drawn to each other, the more reasons for dispute arise. Men are like little children; it is wise to part them in order to prevent fights.[20] The establishment of the United States of Europe, he adds, would require a century, and during this time so many events might occur which would delay the realization of the plan or overthrow what might have been already accomplished. [21] Those considerations led the author of the *Nouvel Essai* to invite the sovereigns of all Christian Powers to examine and put to the test some principles which he states in his fundamental preliminary articles. He thinks that their acceptance would further co-operation among the European States and lead to the final pacification of this continent.

All Christian sovereigns will be invited to form an indis-

[18] *Ibid.*, pp. 1, 6.
[19] *Ibid.*, pp. 22-23.
[20] *Ibid.*, pp. 24-25.
[21] *Ibid.*, p. 24.

soluble Association in which membership may not be revoked and by means of which they will guarantee each other all their possessions and rights based on the last treaties, without prejudice, however, to the legitimate claims which may be brought up in the future and for which provisions will be made hereafter.[22] All the above-mentioned sovereigns will have to renounce, expressly and for ever, the right of taking the law into their own hands and will have to pledge themselves and their successors to submit all their differences and all their claims to the unconditional final judgment of their peers.[23] To this end, there will be established a Council or permanent High Tribunal made up of plenipotentiary delegates representing the associated Powers. To this Council or High Tribunal will be referred all complaints, grievances, and, in general, all disputed claims that a final irrevocable judgment may be passed on them.[24]

No state can have more than one vote in this body the functions of which are either to act as a Council responsible for the preservation of peace or as a tribunal called upon to settle the disputes between nations. The sovereign whose name will be drawn by lot, one month before the expiration of the term of his predecessor, will preside over the Council and the High Tribunal for one year.[25] All the details of the procedure are to be worked out by the Congress which will assemble as soon as the preliminary fundamental articles are accepted by the Powers.[26] Not every dispute will require the action of the High Tribunal. Most of them are to be settled by Mediators. Each of the contending nations will choose among the Powers whose interests are not involved in the dispute two states, one of which must be accepted by the contending party. The two states finally chosen as Mediators will try to settle matters by the way of negotiations. If they fail in this attempt, they will act as Arbiters or as a Court of first instance. If they do not reach an agreement or if one of the contending parties

22 *Ibid.*, p. 2.
23 *Ibid.*, p. 31.
24 *Ibid.*, p. 31.
25 *Ibid.*, p. 39.
26 *Ibid.*, p. 40.

refuses to submit to their decision, the case will be referred to the Council of Plenipotentiaries which, acting as a High Tribunal, will pass judgment by the majority of votes.[27]

To support its decisions which must have the force of law as well as to be able to deal with any Power which would allow itself an act of violence or aggression against a state belonging to the Association, an international army will be created. Each state will have to furnish a contingent of troops according to a quota assigned. This army will be at the unconditional disposal of the Council. In some exceptional cases contributions in money alone will be authorized. Those states which are not large or wealthy enough to be in a position to supply man power or money will not be deprived of the protection of the Association. They can have Agents to defend their interests before the Assembly of Plenipotentiaries; they cannot, however, vote or be members of the Council.[28]

The author thinks that the century in which he lives is apt to solve the problem of the abolition of war. Never before have philosophers exercised such a powerful influence on the minds and behavior of men. The progress of science, the development of commerce, both of which, by their very nature, are not national, but international, are called upon to further in a great degree the ideal of peace:

The spread of the philosophical spirit has slackened the pace of aggressive ambition proving the absurdity of the inordinate desire to exalt oneself through conquests. In former times this longing for military glory made many people lose their heads. The philosophical outlook has destroyed the seeds of religious wars. At the same time the spirit of peace seems to bring together most European nations. This spirit of peace has been enlightened and supported by the genius of commerce and that of finance, the estimates of which prove that war is the gulf that swallows up the greatest part of wealth. The voice of humanity becomes more and more audible.[29]

The author, who seems to be a native of Switzerland, thinks

27 *Ibid.*, pp. 34-35.
28 *Ibid.*, p. 39.
29 *Ibid.*, p. 19.

that France, which he considers to be the intellectual leader of Europe, should take the initiative. At the same time he invites all those who are apt not to confine themselves within the narrow limits of selfish interests to devote their talents, their knowledge, and their energy to the realization of the great ideal of peace.

Four years elapsed after the scheme for world peace offered by Palier de Saint-Germain had been published. France was passing through the severe trials of the Revolution. Near the height of the crisis there appeared in print a plan unique in its kind, that of ANACHARSIS CLOOTS (1755-1794).[30]

Cloots's real given name was Jean Baptiste, but, being inclined to see in religion "a social disease of which one ought to get rid," [31] he renounced his Christian name—"he unbaptized himself"—for such is the term he used—and adopted the name of Anacharsis, the young Scythian, disciple of the Greek philosopher Solon. Like this Scythian, who had left his native steppes, stretching along the northern coasts of the Black Sea, and had gone in search of knowledge to the most civilized country in the ancient world, the young Prussian millionaire, Baron von Klotz, born in the sumptuous castle of Gnadenthal (Western Prussia), looked to France, and particularly to Paris, for knowledge and enlightenment. Although a native German, he had received a French education; under the influence of his uncle, Corneille de Pauw, a renowned Dutch scholar and contributor to Diderot's *Encyclopédie,* he became well acquainted with the ideas of the French philosophers and was a great admirer of Rousseau as well as of Voltaire whom he had the chance to meet later in Paris.

After two years spent at the Military Academy of Berlin, where he attended the lectures of prominent European scholars, he decided, in spite of his admiration for Frederick the Great, the founder of this school, to leave Berlin. Some

[30] *La République universelle* ou *Adresse aux tyrannicides,* l'An quatre de la Rédemption.
[31] *Ibid.,* p. 27.

lines in *L'Orateur du genre humain* give us the thoughts and feelings which led him to this decision:

A brilliant career lay open before me . . . arguments in favor of a lasting happiness silenced, however, the sophisms suggested by restless ambition. . . . To belong to a man, and not to reason . . . to have to carry out orders instead of being guided by one's own judgment in the choice of a residence and course of life . . . I made my decision, and from that moment the whole world was mine.[32]

Cloots left Prussia and traveled extensively for some years. During this period he learned to see in the people he met not Englishmen, Dutchmen, or Germans, but human beings. Then he went to Paris where he espoused with enthusiasm the guiding principles of the French Revolution. "The Revolution was in the brain of philosophers a long time before 1789, like Minerva in the brain of Jupiter," he writes; [33] and in another place: "Will our nephews ever believe that two years were sufficient to produce this marvel, though we had at the same time to clear a ground blocked up by fifteen centuries of savagery?" [34] and again: "The miracle of Jericho seems a natural event after our legislators have been able to destroy in one single night the ramparts of feudalism and old fiscal laws." [35] Cloots' clear creative mind, his fiery eloquence, the daring originality of the leading articles he was contributing to the newspapers and periodicals of the time, made him one of the most prominent members of the Jacobin Club; he was asked to become a French citizen and was elected member of the National Convention. He was one of the Deputies who voted the death of Louis XVI and the execution of the Girondists; he believed fanatically in the necessity of crushing all those who might check the triumphant march of the Revolution.

The idea to the propagation of which he devoted himself

[32] *L'Orateur du genre humain* ou *Dépêches du Prussien Cloots au Prussien Herzberg*, Paris, l'An deux de la Rédemption, pp. 26-27.
[33] *Ibid.*, p. 85.
[34] *Ibid.*, p. 45.
[35] *Ibid.*, pp. 153-154.

and for which he even paid with his life was that of a Universal Republic. Cloots, whose mind was infallibly preoccupied with the task of discovering a way that would lead mankind toward happiness and prosperity, believed he had found it; he began, accordingly, to speak and write on the necessity for all nations to form one Union. He was never tired of emphasizing the point that his Union was not meant to be a universal monarchy, "that assemblage of peoples trampled under the heel of one man" [36] nor a league of independent states tied by ephemeral bonds, but a "confederation of individuals" [37] which would make one nation out of millions of men, the whole population of our earth; this harmony of individual wills could alone offer a guarantee for a perpetual peace:

What ignorance, what savagery to pen ourselves within different political entities vying with each other, while we have the advantage of inhabiting one of the smallest planets of the celestial sphere! [38]

A body does not make war upon itself, and mankind will live in peace when it will form one body, one Nation.[39]

Let us do away with national feudalism since we knew how to get rid of feudal anarchy which had transformed peaceful dungeons into haunts of thieves and murderers! [40]

If there were only one universal state, the map of the world would no longer show a vast number of political bodies every one of which is surrounded, as a rule, by hostile neighbors. History shows that wars are waged mainly by neighbors. There will be no neighbor states in the Universal Republic planned by Cloots, for all borders which separate nations will be declared non-existent. There will be no foreign countries either: "A foreign land; a barbarous expression of which we

---

36 *Voeux d'un Gallophile*, 1786, p. 3. A little further on Cloots writes: "Il faut rougir des paroles 'L'Etat c'est moi.'" [G. Lanson doubts whether Louis XIV ever uttered those words.]

37 *L'Orateur du genre humain*, pp. 145-146.

38 *La République universelle*, p. 7.

39 *Ibid.*, p. 24.

40 *Ibid.*, p. 13.

begin to feel ashamed. . . . There is but one natural border, that between the earth and the firmament!" [41] Cloots finds the expression "my native land" ridiculous; people who indiscriminately use it are ignorant of the fact that the prosperity of one country contributes powerfully to that of other lands.[42] "What is, in reality, a native country?" he asks, and answers: "A piece of land between two rivers and two hills." [43] Rousseau seemed to hold the same opinion; according to him, there are neither French nor German, English nor Spanish peoples, only Europeans: all have the same passions, the same moral principles, the same taste.[44] Cloots goes much farther in his internationalism when he says:

There are not two human races. . . . Do not advance the argument of ignorance; while knowledge is the result of special studies, reason, as a rule, is an appanage of all. Do not bring in the argument of distance: when I see a tyrant in Madrid and another in Petersbourg on the point of dividing between themselves both hemispheres; when a Lama of Rome and another of Mecca make laws for Peru and Malaysia; when the merchants of Amsterdam and London rule over Bengal and the Moluccas; I become aware of the facility with which an Assembly in session in Paris could govern the whole human race.[45]

According to Cloots, perpetual peace among nations presupposes mankind governed by one common constitution the foundation of which could never be shaken, a constitution for which the ideas we connect with the words subjects, allies, enemies, foreigners, bourgeois, peasants, white men, colored men, Catholics, non-Catholics, colonies are unknown. Such a constitution would last for ever.[46]

Men will be what they should be when each one is able to

[41] *Bases constitutionnelles.* . . . pp. 4, 25, 26. Cf. G. Avenel, "A. Cloots, l'orateur du genre humain," 1865, II, 147.

[42] *L'Orateur du genre humain,* p. 106: "Toutes les nations peuvent dire: nous ne sommes rien par nous-mêmes; nous brouterions l'herbe sans les étrangers."

[43] *Voeux d'un Gallophile,* p. 177, "Lettre à M. le Comte de Voison, 6 mars, 1786."

[44] J. J. Rousseau, *Gouvernement de la Pologne,* ch. III-IV.

[45] Cloots, *L'Orateur du genre humain,* p. 142.

[46] *Ibid.,* p. 142.

say: "The world is my native country, the world is mine." [47]
Cloots stresses again and again that his Universal Republic
is not meant to be a federation of independent states: "Let
us prevent the germination of the baneful idea of a federation of adjacent countries. The Abbé de Saint-Pierre invited the incoherent European Powers to establish a strange
and ridiculous Congress which would foment war rather
than establish peace. I am for an absolute leveling, for the
destruction of all barriers which thwart the interests of the
human family." [48] Politics and ethics will be in accordance,
he thought, as soon as, in the place of a great number of national states, there is one nation, comprising the whole human
race.[49] If it is hardly possible, he thought, to speak of general happiness in a state where there are social classes and
corporations strongly marked by a spirit of party, it is even
less possible to hope for the happiness of mankind once we
allow the existence of separate national units. Peace can be
made a reality only through the despotical reign of a universal law which would sum up the expressions of individual
wills.[50]

All those ideas found strong opponents in the Girondists
headed by Roland and Brissot. This party considered the
political organization of the United States, at this time beginning its history of an independent political body, as an
example to be followed. Cloots saw a great difference between the young American Republic, with its sparse population profoundly religious, and France; he was sure that his
adopted country, organized as a federative state, would go
to pieces and become the prey of her neighbors. Strong cen-
tralization was, in his mind, the only way to save France
from disintegration. The Girondists, on the contrary, were
in favor of decentralization. They disagreed also on another
important point: the Girondists were not willing to let Paris
play a greater political rôle than they were ready to allow the
leading towns of the Departments, while Cloots saw in Paris

[47] *Ibid.*, p., 147.
[48] *La République universelle*, p. 17.
[49] *L'Orateur du genre humain*, pp. 137-139.
[50] *Ibid.*, p. 146.

"the great center" of the universe. In his *République universelle* (page 24) he writes: "The commune of Paris will be the place of reunion, the central beacon of the universal community," and on page 48: "Paris is the Vatican of reason; its thunderbolts reach the farthest boundaries of the kingdom." It is essential, the author feels, to have a center which would co-ordinate different opinions, characters, tastes, would struggle against religious, political, and social prejudices, crush egotism and make common interests prevail. The rôle of Paris, as Cloots sees it, is to change the man of any particular region into the man of France, and the man of France into the man of the universe.[51] He speaks also of the part a large city is called upon to play in the life of a country in the following lines:

I have said often and I am repeating again that men when isolated are beasts, when united are gods. Ten thousand small scattered towns are of no significance and cannot achieve anything in the fields of philosophy or science. Make of them one city, and you will be astounded at the result.[52]

The official language of Cloots' Universal Republic is to be French. France, in his opinion, is the only country which is able to make a reality out of his dream of a universal state —the Great Germania, the Brotherhood of Man. There are, he thought, no people in the world who would not be ready to adhere to the *Déclaration des droits de l'homme et du*

[51] *La République universelle*, p. 45.
One might remember in connection with these opinions of Cloots one of the *Thoughts* of Montesquieu: "C'est surtout une grande capitale qui fait l'esprit général d'une nation; c'est Paris qui fait le Français: sans Paris, la Normandie, la Picardie, l'Artois, seraient allemands comme l'Allemagne; sans Paris, la Bourgogne et la Franche-Comté, seraient suisses comme les Suisses; sans Paris, la Guyenne, le Béarn, le Languedoc, seraient espagnols comme les Espagnols. Cf. *Pensées et Fragments inédits*, 1899, "Pensée 318."

[52] *Ibid.*, p. 55.
Cloots loved Paris as much as did Bernardin de Saint-Pierre. Both these men saw in it not only the heart and brain of civilization, the center of practical conveniences and cultural advantages, but they realized the rôle Paris played in the lives of the lonely, the poor, and the unfortunate. Cloots writes: "L'immensité de la Ville [de Paris] est une sauve-garde. On trouve ici un asile contre l'amour-propre offensé, contre les haines des petites villes, contre l'ennui de vivre isolé. Un ci-devant seigneur vient

citoyen, and he tries to prove this by appearing at the bar of the National Assembly on June 28, 1790, the anniversary of the "Serment du jeu de paume," at the head of the group of thirty-six foreigners all wearing their national costumes. He introduced them as the embassy of the Human race and claimed for them a place at the great Festival of the Federation which was to take place on July 14, 1790. It was following this event that people began to call him half jokingly, half seriously "l'Orateur du genre humain."

But Cloots could in no way be satisfied with the mere propagation of his ideas; the dreamer he was in his youth developed under the strain of events into a man of will and action. On November 19, 1793, the National Convention published the following declaration: "The National Convention proclaims in the name of the French nation that it will admit to brotherhood and give assistance to all peoples who wish to regain their freedom." [53] In Cloots' opinion, this was the right moment to take the first step toward the realization of his plan. The lands which France would free from the yoke of foreign countries during her defensive war against the European coalition should be made part of her territory. Cloots entered into close relations with the National Assemblies of the liberated peoples, and his efforts were not lost. The National Assembly of Savoy voted the annexation of this country which became a part of France,

---

oublier à Paris les honneurs qu'on lui refuse. . . . M. le ci-devant baron est enchanté de pouvoir conserver son franc-parler, son franc-calomnier . . . et l'ancienne étiquette de l'inconcevable Cour des Tuileries donne des réminiscences délicieuses aux pauvres hères déblasonnés." (*L'Orateur du genre humain,* p. 42.)

Speaking of Paris, Bernardin de Saint-Pierre writes: "J'aime cette ville non seulement parce que toutes les commodités de la vie y sont rassemblées, qu'elle est le centre de toutes les puissances du royaume . . . , mais parce qu'elle est l'asile et le refuge des malheureux. C'est là que les ambitions, les préjugés, les haines et les tyrannies des provinces viennent se perdre et s'anéantir. Là il est permis de vivre obscur et libre. Là il est permis d'être pauvre, sans être méprisé. L'homme affligé y est distrait par la gaîté publique, et le faible s'y sent fortifié des forces de la multitude." (*Etudes de la Nature,* III, 279.)

[53] A. Aulard, "La Diplomatie du premier Comité de salut public," *La Révolution Française,* 1890, p. 128.

the Department of the Mont-Blanc. For Cloots, the gradual incorporation of different lands appeared to be a starting point towards the abolition of borders. France was to be the center round which the rallying of peoples would take place. The Universal Republic of his dreams would be created, at least in the first stage, by the process of the extension of the boundaries of France through the voluntary incorporation of foreign lands. As a result, "the boundaries of France would necessarily comprise all the universe, all mankind." [54] In a process like this the proper names of the nations should be dropped; in order to make themselves ready for this fusion, all peoples should give up at once the names of their countries and, "since our Association is a true brotherly union, we, the French nation, might readily agree to be called Germans (Germains).[55] Cloots was happy in thinking that his native country with the hereditary castle of Gnadenthal would become part of French territory as soon as the borders of France reached the Rhine:

One object the Court of Versailles should not lose sight of is the extension of the borders of France to the mouth of the Rhine. This river is the natural boundary of Gaul as well as are the Alps, the Pyrenees, the Mediterranean Sea, and the Ocean.[56]

This goal might be attained through clever negotiations, Cloots thought. He was intent on peace between nations, but this did not prevent him from insisting on the necessity for military preparedness and advocating as urgently as did S. Mercier the use of the most terrible and destructive implements against an attacking enemy. "Louis XV," he writes, "refused to take advantage of M. de Lille's invention, the Greek fire, which would in one moment destroy the most powerful fleet."—"So much the better," Cloots thought, "the Greek fire would put an end to war at sea once and forever." [57]

[54] Cloots, *La République universelle*, p. 162, note, and p. 141. Cf. H. Baulig. "A. Cloots . . . ," *La Révolution française*, tome 41; juillet-déc. 1901, p. 344.
[55] "Bases constitutionnelles . . . ," pp. 29-30. Cf. H. Baulig, *op. cit.*, p. 405.
[56] *Voeux d'un Gallophile*, p. 53.
[57] *Ibid.*, p. 149.

As the center of the Universal Republic, Cloots advocated the selection of France, the torchbearer of European civilization and the promoter of the ideas of liberty, equality, and brotherhood which would cement the world into one whole. The fulfillment of this task did not carry with it the right to dominate the rest of the world: "If Geneva should refuse to unite with us, we would ask Geneva if we might unite with her," [58] and further:

I recognize neither French domination nor French constitution. In order to avoid all misunderstandings, I propose that the word "French" be abolished as well as the words Burgundian, Norman, Gascon. An official renunciation would cover us with glory. It would be wise and of good policy to adopt a name which would win over for us a vast neighboring country and, as our Association is a true brotherly Union, the name "Germans" would suit us perfectly.[59]

Cloots prepared the draft of the declaration he wished to see solemnly made by the National Convention on April 23, 1793; it read as follows:

The National Convention, in its desire to put an end to errors, inconsistencies, and contradictory claims of the corporations and individuals that call themselves "sovereign," solemnly asserts under the auspices of the *Declaration of the Rights of Man:*

Art. 1. There is no other sovereign than the human race.

Art. 2. Every individual, every community willing to recognize this luminous and immutable principle will enjoy the right to become a member of our brotherly Association, of the Republic of Men, Germans, Universals.

Art. 3. The admission to membership of remote communities and lands is postponed on account of distance and the difficulties of maritime communications.[60]

Such were the principles, but by what means did the author think to put them into practice?—A legislative body of 1,500-2,000 delegates shall represent the sovereign human race. This Assembly shall elect an Executive Council fully subor-

[58] "Bases constitutionnelles . . . ," see Avenel, *op. cit.,* II, 142.
[59] *Ibid.,* II, 148-149.
[60] *Ibid.,* II, 151-152.

dinated to the Assembly. The judiciary power shall be vested in tribunals similar to those which were functioning in the author's time. He did not see any urgent need for their reorganization.

Religious freedom shall be guaranteed to all citizens; "it removes great obstacles rallying all men at the tribunal of conscience." [61] "Let every one cultivate his field in his own way; let every one worship as he likes. A common law will protect all forms of work and worship." [62] Cloots advanced also purely practical arguments in favor of tolerance; he saw sheer folly in the effort to oppose what one cannot prevent; furthermore, to get rid of all dissenters would mean to make a desert of Europe, Asia, Africa, and America. [63] Personally, he was in favor of a religion based on evidences within reach of all men. [64]

The Departments of the Universal Republic shall enjoy, to a certain extent, the right of self-government, especially in questions concerning their economic welfare; they will take care of their roads, schools, hospitals, jails, and provide for old people and the unemployed.

Cloots writes of all the economic advantages the realization of his plan would bring: taxes for the upkeep of the central government would be practically nil; money which is used, under present conditions, for the army and navy, fortresses, customhouses, diplomatic service, colonies, and war would be saved; hence, poverty would be unknown. Perpetual peace once established, there would be a balance between production and consumption and, owing to free trade, a reasonable distribution of goods. Cloots does not anticipate the possibility of another revolution; he believes that every citizen will do his best to maintain the established order of things; he has the conviction that the constitution designed by him is superior to all preceding ones. The mere fact that his organization will be universal insures it against the faults of narrow provincialism. "I have pored over books contain-

[61] *La République universelle*, p. 22.
[62] *Ibid.*, p. 20.
[63] *L'Orateur du genre humain*, p. 119.
[64] *Voeux d'un Gallophile*, p. 89.

ing various human constitutions; I have found that each one is colored with national prejudices." [65]

What was the reaction of Cloots's contemporaries to his plan? One of the members of the National Convention, Robert, expressed the opinion of the majority when he said:

Let us leave to philosophers the task of studying mankind from all points of view. We are not the Representatives of the human race; therefore, I want the legislator of France to forget for one moment the universe and to center his thoughts upon his own country. Unless we have in us a certain dose of national egotism, we cannot be faithful in fulfilling our duties; we shall work for those who have not commissioned us and forget those whose well-being we can secure. I love all men, particularly free men, but I love the free men of France better than any other men in the universe.[66]

The political party to which Cloots belonged, "les Montagnards" (the Mountain), headed by the all-powerful Robespierre, did not share his viewpoint; they were opposed to the policy of annexation which was arming Europe against their country. Besides, the personal animosity of Robespierre for Cloots was great; what could really be the feelings of a man of boundless ambition and humble origin, a strong nationalist, for Cloots, an aristocrat of great wealth, a favorite of the crowd, an internationalist, and a propagandist of a plan for a universal republic. The dictator decided to get rid of him. A framed-up trial was staged; Cloots was unfairly accused of having taken part in a conspiracy against the French Republic, of being a Prussian spy. He was executed on March 24, 1794.

His scheme for the establishment of a universal republic, being mainly opposed from the national and political point of view, was criticized also for its contradiction of well-known historical facts and found incoherent from the point of view of common human experience. On November 21, 1792, at a meeting of the club of the Jacobins, his scheme was analyzed

[65] "Bases constitutionnelles . . . ," see Avenel, op. cit., II, 142.
[66] Cf. A. Aulard, "La Diplomatie du Comité de salut public," La Révolution Française, tome 18, janv.-juin 1890, p. 134.

by one of the members of the Club, Alexandre Courtois. The latter expressed his readiness to share the author's opinion that all men are brothers, according to the natural law, but he pointed to the distance between them because of the different levels of culture they have reached. He wanted the audience to consider likewise the fact that everything in this world seems to be bound to have a limit, even the power of our brain; that one family is separated from the other, one nation from the other. The unlimited extension of borders, according to Courtois, is not to be desired: when the pulse of life in vast political bodies slows down, they remind one of pools of stagnant water.[67]

Among the late eighteenth-century peace projects Cloots's scheme advocated the most extensive changes. No other plan up to the present day has ever proposed to sweep aside the past so completely, yet all those projects recognized that nations might have been deprived of their rights by treaties and that certain age-old conditions no longer answered the vital interests of a people; they admitted that in such cases some changes were to be made before the *status quo* principle was to be finally established.

[67] Cf. Selma Stern, *A. Cloots, der Redner des Menschengeschlechts*, 1914, p. 200.

CONCLUSION

THE magnitude of development and the power of expression the peace idea had reached in the works of the world-known representatives of French literature, the promise of a new order of things in the sphere of international life implied in the French projects for world organization, exerted a far-reaching influence. England and Germany proved the most responsive countries.

In 1789 Jeremy Bentham's *Principles of International Law* appeared in print. In the fourth chapter of his work we find a project for perpetual peace. It suggests the establishment of a diplomatical assembly with two deputies from each European state. This assembly would act as a tribunal in case of conflicts between peoples; the assembly would prevent any attempt at secret diplomacy in which Bentham, like Crucé and the Abbé de Saint-Pierre, saw the main cause of conflicts. Bentham insists on the publicity of treaties. With regard to military sanctions, he shows some hesitation: he thinks them undesirable and impractical; he would like to see them replaced by pressure of a political or economic character; besides, firmly believing in the force of public opinion, he expects from the parties a voluntary submission to the decision of the tribunal. To make the peace idea bear fruit, it is sufficient, according to him, to find a line of common utility between peoples, instead of trying to touch their hearts. Bentham's name is closely connected with the doctrine of utilitarianism which the Abbé de Saint-Pierre seems first to have applied to the question of peace.

The year 1795 saw the publication of Immanuel Kant's *Zum ewigen Frieden.* Like the French pacifists, he saw the need for the establishment of a union of European states, whose territories could under no conditions pass from one Power to another. Like Rousseau, he was not in favor of large political bodies, since laws, he thought, always lose in energy what government gains in extent. Diversity of language and religion, he saw, were nature's means of preventing nations from mixing one with another. Like Rousseau, he refused to admit the possibility of peaceful international relations until all European states adopted a republican form of government.

The first real attempt to substitute juridical sanctions for those of mere force was made at the end of the nineteenth century. In 1899, on the initiative of Nicholas II of Russia, twenty-six European states delegated plenipotentiaries to a conference at The Hague in order to discuss the means of assuring a lasting peace. This conference had for result the establishment of The International Court of Arbitration which, in its main lines, recalled the system proposed by Pierre Dubois in his *De recuperatione Terre Sancte* (1305-1307).

The second Peace Conference at The Hague in 1907, attended by the representatives of forty-four states, recognized the right of each party in the dispute to apply to the International Court of Arbitration independently of the other party or parties. The establishment of this first World Court was in fact the first practical achievement in the sphere of international relations.

In 1919 the League of Nations came into existence. The close relationship between its Covenant and the *Projet de paix perpétuelle* of the Abbé de Saint-Pierre is striking; no wonder, since both were the outgrowth of plans for international organization with which, after they had originated in France, so many minds in different countries were preoccupied.

Pacifist thought in France during the seventeenth and eighteenth centuries was essential to these later movements. It had followed two main directions: one of them was characterized by the effort to create a league of states with a central governing body whose main task was to prevent conflicts among the member states and to settle disputes through a court

of arbitration.   The other was a part of the general liberal-
ization of ideas which characterized the great writers of the
Age of Enlightenment.

With the ideal of the triumph of justice over force always
present in their minds, the creators of political schemes tried
to discover universal principles upon which the structure of a
society of peoples might be erected.   The great goal was peace
among the members of this society; however, this peace was
to be established and maintained so as not to imperil something
which in the opinion of all those writers, was and is more
precious than peace, namely, national independence, the right
of a people to preserve the integrity of its territory and to
shape its life according to its ideals.   This outlook led toward
the rejection of the slogan "no war under any conditions whatever, peace at any price."   In regard to their own country, the
authors of political schemes were fully conscious that, in considering national defense not only the right but the sacred duty
of a citizen, they were defending, besides the interests of the
people of France, universal values embodied in French civilization.   Accordingly, the necessity for preparedness against
eventual aggression was stressed in every political plan.   All
assertions that it is impossible to distinguish between defensive
and offensive war, all conversations about and proposals for
disarmament met in France at all times the invariable answer:
"No disarmament without security."   "Nous ne sommes pas
encore au moment des embrassements fraternels dans la vieille
Europe," as A. Briand once said.

Since the best way to avoid war is to discuss the situation
beforehand, all French peace projects insisted upon the establishment of a central political body of delegates from each individual state.   They emphasized that this body should be
permanent and its activity continuous so that difficulties arising in the sphere of international life might be discussed and
solved before overwhelming trouble broke out.   From the
fourteenth century on, the desiderata of most French political
writers have been: obligatory membership for every European
state in the league of nations and compulsory recourse to arbitration.   Since the absence of sanctions makes any decision
of a tribunal void, all of them insisted on the necessity of plac-

ing an armed force at the disposal of the council of representatives.

Such were the leading ideas of French plans during the seventeenth and eighteenth centuries. Individual schemes presented few distinguishing characteristics. However, a stronger trend from idealism to a more practical approach to realistic problems became evident as the years went by. The suggestion to regain the Holy Land, offered by Dubois (1305-1307) as a common goal to unite the Christian nations, is characteristic of a comparatively early period. If we find Sully also advocating war against infidels (1638), his reasons were quite different: he simply desired to protect Europe against Asiatic invaders. As for the political writers who came after him, we hear from them no further mention about war against non-Christians. The latter were being accepted as allies or as regular members of the leagues of states which were being proposed. The importance of giving to those leagues a universal character was already emphasized in Crucé's *Le Nouveau Cynée* (1723) as well as in some later plans, those of the Abbé de Saint-Pierre (1713), Gargaz (1782), and Cloots (1792). Practical considerations alone compelled the other writers of the eighteenth century to center their attention upon the establishment of strictly European leagues. If Cloots insisted upon declaring French as the official language and Paris as the capital of his Universal Republic which he saw coming to life through gradual voluntary incorporation of different countries into France, one must recognize therein simply a process of formation of his World Union, a process in which the word France as well as all other national names were expected to disappear. While the idea of the hegemony of France could be inferred in two early plans, those of Dubois and Sully, all other originators of political projects showed no tendency to let France domineer over the other countries.

With the exception of Cloots, all those writers planned for the establishment of leagues of national, independent, sovereign states, and this in spite of the variety of names they indiscriminately used to designate their organizations.

Sully thought that the era of perpetual peace would follow a final war which would reconstruct the map of Europe ac-

cording to the principle of nationality. His plan provided for
the division of the continent into states of more or less equal
size and abundance of natural resources. Most French plans,
on the contrary, took the *status quo* for their starting point.
Goudar, Gargaz, the unknown author of the plan of 1782, and
Palier de Saint-Germain admitted but a partial *status quo;*
they asserted that the establishment of lasting peace must have
for prerequisite the restoration of rights of those peoples that
have suffered from injustice.

One vote for each member-state was the system the majority of authors agreed upon. Sully, however, was disposed
to favor France, Spain, Germany, England, and the Holy See,
since they had larger populations and more power, while the
anonymous project of 1782 made the four Great Powers
(France, Austria, Spain with Portugal, and Prussia with
Poland) the guarantors of peace and at the same time the
supreme arbiters of Europe.

The anonymous author of 1745 and especially Rousseau
stressed the importance of the establishment of federations of
small states; these, enabling the peoples to oppose their joined
force to eventual attacks of the mighty, would restrain the ambition and the aggressive spirit of the latter.

Looking for means toward the abolition of war, Dubois,
Crucé, Sully, the author of the project of 1745, and Gargaz
wondered whether the establishment of freedom of commerce
on land and sea throughout the world might not bring about
lasting peace. Voltaire, for his part, seemed to find this expectation very naïve; he refused to admit that an activity based
on competition, as trade is, could contribute to the pacification
of the world.

The merit of pointing out concrete means for solving a
problem of such great importance and difficulty as that of the
establishment of peace among nations was enhanced in seventeenth and especially in eighteenth-century France by the talent
of her great writers. Their skill in giving a striking picture of
the horrors of war and their wit in disclosing and emphasizing
its futility have hardly ever been surpassed.

An abstract system, [Seeber writes] a theoretical idea of justice, an economic theory, a political system do not become vitally active until they are popularized and vivified by writers gifted with that amount of passion and feeling. . . .[1]

Passion and feeling, as shown in the works of French writers, gained in intensity the closer was the advent of the Revolution. In the particular field of social and foreign relations, they inspired the great French writers to create a public opinion destructive to the spirit of conquest, religious intolerance, and racial prejudices that generated civil and foreign wars. Mistrusting the possibility of direct influence upon monarchs and statesmen, those writers aroused in the public the desire that the policies of the people be substituted for those of the sovereigns. They made French literature reign undisputedly over the minds of men. "What has been achieved, has been achieved through books," Voltaire used to say; "never will anything useful, good, important, great be achieved but through books." The "books" written by French philosophers of the century of the enlightenment were so important that they became intellectual food for their contemporaries. Their influence is felt in the speeches of the orators during the time of the Revolution:

O nations! [Volney exclaims] Let us banish all tyranny and all discord; let us form but one society, one great family; and, since human nature has but one constitution, let there exist in future but one law, that of nature; one code, that of reason; one throne, that of justice; one altar, that of union.

You will not allow millions of people to become mere playthings in the hands of some of their fellowmen and you will restore dignity and rights to nations! [2]

Those ideals also begin to inspire foreign writers. The German poet and philosopher J. G. Herder (1744-1803), in his *Briefe zur Beförderung der Humanität* (1793-97) speaks of seven mental attitudes (*Gesinnungen*) which, if deeply

---

[1] E. D. Seeber, *Anti-slavery Opinion in France During the Second Half of the Eighteenth Century*, 1937, Preface.

[2] *The Ruins*, transl. by * * * in 1828, p. 93.

rooted in the minds and hearts of men, could not fail to bring peace upon earth:

1. The hatred of war inseparable from the conviction that defensive war alone can be regarded as legitimate.

2. The refusal of our soul, our conscience to worship military glory and the genius of a conqueror.

3. The profound conviction that the greatness of a reign or a government does not reside in the ability to extend the territory of the dominion.

4. A high ideal of patriotism that would stimulate in every citizen the efforts to make his own country noble, prosperous, civilized, happy and would at the same time restrain him from interfering with matters concerning the internal life of other nations.

5. The steady desire for co-operation, for a close union which would make nations ready to protest together against any unlawful action of which a member state might be found guilty. [It is, however, necessary to mention that Herder was strongly opposed to military sanctions, as was also Kant.]

6. The recognition of freedom of seas and rivers demanded by our sense of justice.

7. The recognition of the duty to spread the light of knowledge among men; for a cultured nation an olive branch means more than a laurel wreath.[3]

Herder had the greatest admiration for the French philosophers. He was proud of being regarded as their disciple. He spoke, furthermore, with the most sincere sympathy of the Abbé de Saint-Pierre, saying: "I preach eternal peace as though I were an apostle of the Abbot Saint-Pierre . . . ."

As though to carry further the watchwords of the French philosophers, America, in turn, entered the scene. In letters Washington wrote to Lafayette we read:

. . . as a citizen of the great republic of humanity at large . . . I consider how mankind may be connected like one great family in fraternal ties. I indulge a fond, perhaps an enthusiastic idea that . . . nations are becoming more humanized in their

[3] Cf. J. G. Herder, *Werke*, Leipzig, IV, 518-528, "Briefe zur Beförderung der Humanität," and "Zum ewigen Frieden."

policy, that the subjects of ambition and causes for hostility are daily diminishing . . .[4]

. . . but we do not wish to be the only people who may taste the sweets of an equal and good government. We look with an anxious eye to the time when happiness and tranquillity shall prevail in your country, and when all Europe shall be freed from commotions, tumults, and alarms.[5]

We have sowed seeds of Liberty and Union that will spring up everywhere upon earth. Some day, taking its pattern from the United States, there will be founded the United States of Europe.[6]

The universal importance of the American Revolution was in the fact that great humanitarian principles were put into practice, those principles which were affirmed with great power in the works of French writers of the Age of Enlightenment. True to their cosmopolitan outlook, the French philosophers stressed the idea that there is no chosen people, no superior race, no master nation, and that all groups should be equally called upon to collaborate in order to bring about the universal brotherhood of man. From whatever angle we analyze the rôle they played in the stormy life of the European nations, we must admit that they exerted a unifying influence. Joining their efforts with those of the creators of peace projects, they examined the issues of war and peace from all points of view: humanitarian, religious, rationalistic, and economic. They knew how to inspire men with ideals of peace and thereby they indeed "exercised a function and fulfilled a mission." [7]

[4] See *G. Washington's Writings* collected and edited by W. Ch. Ford, 1890, XI, 56, "Letter of Washington to Lafayette of Aug. 15, 1786."
[5] *Ibid.*, XII, 59, "Letter of July 28, 1791."
[6] Cf. J. Hodé, *op. cit.*, p. 168.
[7] V. Hugo, *Oration on Voltaire* on May 30, 1878, transl. from French by James Parton.

BIBLIOGRAPHY

BIBLIOGRAPHY

SOURCE MATERIAL[1]

AUBERT, Guillaume. *Oraison de la Paix et les Moyens de l'entretenir.* Paris, 1559.

BALZAC, Guez de. *Le Prince.* Toussaint du Bray, 1631.
———. *Socrate chrétien.* Courbé, 1652.
———. *Dissertations chrétiennes et morales, politiques et critiques.* Paris, L. Billaine, 1665.

BAYLE, Pierre. *Pensées diverses sur la comète,* 2 vol., éd. Prat. Paris, Hachette, 1911-1912 [1682].
———. *A Philosophical Commentary on These Words of the Gospel: "Compel them to come in that My House may be full,"* 2 vols., tr. from French. London, 1708 [1686].
———. *Dictionnaire historique et critique,* 16 vol., éd. Beuchot. Paris, Desoer, 1820 [1697].
———. "Unpublished Letters," ed. by J. L. Gerig and G. L. van Roosbroeck. *Romanic Review,* vols. XXII-XXV, years 1931-1934.

BENTHAM, Jeremy. *A Plan for an Universal and Perpetual Peace* with an Introduction by C. John Colombos. London, Sweet and Maxwell, 1937 (Grotius Society Publications, No. 6) [1789].

BOILEAU-DESPRÉAUX, Nicolas. *Oeuvres,* 4 vol., éd. Berriat Saint-Prix. Paris, Langlois, 1830 [1666].

BOSSUET, Jacques-Bénigne, évêque. *Oeuvres,* 4 vol. Paris, Didot, 1852 [1736].

Bulletin of the Bureau of Rolls and Library of the Department of State, vols. 6, 8, 10.

Causes politiques secrètes ou *Pensées philosophiques sur divers évènements qui se sont passés depuis 1763 jusqu'en 1772,*

---

[1] The dates of the first editions are given in brackets, when later editions have been referred to.

suivies d'un Projet de Haut-Pauvoir-Conservateur dirigé par les quatre grandes Puissances de l'Europe. Par un Ministre d'Etat qui ne se soucie plus de l'être. Ouvrage traduit de l'anglais sur la sixième édition. Londres. Aux dépens du Lord North. M.DCC.LXXXII. MLA Microfilm, No. 420F, 1938, Library of Congress.

CLOOTS, Jean-Baptiste (Anacharsis). *Voeux d'un Gallophile.* Amsterdam, 1786.

――――. *L'Orateur du genre humain* ou *Dépêches du Prussien Cloots au Prussien Herzberg.* L'An deux de la Rédemption.

――――. *La République universelle* ou *Adresse aux tyrannicides.* Paris, chez les Marchands de Nouveautés, l'An quatre de la Rédemption.

――――. *Bases constitutionnelles de la République du genre humain* (le deuxième discours d'A. Cloots à la Convention Nationale, le 24 avril, l'An deux de la République une et indivisible). Bibl. Nation., le 38/234.

COMMINES, Philippe de. *Mémoires,* éd. Lenglet du Fresnoy. Londres, 1747.

CONDILLAC, Etienne-Bonnot, Abbé de. *Oeuvres,* 23 vol. Paris, Houel, 1798.

CONDORCET, Antoine Nicolas Caritat, Marquis de. *Oeuvres,* 12 vol., éd. Condorcet, O'Conoor et Arago. Paris, 1847-49 [An XIII].

――――. *Outlines of an Historical View of the Progress of the Human Mind.* London, 1795.

――――. *Esquisse d'un tableau historique des progrès de l'esprit humain,* texte revu et présenté par O. H. Prior. Paris, Boivin, 1933.

――――. "Vie de Turgot," voir Condorcet, *Oeuvres,* 1847-49, t.V.

CRUCÉ, Emeric. *Le Nouveav Cynée* ou *Discours d'Estat représentant les Occasions et Moyens d'establir une Paix Générale et la Liberté du Commerce par tout le Monde. Aux Monarques et Princes Souverains de ce temps.* Em. Cr. Par. A Paris, chez Jacques Villery, au Palais sur le Perron Royal. M.D.C.XXIII. Avec Privilège du Roy.

――――. *Le Novveav Cynée,* ed. with an Introduction and translation into English from the original French text of 1623 by Th. W. Balch. Philadelphia, Allen, Lane, and Scott, 1909.

CYRANO DE BERGERAC. "Les Estats et Empires de la Lune [1659] et Les Estats et Empires du Soleil [1662]." See *Les*

Oeuvres libertines de Cyrano de Bergerac, 2 vol., éd. F. Lachèvre. Paris. Champion, 1921.

DESCHAMPS, L. M. (Dom). *Le Vrai Système* ou *Le Mot de l'énigme métaphysique et morale*, publié sous le patronage de la Société des textes français modernes par Jean Thomas et Franco Venturi. Paris, Droz, 1939.

DIDEROT, Denis. *Oeuvres*, 20 vol., éd. Assézat et Tourneux. Paris, Garnier. 1875-79 [1773].

——. *Pages choisies*. Paris, Armand Collin, 1921.

——. *Encyclopédie*, 36 vol., Lausanne et Berne, chez les Sociétés typographiques, 1780-82 [1751-1772].

——. *Pages inédites contre un tyran.* Introduction par Franco Venturi. Paris, GLM, 1937. (Le manuscrit original, sous le titre de *Lettre de M. Denis Diderot sur l'Examen de l'Essai sur les Préjugés* [1771], se trouve à la Bibliothèque Nat. sous la cote Nouv. Acquisitions Françaises, 6203, f. 35-44.)

DUBOIS, Pierre. *De recuperatione Terre Sancte*, éd. Ch. V. Langlois. Paris, Picard, 1891 [1611].

FÉNELON, François de Salignac de La Motte. *Oeuvres*, 3 vol., éd. Lefèvre. Paris, 1835 [1787-92].

——. *Adventures of Telemachus*, tr. by Dr. Hawkesworth, ed. by O. W. Wight. Boston, Houghton Mifflin, 1881.

——. *Les Aventures de Télémaque*, éd. Cahen. Paris, Hachette, 1923.

——. *Proper Heads of Self-examination for a King.* London, 1747.

FONTENELLE, Bernard le Bouvier de. *Oeuvres*, 12 vol. Amsterdam, 1764.

FRANKLIN, Benjamin. *Writings*, ed. by A. H. Smyth. New York, Macmillan, 1905-1907.

"French Disarmament Plan." *Series of SDN Publications*, No. 58, Nov. 14, 1932.

GAILLARD, Gabriel-Henri. "Des Malheurs de la guerre et des Bienfaits de la paix," *Mélanges académiques, poétiques, littéraires, critiques et historiques.* Paris, Agasse, 1806.

GARGAZ, Pierre-André. *A Project of Universal and Perpetual Peace* . . . printed by B. Franklin at Passy in the year 1782. Here reprinted, together with English version, introduction, and typographical note by G. S. Eddy. New York, G. S. Eddy, 1922.

GOUDAR, Ange. *La Paix de l'Europe ne peut s'établir qu'à la suite d'une longue trêve* ou *Projet de pacification générale combiné par une suspension d'armes de vingt ans entre toutes les Puissances politiques.* Par M. le Chevalier G———. Chez Chatelain, Amsterdam, 1757.

GROTIUS, Hugo. "De Jure Belli ac Pacis." Selections transl. with an Introduction by W. S. M. Knight. *The Grotius Society Publications,* t. 3.

HELVÉTIUS, Claude-Adrien. *Oeuvres,* 14 vol., éd. Didot. Paris, 1795.
———. *Collection des plus belles pages.* Paris, Mercure de France, 1909.

HERDER, J. G. *Werke,* Leipzig (n.d.).

HOLBACH, Paul-Henri-Dietrich, Baron d'. *La Politique naturelle,* Londres, 1773.
———. *Eléments de la morale universelle.* Paris, 1790.
———. *La Morale universelle,* 2 vol. Paris, Masson et fils, 1820 [1776].
———. *Le Système social.* Paris, 1822 [1773].

KANT, Immanuel. *Zum ewigen Frieden.* Königsberg, Nicolovius, 1795.
———. *Fundamental Principles of the Metaphysic of Ethics,* transl. by Th. K. Abbott. New York, Longmans, 1929.

LA BRUYÈRE, Jean de. *Oeuvres,* éd. Servois, 3 vol. Paris, Hachette, 1865 [Les Caractères, 1688].
———. *The Characters of the Age,* made English by several hands, London, 1705.
———. *The Characters,* tr. by H. van Laun. London, 1885.

LA FONTAINE, Jean de. *Oeuvres,* 11 vol., éd. Régnier. Paris, Hachette, 1892 [Les Fables, 1668].

LA HARPE, Jean-François de. *Oeuvres,* 6 vol. Paris, Pissot, 1778.
———. *Cours de littérature,* 3 vol. Paris, Didot, 1840 [1825-26].

LA-MOTHE-LE-VAYER, François de. *Oeuvres,* 7 vol., imprimées à Pfoerten chez Siffard en 1756, et se trouvent à Dresdes chez M. Groell [1654].

LINCOLN, Abraham. *Oration at Gettysburg,* Nov. 19, 1863.

MABLY, Gabriel Bonnot, Abbé de. *Oeuvres,* 12 vol. Lyon, Delamollière et Falque, 1796 [An III].

MERCIER, Louis-Sébastien. *Discours sur les malheurs de la ¡guerre,* 1766.

——. *Mon Bonnet de nuit,* 4 vol. Neufchâtel, Imprimerie de la Société typographique, 1784?.

——. *Nachtmütze,* 4 vols. tr. from French. Berlin, 1784-86.

——. *Songes et Visions* (Songes philosophiques). Amsterdam, 1788-89.

——. *L'An deux mille quatre cent quarante,* 3 vol. Paris, 1791 [1770].

Moniteur, No. du 21 mai 1790.

MONTESQUIEU, Charles de Secondat, Baron de la Brède et de Montesquieu. *Oeuvres,* 8 vol., éd. Lefèvre. Paris, 1826 [Londres, 1757].

——. *Complete Works,* London, 1777.

——. *Pensées et Fragments inédits,* éd. du Baron Gaston de Montesquieu. Bordeaux, Gounouilhou, 1899.

NECKER, Jacques. *Oeuvres,* 15 vol., *éd. de Stael.* Paris, Treuttel et Würtz, 1820-21.

——. *De l'Administration des finances de la France,* 3 vol. Dijon et Bordeaux, 1784.

PALIER de SAINT-GERMAIN. *Nouvel Essai sur le Projet de paix perpétuelle.* En Suisse, 1788 (Lausanne, B. M.). MLA Microfilm No. 453F, 1938, Library of Congress.

PASCAL, Blaise. *Oeuvres,* 3 vol., Biographie et Introduction par F. Strowski. Paris, Ollendorff, 1923 [1779].

——. *Pensées,* éd. L. Brunschvicg. Paris, Hachette, 1904 [1670].

——. *Pensées et Opuscules,* éd. L. Brunschvicg. Paris, Hachette, 1922.

——. *"Pensées",* tr. from the edition of Léon Brunschvicg by William Finlayson Trotter. See *Everyman's Library* (1931) ed. by Ernest Rhys and published by E. P. Dutton & Co., Inc., New York.

PENN, William. *An Essay Toward the Present and Future Peace of Europe.* The Second American Peace Society, Washington, D. C., 1912 [1696].

Projet d'un nouveau système de l'Europe, préférable au système de l'équilibre entre la Maison de France et celle d'Autriche, s. l. 1745. (K. b. B., München). MLA Rotograph, No. 471, 1938, Library of Congress.

RACINE, Jean. *Oeuvres*, 8 vol., éd. Mesnard. Paris, 1865-73
[1675-76].

RAMSAY, A. M. *The Life of François de Salignac de La Motte
Fénelon.* London, 1723.

RAYNAL, Guillaume, Abbé. *Histoire philosophique et politique
des Isles françaises dans les Indes occidentales.* Lausanne,
chez Pierre Heubach et Cie, 1784 [1770].

————. *A Philosophical and Political History of the Settlements
and Trade of the Europeans in the East and West Indies.*
Dublin, 1784.

ROUSSEAU, Jean Jacques. *Oeuvres*, 4 vol., éd. Furne. Paris,
1835-39 [1782-90].

————. *Oeuvres*, 15 tomes en 12 vol., éd. Volland. Paris et
Genève, 1790.

————. *Political Writings*, 2 vols. ed. from the original manuscripts and authentic editions, with Introductions and notes by
C. E. Vaughan. Cambridge (England), Univ. Press, 1915.

————. *A Lasting Peace* and *The State of War,* transl. by C. E.
Vaughan, London, Constable, 1917.

————. *L'Etat de guerre et le Projet de paix perpétuelle,* ed.
with a Foreword by G. P. Putnam and an Introduction by
Schirley Patterson. New York, The Knickerbocker Press,
1920.

————. *A Project for Perpetual Peace,* tr. from the French,
with a Preface by the translator. London, 1761.

————. *The Social Contract,* tr. from French with an Introduction by Henry Tozer. London, Allen, 1924.

SAINTARD.[2] *Le Roman politique sur l'état présent des affaires
de l'Amérique ou Lettres de M * * * à M * * * sur les moyens
d'établir une paix solide et durable dans les Colonies et la
Liberté générale de Commerce Extérieur.* Amsterdam, 1756.

SAINT-EVREMOND, Charles de Marguetel. *Oeuvres,* éd. Ch. Giraud, 3 vol. Paris, Techener, 1865 [1706].

SAINT-PIERRE, Bernardin de. *Etudes de la nature,* 3 vol. Paris,
Didot, 1784.

SAINT-PIERRE, Charles-Irénée-Castel, Abbé de. *Projet pour
rendre la paix perpétuelle en Europe,* 2 vol. Utrecht, A. Schou-
ten, 1713.

————. *Op. cit.,* troisième volume, Lyon, Deville, 1717.

[2] No data concerning his name, the place of his birth and death.

————. *Abrégé du Projet de paix perpétuelle.* Rotterdam, Beman, 1729.

————. *A Project for Setting an Everlasting Peace in Europe,* tr. from French, London, 1714.

———— *Annales politiques* (1658-1740). Paris, Champion, 1912.

————. *Oeuvres,* 16 tomes en 10 vol. Rotterdam, Beman, 1729-41.

Soupirs (Les) de la France esclave. Amsterdam, 1689.

SULLY, Maximilien de Béthune, Baron de Rosny, Duc de. "Mémoires des Sages et Royales Oeconomies d'Estat, Domestiques, Politiques et Militaires de Henry le Grand," *Nouvelle Collection des Mémoires relatifs à l'histoire de France,* par Michaud et Poujoulat. Paris, Didier, 1854 [1638].

TURGOT, Anne-Robert-Jacques. *Oeuvres,* 2 vol., éd. Daire. Paris, Guillaumin, 1844 [1808-11].

————. *On the Progress of Human Mind,* tr. from French. The Sociological Press.

VAUBAN, Sébastien Le Prestre. "La Dîme royale," see Daire, *Economistes financiers du 18e siècle.* Paris, 1844.

VAUBAN. *Oisivetés et Correspondance,* 2 vol., éd. de Rochas d'Aiglun. Paris, Berger-Levrault, 1910.

VOLNEY, Constantin François Chasseboeuf, Comte de. *The Ruins or Meditation on the Revolution of Empires,* tr. under the immediate inspection of the author from the sixth Paris edition. New York, 1828.

VOLTAIRE, François Marie Arouet de. *Oeuvres,* 52 vol., éd. Moland, Paris, Garnier, 1877-85.

————. *The Works,* 22 vols. in contemporary version by W. F. Fleming. Illustrations (168) by the craftsmen of St. Hubert Guild. New York, 1901.

————. *Candide and other romances,* transl. by Richard Aldington, 1923.

————. *The tragedy of Zara* (Zaïre), tr. by Aaron Hill, 1776.

————. *Complete Works of M. de Voltaire.* London, 1742.

————. *Voltairiana,* 4 vols., selections from Voltaire, tr. into English by Mary Julia Young. London, 1805.

WASHINGTON, George. *Writings* collected and edited by W. Ch. Ford, 14 vols. The Knickerbocker Press, 1890.

WILSON, Woodrow. *Messages, discours, documents diplomatiques relatifs à la guerre mondiale,* tr. from English by Désiré Roustan. Paris, Bossard, 1919.

CRITICAL WORKS CONSULTED

ALLEN, Devere. *The Fight for Peace.* New York, Macmillan, 1930.

ANGELL, Norman. *The Great Illusion.* New York, The Knickerbocker Press, 1913.

ASCOLI, G. "Voltaire," *Revue des Cours et Conférences,* 1923-24.

AULARD, Alphonse. *Etudes et Leçons sur la Révolution française,* série 9, ch. 2 (Le forçat Gargaz). Paris, Alcan, 1901-24.

————. "La Diplomatie du premier Comité de salut public," *La Révolution Française,* tome 18, janvier-juin 1890.

————. "La Diplomatie du Comité de salut public," *La Révolution Française,* tome 18, janvier-juin 1890.

AVENEL, Georges. *A. Cloots, l'orateur du genre humain,* 2 vol. Paris, Librairie internationale Lacroix . . . , 1865.

BALCH, Th. W. *Emeric Crucé.* Philadelphia, Allen, Lane, and Scott, 1900.

BARNI, Jules. *Histoire des idées morales et politiques en France au 18e siècle,* 3 vol. Paris, Baillère, 1865.

BARROUX, Robert. "Un Projet de fédération européenne," *Revue d'histoire diplomatique,* année 47, 1933.

BAULIG, Henri. "A Cloots avant la Révolution," "A. Cloots théoricien et journaliste," "A. Cloots conventionnel." *La Révolution Française,* tome 41, juillet-décembre 1901.

BEALES, A. Ch. F. *The History of Peace.* New York, The Dial Press, 1931.

BÉCLARD, Léon. *L.-S. Mercier avant la Révolution.* Paris, Champion, 1903.

BERSOT, Ernest. *Etudes sur le 18e siècle.* Paris, Durand, 1855.

BONFILS, Henri. *Manuel de droit international public.* Paris, Fauchenille, 1912.

BRIAND, Aristide. *Paroles de paix.* Paris et Bruxelles, Figuière, 1928.

BUTLER, Nicholas Murray. "Introduction" to Kant's *Perpetual Peace.* Los Angeles, 1932.

BUTLER, Sir G. G. *Studies in Statecraft.* Cambridge, England, The Univ. Press, 1920.

CAHEN, Léon. *Condorcet et la Révolution française.* Paris, Alcan, 1904.

CARO, Elme. *La Fin du 18e siècle: Etudes et Portraits,* 2 vol. Paris, 1881.

CAZES, Albert. *Pierre Bayle; sa vie, ses idées, son influence, son oeuvre.* Paris, Dujarric, 1905.

CHÉREL, A. *Fénelon au 18e siècle en France.* Paris, Hachette, 1917.

COHEN, Morris R. *Reason and Nature.* New York, 1931.

COMTES de PATRIS. "Fénelon précurseur de la Société des Nations," *Revue d'histoire diplomatique,* année 39, 1925.

CONSTANTINESCU-BAGDAT, Mme. Elise. *De Vauban à Voltaire.* Paris, Presses universitaires, 1924.

CUSHING, M. P. *Baron d'Holbach.* Lancaster, The New Era Printing Company, 1914.

DAMIRON, J. P. *Mémoires pour servir à l'histoire de la philosophie au 18e siècle,* 3 vol. Paris, 1858.

DELVOLVÉ, Jean. *Essai sur Pierre Bayle.* Paris, 1906.

DEMAHIS, Etiennette. *La Pensée politique de Pascal.* Saint-Amand (Cher), Imprimerie Bussière, 1931.

DENIS, Jacques. "Sceptiques et Libertins de la première moitié du 17e siècle," *Mémoires de l'Académie de Cahen,* 1884.

DEROCQUE, Gilberte. *Le Projet de paix perpétuelle de l'Abbé de Saint-Pierre comparé au Pacte de la SDN.* Paris, Rousseau, 1929.

DESNOIRESTERRES, G. *Voltaire et la Société française au 18e siècle.* Paris, Didier, 1871-76.

DROUET, Joseph. *L'Abbé de Saint-Pierre: l'homme et l'oeuvre.* Paris, Champion, 1912.

DRUON, H. "De l'Enseignement politique donné par Bossuet et Fénelon." *Mémoires de l'Académie de Nancy,* 1888, séries 5-6.

DU PONT de NEMOURS, P. S. *Mémoires sur la vie et les ouvrages de Turgot.* Paris, 1782.

DUPUIS, Charles. "Les Antécédents de la Société des Nations," *Institut de France,* 89, janvier-juin 1929.

FAGUET, Emile. *Le Dix-huitième siècle.* Paris, Lecène et Oudin, 1890.

———. *La Politique comparée de Rousseau, Montesquieu et Voltaire.* Société Française d'Imprimerie et de Librairie, 1902.

————. "L'Epoque de Voltaire (1730-50)." "L'Epoque de Rousseau et de Voltaire (1750-78)." *Histoire générale de la France* publiée par Lavisse et Rambaud. Paris, Colin, tome VII, 1896.

FERNESSOLE, Pierre. "Bossuet et la Guerre," *Etudes,* 143, avril-juin, 1915.

FEUGÈRE, Anatole. *L'Abbé Raynal.* Angoulème, Imprimerie ouvrière, 1922.

FRIED, Alfred. *Handbuch der Friedensbewegung.* Berlin und Leipzig, Friedens-Warte, 1911-13.

FROGER-DOUDEMONT, R. "A la Recherche de la sécurité," *La Paix,* 1931.

————. "La Stérilisation de la victoire," *La Paix,* 1932.

GAIFFE, F. *L'Envers du grand siècle.* Paris, Michel, 1924.

GARCIN, Eugène. "Jean Jacques Rousseau dans la Révolution," voir Grand-Carteret, *J. J. Rousseau jugé par les Français d'aujourd'hui.* Paris, Didier, 1890.

GUERRIER. *L'Abbé de Mably moraliste et politique.* Paris, Vieweg, 1886.

HAVENS, G. R. *Voltaire's Marginalia on the Pages of Rousseau. A Comparative Study of Ideas.* The Ohio State University, 1933.

HENDEL, Ch. W. *J. J. Rousseau moralist.* New York, Oxford University Press, 1934.

HERMAND, Pierre. *Les Idées morales de Diderot.* Paris, Les Presses univers., 1923.

HEYBERGER, Anna. *Jean Amos Comenius* (Komensky), *sa vie et son oeuvre d'éducateur.* Paris, Champion, 1928.

HODÉ, Jacques. *L'Idée de fédération internationale dans l'histoire.* Paris, Vie universitaire, 1921.

HODGSON, W. B. *Turgot.* London, 1870.

HORNUNG, Joseph. *Les Idées politiques de Rousseau jugées par les Genevois.* Genève, Sandez, 1879.

HUBERT, René. *D'Holbach et ses amis.* Paris, Delpeuch, 1928.

HUGO, Victor. *Oration on Voltaire* on May 1878, the hundredth anniversary of his death, tr. by James Parton.

JACQUART, Jean. *L'Abbé Trublet critique et moraliste.* Paris, Picard, 1926.

JANET, Paul. *Histoire de la science politique dans ses rapports avec la morale.* Paris, Alcan, 1913.

JULIEN, E. L., évêque d'Arras. "Bossuet," le troisième centenaire de sa naissance, 27 septembre 1927, *Correspondant*, 99, vol. 309, oct.-déc. 1927.

KAMPF, Helmut. *Pierre Dubois und die geistigen Grundlagen des französischen Nationalbewusstseins um 1300.* Berlin und Leipzig, Teubner, 1935.

KAYE, F. B. *The Fable of the Bees* (1714), critical edition of Mandeville's work with Introduction, 2 vols. Oxford, The Clarendon Press, 1924.

KAYSER, W. *Rousseau, Kant, Herder über den ewigen Frieden.* Leipzig, 1916.

KEIM, Albert. *Helvétius.* Paris, 1907.

KUKELHAUS, Theodor. *Der Ursprung des Planes vom ewigen Frieden in den Memoiren des Herzogs von Sully.* Berlin, 1893.

LACROIX, Lucien, Mgr. "Un Apôtre de la paix : l'Abbé de Saint-Pierre." *La Grande Revue,* mai 1919.

LANGE, Maurice. *La Bruyère, critique des conditions et des institutions sociales.* Paris, Hachette, 1909.

LANSON, Gustave. *Voltaire.* Paris, Hachette, 1910.

———. "Fénelon." *Revue des Cours et Conférences,* 8 avril, 1909.

———. "Origines et premières manifestations de l'esprit philosophique dans la littérature française de 1675 à 1748." *Revue des Cours et Conférences,* 1907-1909.

———. *L'Idéal français dans la Littérature de la Renaissance à la Révolution.* Paris, Bibliothèque de "La Civilisation française," 1927.

LANZAC de LABORIE. "L'Apôtre de la paix perpétuelle : L'Abbé de Saint-Pierre," ; *Revue hebdomadaire,* mai 1919.

LASSUDRIE-DUCHENE. *J. J. Rousseau et le Droit des gens.* Paris, Jouve, 1906.

LE FOYER, Lucien. "L'Union fédérale européenne." *La Paix,* 1930.

LEMAITRE, Jules. *Fénelon.* Paris, Fayard, 1910.

LICHTENBERGER, A. *Le Socialisme au 18e siècle.* Paris, Alcan, 1895.

LIGHT. *La Paix créatrice,* 2 vol. Paris, Rivière, 1934.

LIPSCHUTZ, M. *Montesquieu als Geschichtsphilosopher.* Strasbourg, Les Editions universitaires, 1927.

Louis-Lucas, Pierre. *Un Plan de paix générale et de liberté de commerce au 17e siècle: Le Nouveau Cynée d'Emeric Crucé.* Paris, Tenin, 1919.

Lovejoy, A. O. "The Parallel of Deism and Classicism." *Modern Philology,* vol. XXIX, No. 3, Febr. 1932.

Madelin, Louis. "Le Crépuscule de la Monarchie," *Revue hebdomadaire,* année 45, février 1936.

──────. "Le Premier Son de cloche de la Révolution (1743-54)," *Revue des Deux-Mondes,* 1924.

Markovitch, Milan. *J. J. Rousseau et Tolstoï.* Paris, Champion, 1928.

Marriott, Sir John A. R. *Commonwealth or Anarchy? A Survey of Projects of Peace from the 16th to the 20th Century.* London, Allan, 1937.

Martin, Kingsley. *French Liberal Thought in the 18th Century. A Study of Political Ideas from Bayle to Condorcet.* Boston (Engl.), Little, Brown and Co., 1929.

Mead, E. D. *The Grand Design of Henry IV.* Boston, Ginn, 1909.

Melamed, S. M. *Theorie, Ursprung und Geschichte der Friedensidee.* Stuttgart, 1909.

Meulen, Jacob ter. *Der Gedanke der internationalen Organisation in seiner Entwicklung.* Haag, Nijhoff, 1917.

Morley, John. *Jean Jacques Rousseau,* 2 vols. New York, Macmillan, 1886.

──────. *Voltaire.* London, Macmillan, 1923.

──────. *Diderot and the Encyclopedists.* New York, Macmillan, 1891.

Mornet, Daniel. *La Pensée française au 18e siècle.* Paris, Colin, 1926.

──────. *Les Origines intellectuelles de la Révolution française* (1715-87). Paris, Colin, 1933.

Novicow, I. A. *La Fédération de l'Europe.* Paris, Alcan, 1901.

Osterlow, Richard. *Fénelon und die Anfänge der literarischen Opposition gegen das politische System Ludwigs XIV.* Göttingen, 1913.

Owen, John. *The Sceptics of the French Renaissance.* New York, Macmillan, 1893.

Paix (La) et l'Enseignement pacifiste: leçons professées à l'Ecole des Hautes Études Sociales par d'Estournelles de Constant,

Richet, Novicow, Maumus, E. Bourgeois, G. Lyon, Passy et Weiss. Paris, Alcan, 1904.

PATCHETT, E. W. "Pascal and Scepticism," *Spec. Relig.*, Oxford Press, 1929.

PELLISSIER, Georges. *Les Ecrivains politiques au 18e siècle en France avant la Révolution.* Paris, Weille et Maurice, 1882.

———. *Voltaire philosophe.* Paris, Colin, 1908.

PELLISSON, M. *Les Hommes de lettres au 18e siècle.* Paris, Colin, 1911.

POWICKE, F. M. "Pierre Dubois : a Mediaeval Radical." *Histor. Essays,* London, 1902.

RENAN, Ernest. "Pierre Du Bois légiste," *Histoire littéraire de la France,* tome XXVI, pp. 491ff. Paris, Didot.

ROBINSON, Howard. *Bayle the Sceptic.* New York, Columbia Univ. Press, 1931.

ROCHAS d'AIGLUN de. "Discours prononcé à l'inauguration du monument de Vauban à Bazoches le 26 août 1900," *Revue scientifique,* séries 4-14, janvier-décembre 1900.

RODET, Henri. *Le Contrat social et les idées politiques de J. J. Rousseau.* Paris, Rousseau, 1909.

ROUSTAN, Marius. *The Pioneers of the French Revolution,* tr. from French by F. Whyte. London, 1926.

SABRIÉ, J. B. *Les Idées religieuses de Guez de Balzac.* Paris, Alcan, 1913.

SALTYKOW, Wera. *Die Philosophy Condillac's.* Bern, Sturzenegger, 1901.

SCHAPIRO, J. Salwyn. *Condorcet and the Rise of Liberalism.* New York, Harcourt, Brace, and Co., 1934.

SCHUCKING, Walther. *Die Organisation der Welt.* Leipzig, 1909.

SCHWITZKY, Ernst. *Der europäische Fürstenbund Georgs von Podiebrad; ein Beitrag zur Geschichte der Weltfriedensidee.* Marburg, Ebel, 1907.

SÉE, Henri. *Les Idées politiques en France au 18e siècle.* Paris, Hachette, 1920.

SEEBER, E. D. *Anti-Slavery Opinion in France during the Second Half of the 18th Century.* Baltimore, The Johns Hopkins Press, 1937.

SEROUX d'AGINCOURT. *Exposé des Projets de paix perpétuelle de l'Abbé de Saint-Pierre et de Henri IV, de Bentham et de Kant.* Paris, Jouve, 1905.

Siégler-Pascal, S. *Un Contemporain égaré au 18e siècle: les Projets de l'Abbé de Saint-Pierre.* Paris, Rousseau, 1900.
Smith, Horatio E. *The Literary Criticism of Pierre Bayle.* Albany, The Brandow Printing Co., 1912.
Sorel, Albert. *Montesquieu,* tr. from French by M. and E. Anderson. Chicago, McClurg, 1892.
Stern, Selma. "A. Cloots, der Redner des Menschengeschlechts. Ein Bietrag zur Geschichte der Deutschen in der französischen Revolution," *Historische Studien.* Berlin, Ebering, 1914.
Streit, C. K. *Union Now.* New York and London, Harper and Brothers, 1938.

Texte, Joseph. *Jean Jacques Rousseau and the Cosmopolitan Spirit in Literature,* tr. from French. New York, Macmillan, 1889.
Torrey, Norman L. *Voltaire and the English Deists.* Yale Univ. Press, 1930.
———. *The Spirit of Voltaire.* New York, Columbia Univ. Press, 1938.
———. *Voltaire and the Enlightenment;* selections from Voltaire newly translated, with an Introduction. New York, Crofts, 1931.
Tourneux, M. *Diderot et Catherine II.* Paris, Lévy, 1899.

Vaillat, Léandre. "Vauban," *National Review,* Jan.-June, 1933.
Vesnitch, M. R. "Emeric Crucé," *Revue d'histoire diplomatique,* 1911.

Wickelgren, F. L. "La Pensée de La-Mothe-Le-Vayer," *F. Quar.* V, 1923.
Wickwar, W. H. *Prelude to the French Revolution.* London, Allen and Unwitt, 1935.

York, Elizabeth. *Leagues of Nations Ancient, Mediaeval, and Modern.* The Swarthmore Press, 1919.

Zeck, Ernst. Der Publizist Pierre Dubois. Berlin, 1911.

INDEX

INDEX